KHARTOUM AT NIGHT

D1496285

KHARTOUM AT NIGHT

Fashion and Body Politics in Imperial Sudan

MARIE GRACE BROWN

Stanford University Press
Stanford, California

Stanford University Press
Stanford, California

©2017 by the Board of Trustees of the Leland Stanford Junior University.
All rights reserved.

This book has been partially underwritten by the The Susan Groag Bell Publication
Fund in Women's History. For more information on the fund, please see www.sup
.org/bellfund.

Printed in the United States of America on acid-free, archival-quality paper

Library of Congress Cataloging-in-Publication Data

Names: Brown, Marie Grace, 1982- author.
Title: Khartoum at night : fashion and body politics in imperial Sudan /
Marie Grace Brown.
Description: Stanford, California : Stanford University Press, 2017. | Includes
bibliographical references and index.
Identifiers: LCCN 2016052537| ISBN 9781503601529 (cloth : alk. paper) |
ISBN 9781503602649 (pbk. : alk. paper) | ISBN 9781503602687 (ebook)
Subjects: LCSH: Women—Sudan—Social conditions—20th century. | Women's
clothing—Sudan—History—20th century. | Women—Political activity—Sudan—
History—20th century. | Fashion—Political aspects—Sudan—History—20th century.
| Human body—Political aspects—Sudan—History—20th century. | Sudan—Politics
and government—1899–1956.
Classification: LCC HQ1793.5 .B76 2017 | DDC 320.082/09624—dc23
LC record available at https://lccn.loc.gov/2016052537

Typeset by Bruce Lundquist in 10.25/15 Adobe Caslon Pro

"I need to understand how a place on the map is also a place in history within which . . . I am created and trying to create."
Adrienne Rich, "Notes towards a Politics of Location" (1984)

CONTENTS

FIGURES

ACKNOWLEDGMENTS

Scholars use citations so that others may trace their evidence and arguments. But an eager researcher following the sources listed in the back of this volume would only get so far. For this book was made possible by a village of friends, colleagues, archivists, and strangers, whose encouragement, assistance, and kindness defy formal citation.

When I look back on my time in Sudan, I am truly humbled by the warmth and generosity of spirit of the people I met. Anyone who has conducted research abroad knows that even the most minor victories are often hard won. So many people, some of whom were near-strangers, went out of their way to offer help, and I regret that I cannot name them all. Drs. Gasim Bedri and Nafisa M. Bedri of the Ahfad University for Women sponsored both of my visas to Sudan and smoothed my entrance into university and government archives. In 2010, the coordinated efforts of Ali Ali-Dinar and Ambassador Akec Khoc helped to push a nervous graduate student's visa approval through at the last minute. Thank you to the staff at the National Records Office in Khartoum for accommodating a researcher with multiple interests. Thank you to the Institute of African and Asian Studies at University of Khartoum and in particular Khalid Abdalla of the Folklore Archive for opening their collections to me.

Outside the archives, Imam Gasmelseed, Kamal Ahmed, Hassan Abdelrahman, and Nagwa Mohmed Suliman all displayed enthusiasm for my work and, far more importantly, gave generously of their time to introduce me to their country. Dr. Ismail Elkhalifa Suleiman and his family deserve special recognition for their kindness: Ihsan Ismail Adam Hassan filled me with good food, and Abdel Muhsin features in one of my favorite memories, of driving through Khartoum singing Adele's "Rolling in the Deep." I am grateful for the winds of chance that led me to bump into Sister Maryam outside St. Matthews Cathedral and the resulting glimpses of Khartoum that I had not seen before. My most heartfelt thanks to Dr. Nafisa Ahmed el Amin, Sittana Bedri, and Griselda el Tayib for sharing their stories with me. No matter where my day took me, in the evenings I returned to the incomparable hospitality of two generations of the Pagoulatos family and their staff at the Acropole Hotel. They made me feel like family from the very first; and the warmth that lit the hotel was matched only by the vibrancy of its iconic blue shutters.

In England, the Sudan Archive at Durham University is a delightful and sunny place to work. And no one could ask for more patient or responsive archivists than Jane Hogan, Francis Gotto, and Mike Harkness.

Historical research is a surprisingly expensive endeavor. Funding for the above travel and research as well as critical leave from teaching was made possible by generous grants from the American Association of University Women, the University of Kansas, the Mellon Mays Foundation, the Social Science Research Council, and the Woodrow Wilson National Fellowship Foundation.

I have been fortunate to begin my career at the University of Kansas, where I am surrounded by lively and supportive colleagues. Paul Kelton introduced me to the workings of an academic department and was a steadying presence across the hall. Kim Warren read portions of this book and offered helpful feedback. Megan Greene graciously and thoughtfully read the entire manuscript twice and was always on call to answer any question. Katherine and Jonathan Clark offered royal accommodations and relaxation when the British archives proved too much. Tony Rosenthal had a sixth sense about knowing just when I needed to be taken out to lunch. Brad Osborn proved an unexpected but very much welcome companion on this publishing journey. And Benjamin Rosenthal never once doubted me or this project.

Comments and suggestion from the anonymous readers at Stanford University Press made this a better book. Many thanks to my editor, Kate Wahl, whose advice early on helped to shape this project and whose encouragement at the end kept me going. Thanks as well to Cassi Pittman and LaToya Tavernier, who both spent seven years keeping me accountable to this work. Portions of chapter five and the conclusion were previously published in "Fashioning their Place: Dress and Global Imagination in Imperial Sudan," *Gender & History* 26 (2014); I appreciate the opportunity to expand on those arguments here.

A decade's worth of thanks to Eve Troutt Powell, who continues to teach me what it means to be a scholar, a colleague, and a woman of color.

A final word of gratitude for my mother: who never said "no," and taught me to work for, and expect only, the best.

NOTE ON TRANSLITERATION

For the ease of the general reader, this book follows a simplified form of transliteration as outlined by the *International Journal of Middle East Studies*. All diacritical critical marks have been omitted except for the Arabic letters *'ayn* (') and *hamza* (') when they occur in the middle or at the end of words. Where they exist, I have used accepted English spellings of common words, people, and places (such as *sayyid* and Khartoum). I have also anglicized plural forms of certain Arabic words by adding an *s* to the end (for instance, *tobe*s and *daya*s). Sudanese place names are spelled according to British usage of the period. All translations are my own.

KHARTOUM AT NIGHT

MAP 1. The Anglo-Egyptian Sudan

INTRODUCTION

Photograph SAD 540/1/80 (Fig. 1) is one of over four hundred pictures of early twentieth-century Sudan captured by a man named D. Clifton. It is labeled, in Clifton's hand, "One of my neighbors, Khartoum." Little is known about D. Clifton. He has no records of his own in the Sudan Archive at Durham University that now houses his photographs. In fact, SAD 540/1/80 came to the archive by accident as part of the papers of Kenneth Henderson, a prominent government official, who purchased Clifton's pictures at a saleroom. Even less is known of the stately woman in the photograph. Her face is weathered, with a hint of a smile. She stands composed, her hands loosely cradling an unidentified bundle. And though she looks to be on her way somewhere, she pauses for Clifton to take her picture. She is wary of neither the camera nor the man behind it.

Many imperial photographs from the late nineteenth and early twentieth centuries aimed to capture colonized people in their "native" habitats, whether that was a particularly wild landscape or a primitive-looking home. Here, the scene behind the woman is notably sparse; there are no clues to her location, surroundings, or place in the world. Clifton, however, provides all the context necessary: the woman is his neighbor. We can only guess at how well the two knew each other, or even if they had exchanged names. Indeed, imperial and local conventions would have dis-

FIGURE 1. "One of my neighbours, Khartoum," ca. 1900–1920, SAD 540/1/80 (K. D. D. Henderson Collection). Copyright Durham University. Reproduced by permission of Durham University Library.

couraged a British man and a Sudanese woman from extensive socializing. Yet the confidence in the woman's gaze and the intimacy of Clifton's caption indicate a certain level of recognition, if not familiarity. The two were neighbors, largely unknown to history, brought together by the unpredictable currents of empire.

This is not the story of D. Clifton, but of his neighbor and the thousands of northern Sudanese women like her whose lives were altered under imperial rule. For such women, empire was not a far-off place, nor was it limited to the administrative machinations in colonial offices. Empire was lived at close range, with an intimacy akin to that of neighbors.

៙

In 1898, just a few years before Clifton took his first photographs, a determined contingent of Anglo-Egyptian troops, led by Lord Herbert Kitchener, conquered Sudan. A neglected territory on the outskirts of the Ottoman Empire, Sudan itself held little appeal for the British. The value of its occupation lay in the country's geographic position as a bulwark against any political unrest moving northward into Egypt and as a critical link in Britain's dreamed-of north-south line of influence from Cape Town to Cairo. As for the Egyptians, they were eager to reclaim control over a territory they had long held to be an extension of their own. Together, the two foreign powers entered into an uneasy and uneven partnership for governing Sudan that would last until 1956. In addition to this dual control, it was clear from the start that Sudan would not be like other British imperial holdings. It could not boast of tight links to the Indian Ocean trade, like Kenya, the opportunity for missionary work in South Africa, or the romantic allure of India. Instead, the Foreign Office deemed Sudan a hardship post, best suited for athletic bachelors who preferred the rigors of the trek to the comforts of home.

The country that they ruled was geographically and culturally diverse, making the application of universal policies difficult and resulting in uneven imperial legacies. Most of the government's energies were concentrated in the northern and central regions of Sudan, anchored by the capital cities of Khartoum and Omdurman and a relatively homogenized Arab-Muslim culture. The people who lived in the major cities and surrounding areas developed an even stronger cultural identity, one that was urban, middle-class, and socially conservative but open to certain aspects of Western education, governance, and material culture. The women who were part of this emerging society are the subjects of this book.

Following the common strategy of divide and conquer, imperial policies further exaggerated Sudan's cultural and ethnic differences. In the late 1920s, a series of legislative acts known as the "Southern Policy" drew a boundary line between north and south, splitting the country into artificial, asymmetrical categories of Arab vs. African and Muslim vs. Christian and leaving its southern portion at a political and economic disadvantage. Upon independence in 1956, northern Sudan, led by the government in Khartoum, emerged as the hegemonic power. The legacies of this north-south split dominated post-independence politics and served as a backdrop for two civil wars. The divide between the two regions crystallized in 2011 when, in a highly anticipated referendum, the southern Sudanese overwhelmingly voted to secede from the north and form an independent country, the Republic of South Sudan.

Even before the referendum, scholars had inherited these constructed divisions in the way we write and talk about Sudan. The terms *north* and *south* are inadequate to describe the ethnic, geographic, and cultural diversity (east to west; rural and urban; desert, riverain, swamp, and grassland) that continues to exist in the two countries. Nevertheless, the Arab-Islamic identity that developed in Khartoum and Omdurman in the late nineteenth and early twentieth centuries is identified as "northern" Sudanese culture. For the sake of brevity and consistency, I will do the same. However, I ask that the reader keep in mind that identities were in flux during the imperial period and that for many people, the far more pressing question was how to maintain closely held values and a sense of self in the face of foreign occupation.

Many books detail Sudan's time under imperial rule and the country's struggle for independence; few, however, examine the lives of Sudanese women during this period of upheaval and change. The standard political histories of Sudan rarely address women, except as subjects of government policy.[1] Conversely, works that take women as their central focus are episodic in nature, limiting themselves to a single event or topic such as girls' education, female genital cutting, or women's activism, and make little attempt to incorporate women's experiences into the larger framework of Sudan's national history.[2] This unevenness in scholarship is not surprising, for there are very few historical documents authored by Sudanese women. In the first half of the twentieth century, formal education for men and women was limited. Only a small minority of women could read and write and even fewer left written records of their lives. Low levels of literacy compounded with Sudan's strict harem culture have led previous scholars to alternately claim that women's history cannot be known, or cast women in the role of a Greek chorus, echoing the voices of their fathers, husbands, and brothers. However, Sudanese activist Nafisa Ahmed el Amin, who came of age in the late 1940s, cautions, "Women's [political] awareness was higher than their education."[3] Her assurances suggest that women's political voices were there—if one only knew where to look.

Locating and making use of this awareness would require a different type of historical work. As Sarah Deutsch describes her search for women's urban experiences in nineteenth-century Boston, "At first I looked . . . where I had been trained to look for men's theories of city form, in explicitly theoretical texts or in sentences that started, 'The city is . . . ' I did not find them. Instead women revealed their reconceptions of the city in the ways they wrote about moving through it, in the practices of their organizations, and in their daily lives."[4] Similarly, Sudanese women did not leave records stating, "Imperialism is . . . " Instead, they articulated their complex understanding of empire in the ways they moved through the capital city, Khartoum, in the clothes they chose to wear, and in the adjustments made to their daily habits. Here was the broad political awareness that Nafisa Ahmed was referring to: expressed not in words, but in gestures and postures. Women's small, individual movements afforded glimpses of broader sociopolitical engagement. Disciplinary prejudices have prevented us from recognizing political consciousness and expression in areas other than written texts. In contrast, this book treats northern Sudanese women's bodies as records of imperial experience and, in doing so, seeks to bring the voices of Nafisa and her peers out from the chorus and onto center stage.

∼

Two overlapping arguments about bodies, movement, and place form the core of this book. First, the experience of empire was intimately expressed on and through Sudanese bodies. Imperialism was immensely personal—a visceral reality as much as a political system. In much the same way that Clifton stopped his neighbor, positioned her within his camera lens, and captured her image, the civilizing and political missions of imperialism interrupted and rerouted Sudanese women's lives on a much larger scale.

Here I am inspired by a recent turn in interdisciplinary feminist scholarship that analyzes global structures and intimate behaviors side by side. As explained by Geraldine Pratt and Victoria Rosner, "the global and the intimate" are overlapping rather than opposing forces. Read together, they collapse and reconfigure standard measures of scale and disrupt "grand narratives" with "the specific, the quotidian, the affective, and the eccentric." Put simply: attention to that which is closest in gives new shape to large, familiar stories. Intimacy is often associated with "feminine" domains such as sex, domesticity, emotion, and attachment, but it should not be mistaken for benevolence, affection, or authenticity. It is, in fact, "infused with worldliness" and bound up with context-specific relationships of inequality, power, and violence.[5] Imperial rule relied on coercion, brutality, and oppression. The cost of progress and opportunity was often discord and division. These multiple effects of empire were not abstractions, but tangible phenomena impressed on Sudanese bodies. Indeed, the power that Clifton exercised over his neighbor was played out again and again in marketplaces, schools, kitchens, bedrooms, and even the private moments of birth. Bodies translated imperial philosophies into close, physical realities.

A generation of scholars of gender and empire has produced a rich corpus of work demonstrating the ways in which asymmetrical relationships of gender and sexuality were fundamental in making and maintaining imperial power. Women's bodies, in particular, served as charged nodes of contact.[6] Contemporary artists, novelists, and explorers cast uncharted terrain and blank spaces on the map as feminine virgin landscapes, awaiting men's efforts of discovery, domestication, and cultivation. Today some scholars have extended this metaphor further to argue that white men's sexual conquest (both real and imagined) of brown women offered a precise parallel for the violent dominance of the imperial system as a whole.[7] Moving from metaphor to actual structures, Ann Stoler has shaped much of the scholarly conversation with her arguments that imperial authority (with its attendant racial distinctions) was constructed on gendered terms. She states, "The very categories 'colonizer' and 'colonized' were secured through forms of sexual control."[8] Yet, dominance and control just as often took other forms, which, though nonsexual, were no less intimate. Under the guise of a civilizing mission, administrators pursued an unrelenting interest in the colonized body, legislating how it would be nourished and clothed, whether it was to be considered clean and healthy or dirty and diseased, and which of its children would be recognized. These modes of control were powerful and pervasive because they were applied "at the level of detail . . . not by restricting individuals and their actions but by producing them."[9] Disciplining the body at the closest level, producing and guiding its actions, was just as central to imperial rule as economic hegemony, military might, and imposed governing institutions. Power, however, never moves in just one direction. Although bodies behaved well in theory, in practice they were "arena[s] of colonial bargaining and strife, translation and mixtures."[10] If the body was a site on which government policies played out, it was also where imperial power reached its limit and colonized voices asserted themselves.

In search of "translations and mixtures," this book follows an ongoing call in gender and world history for us to zoom in closer: to look past the rhetorical and structural relationships of gender, sex, and power and inquire how colonial and colonized bodies actually felt and experienced these systems. By treating the fleshed body as a historical subject in its own right, we gain a greater understanding of the materiality and everyday effects of large social and political systems.[11]

Contrary to what one might expect, there is nothing universal or un-biased in the ways our bodies move. Even the most basic human actions such as sitting, walking, jumping, or throwing a ball are historically and culturally specific "techniques of the body," varying across nations, social classes, and time.[12] In short, our physical habits are not natural or auto-matic, but the result of carefully taught social processes. Thus, techniques and movements are not much different than other marks of identity found on our bodies. As described by anthropologists, our skin serves as a visible "frontier" between our individual and communal selves, on which society's rules are taught, enacted, and, oftentimes, refused.[13] How our bodies and our behaviors conform to, or reject, these expectations maps both our dif-ference and our belonging. Some aspects of this "frontier," such as race, sex, ethnicity, and caste, are relatively fixed. Other body marks like tattoos, piercings, and hairstyles are changeable. Similarly, many of our daily be-haviors have become ingrained and unconscious while others are the result of highly strategic choices. Bodily practices make our political praxis vis-ible. Combined, body marks and techniques all work to plot our distinct sociopolitical position and our sense of place, within our own communities and the world at large.

The focus on real, tangible bodies introduces drama and kineticism to the imperial narrative. It overturns assumptions that imperial agents, most often European men, were the only ones capable of action or movement, while colonized people and spaces remained fixed and static. In their work on mobility, subjectivity, and empire, Tony Ballantyne and Antoinette Burton argue that though historical subjects did not "literally feel the ground moving beneath their feet [they acted] as if its rifts and fissures, its uneven and unstable surfaces, were part of the regular (albeit anxiety-inducing) business of empire."[14] This sense of motion and connection to unsteady terrain is particularly valuable for understanding marginalized subjects like Sudanese women, where a lack of preserved historical infor-mation threatens to uncouple their lives from specific historical contexts and set them adrift in an amorphous, unknowable past. Counterintuitively, perhaps, when we recognize women as moving subjects we are able to ground them more firmly in existing historical landscapes.

Thus the themes of location and uneven terrain frame the second argument of this book. I contend that the body and its adornments are as much an indicator of where we are as of who we are. In Sudan in the twentieth century, imperialism disrupted existing body techniques and habits. Anglo-Egyptian rule reinforced existing gender divisions and hierarchies, but also directed new modes of dressing, washing, birthing, and walking. Like Clifton's neighbor, Sudanese women gazed back: responding, resisting, and adapting to the changes brought by empire. With the world shifting beneath their feet, women used their bodies to calibrate and register their positions within overlapping systems of protected domesticity, empire, nationalism, and modernization. Coming of age in this time of transition and excluded from standard forms of political participation, a pioneering generation of young urban women used a careful choreography of bodies, behaviors, and dress to articulate and make meaning of the rapidly changing world around them.

Motion, then, is at the heart of this story. Each chapter turns on women's complementary forms of movement—within their own skins and across newly constructed imperial space. Medically trained midwives rush to a delivery; schoolgirls find discipline in new uniforms; activists navigate dangerous city streets; and consumers search Khartoum shops for the latest fashions. In following these active bodies, we begin to construct the worlds of politics and pleasures in which northern Sudanese women lived.

Women's moving bodies were wrapped in a unique form of dress, the *tobe*.[15] Meaning "bolt of cloth," a tobe is a rectangular length of fabric, generally two meters wide and four to seven meters long. It is worn as an outer wrapper whenever women are outside their homes or in the company of unrelated males. The tobe's origins date back to the late eighteenth century when prosperous merchants in Darfur clothed their wives and daughters in large swaths of fine imported linen, muslin, and silk as a sign of their wealth and prestige.[16] As markets expanded and prices dropped,

the range of fabrics increased, so that by the twentieth century tobes of
varying quality were imported from Egypt, India, England, and Japan.
Those who still could not afford the high cost of imported fabrics turned
to a locally produced, roughspun cotton known as *damuriyya* as a substi-
tute. With women across classes wearing the tobe, it shifted from a luxury
item to an everyday garment closely associated with domesticity and gender responsibility. Girls received their first tobes at the onset of puberty;
husbands bought tobes for their brides-to-be; and women again received
gifts of tobes on the occasion of the birth of each child. This simple piece
of clothing conveyed multiple messages. As an imported garment, it proclaimed a woman's connection to an expansive global economy, far beyond
the boundaries of her town. As a gift connected to fertility and reproduction, the tobe was a visible sign of women's most private acts. And as the
preferred uniform of teachers and nurses in the twentieth century, the tobe
allowed newly professional women to craft an image of progress tempered
by modesty and tradition.

Fashion, like the body, is an indicator of self and place. As an extension of the body's surface, clothing conveys status, values, and belonging.
But fabric is more fluid than flesh; as a result, clothing styles and adornment are far more adaptive and responsive to rapid social and political
change. It is no surprise, then, that in imperial contexts fashion was a
prime site for creation and negotiation. Scholars of dress, particularly in
Africa, have vividly illustrated how expanding markets, urbanization, imported measures of modernity and morality, and the introduction of the
Singer sewing machine all dramatically altered existing rules of fashion
and adornment.[17] Imperial reformers imposed standards of modest dress,
along with strong soap, to discipline exposed and dirty bodies. Africans
playfully responded with inventive (mis)uses of European styles to create
expressive hybrid identities and imagine new senses of self.

Women's fashion in Sudan followed a different trajectory. Compared
with their neighbors, Sudanese women were relatively resistant to Western fashions. Many considered the dresses they saw British women wear
to be immodest or indecent. Instead, European-style clothing (especially

undergarments) came into use gradually through the intermediaries of Egyptian and Syrian women in Sudan.[18] No matter what they wore underneath, in public women continued to wear the tobe—an entirely Sudanese fashion not shared by other women. The embrace of their traditional tobe did not mean that Sudanese women were any less imaginative in their use of fashion. In fact, the word *traditional* as it is commonly understood when referring to dress is a misnomer here. The tradition that women evoked in their tobes was not a period of isolation, but a centuries-long history of luxury, fertility, and transnational trade. Events under Anglo-Egyptian rule added further meaning to the tobe. Unlike other places in the empire, where "native" clothing was roundly condemned, British administrators in Sudan viewed the tobe as a dignified and modest form of dress. As a result, tobes became critical components of modernizing projects such as girls' education, medical training, and even political action. Thus it was the tobe, and not Singer-sewn dresses, that most closely modeled the opportunities, changes, and refashioning brought by imperialism.

There was one other aspect of the tobe that made it a particularly meaningful vehicle for women's voices and imaginations: each garment carried a name. The best-quality tobes in the first half of the twentieth century were white or very light pastel. Each new season brought subtle shifts in the pattern of dots, stripes, tufts, or borders that decorated the fabric. And each new style was matched with a creative name. Chosen informally by male merchants and their female customers, names highlighted the desirability of the fabric or commemorated popular items of interest, including political leaders, celebrity marriages, and national achievements.

The title of this book, *Khartoum at Night*, is taken from the name of a popular 1950s tobe. It is used here to convey the sentiments of possibility, momentum, rupture, and danger that characterized Sudan's imperial period. At the turn of the twentieth century, Khartoum was an abandoned city, wracked by warfare and famine and populated with mud-brick buildings alongside sewage ditches. By the 1950s, the capital city was a cosmopolitan node of empire complete with a university, dance halls, cinemas, parks, and shops filled with high-end European goods. It was also home to the largest Communist party in Africa, a visible corps of women activists, and the best-educated teachers and nurses in the country.

For the historian, evocative and topical tobe names stand as a remarkable and yet largely unacknowledged record of Sudanese women's lives. They are rich and concrete examples of the interweaving of bodies and politics. Most importantly, the editorial function of tobe names counters presumptions that "the public" and "the political" are entirely male spaces. Instead, the pleasure that women took in the latest fashions was woven inextricably into shifting political and social landscapes. Wrapped in their creatively named tobes, Sudanese women navigated the complexities of imperial rule just as they did the sharp corners of Khartoum's changing streets.

⌒

Finding women's bodies and gestures in traditional archives poses a particular set of challenges. The body's role in constructing our identity and defining our place is at once too large and too mundane to capture on the page. Where evidence of the body does exist, it is often marginalized as anecdotal and thus outside "real" history. In her work *Dwelling in the Archive*, Antoinette Burton criticizes historians' persistent "temptation to ghettoize women's memories" as mere "memorabilia." Instead, Burton contends that women use domestic space (and here I would add, domestic bodily practices) as an archival source from which "to construct their own histories and through which to record the contradictions of living."[19] This is not a call to abandon the archive, but to mine and supplement it in creative ways: to recognize that intimate spaces and intimate practices honor stories and experiences not recorded elsewhere.

In writing this book I went in search of women not as objects of discussion, but as active subjects making their way through complex, uneven sociopolitical space. In some texts, such as a political cartoon about shopping, women's bodily experience leapt from the page. Other sources proved more elusive; it took a second reading to realize that a teacher's critique of a mathematics lesson was also a judgment about dirt and discipline. These traditional sources are joined by an "archive" of remembered tobe names. Assembled together, these names form a collective accounting, a narrative, of women's aspirations, values, and experiences under imperial rule. By way of illustration, each chapter in this book is titled with the name of a tobe or a reference to tobes that exemplifies the period under discussion. They serve as a structural reminder of the critical value of the body and adornment in narrating and memorializing Sudanese women's history. Threading such disparate sources together is simultaneously exciting and slippery; I have done my best to construct broad, textured arguments while remaining, as Natalie Zemon Davis instructs, "held tightly in check by the voices of the past."[20] The resulting narrative is necessarily fragmented—woven more tightly in some areas than in others.

A final example serves to show how women's histories are so often body stories. In one of my earliest conversations with Nafisa Ahmed el Amin, she poignantly referred to the first time she spoke in a public gathering as the moment of her "unveiling." At a meeting at Gordon Memorial College in February 1952, Nafisa Ahmed raised her hand to speak. Wrapped in her tobe, which covered her head, body, and the bottom half of her face, Nafisa realized that her voice could not be heard; she lowered the fabric from her mouth and began to speak. When finished, she raised her tobe back over her mouth and quickly sat down. Sixty years later, Nafisa laughed and laughed as she acted out this story for me. She went through the motions in part to demonstrate the absurdity of it all, but also to perform her strong corporeal memory of that day. The desire to speak her mind gave this young activist the courage to reveal her face. Yet once Nafisa had spoken, she covered herself again. These are the "contradictions of living" of which Burton speaks. And it is only by seeing them play out on the body that we understand their full effect.

Moving between texts and textiles, this book recounts a history of Sudanese women in a language of signs and symbols that held particular resonance for the women themselves. This analysis of bodies and dress demonstrates that women like Nafisa Ahmed and D. Clifton's neighbor experienced and interpreted the vast social, political, and economic systems of empire in intimate ways. The result is a rich and colorful narrative of mobility, danger, beauty, and global connection not fully found in the pages of any written document. Following the paths that they traveled from home to schoolhouse to city streets, *Khartoum at Night* seeks to honor the ways in which Sudanese women told their own stories in the swing of their hips and the tucks and folds of their clothes.

(CHAPTER 1)

THE POST OFFICE PEN

The Imperial Mission

In 1907 in a tiny classroom in the small town of Rufaʿa, seventeen young girls were reading and writing nonsense words. They belonged to the initial class of the Rufaʿa Girls' School, a bold experiment to determine if formal education in reading, writing, and arithmetic was appropriate for Sudanese girls. Because the students had no previous knowledge of the written alphabet, their headmaster, Sheikh Babikr Bedri, devised a primer that introduced groups of similar letters and combined them into "words" so that his pupils could practice pronouncing each sound. When the girls had learned just eleven letters, Ernest Dickinson, the governor of the province, paid the school a visit. The young students carefully and proudly recited what they had learned. Luckily for Bedri and his experiment, Dickinson himself knew little of the Arabic alphabet. He wrote in amazement to the Director of Education that after just a few weeks of schooling, the Rufaʿa girls already knew how to read and write![1]

Several forces combined to make this moment possible, not the least of which was the ambition of Sheikh Babikr Bedri, a merchant and veteran of the Mahdi's army. It was opportune that his vision for girls' education matched the imperial mindset of civilizing reform.[2] Invisible behind the high walls of the harem and the folds of their tobes, Sudanese women were thought to be particularly oppressed. Bringing women and girls out of the shadows and educating them in the basics of literacy, arithmetic, and modern domestic habits formed a central pillar of Britain's administration of Sudan. The imperialists were joined in their project by a nascent group of progressive reformers like Bedri, who argued that women's segregation from social and political spheres was detrimental to the strength of modern nations. Although their tactics often diverged, both imperialists and reformers agreed that women and their bodies, hidden or seen, educated or illiterate, healthy or ill-formed, stood as a measure of society's modernity and civility as a whole. Crucially, it was the British imperialists and not the Sudanese who set the standards of visibility, education, and bodily integrity. And, as with Dickinson's unfamiliarity with the basic Arabic lesson, misunderstandings and mistranslations abounded. Nevertheless, the seventeen young girls in Rufaʿa were undeniable evidence that imperial interest in redirecting and redeeming the lives of Sudanese women had begun.

GORDON'S SUDAN

For much of the nineteenth century, Sudan was one of the most distant provinces of the Ottoman Empire. It was administered via the Khedive of Egypt, itself a part of the Ottoman lands. The vast territory was a difficult province to rule; harsh geography and incredible ethnic and linguistic diversity prompted control through force, rather than diplomacy. Government corruption was endemic. In the last decades of the nineteenth century, as Egypt and much of the rest of Ottoman Empire were undergoing an intense period of modernization and social and economic restructuring, Sudan stagnated under heavy taxation and lost livelihoods due to the abolition of the slave trade. An opportunity for change came in 1879, when, after driving his country to bankruptcy, Khedive Ismail of Egypt was deposed in favor of his son, Muhammad Tawfiq. It was as clear to the Sudanese as the Egyptians that young Tawfiq would be no more than a puppet for foreign interests, namely Great Britain and France. With the Egyptian Government weakened and distracted, the time seemed ripe in Sudan for revolt.

In 1881, a noted religious ascetic named Muhammad Ahmed ibn Abdallah proclaimed himself to be "al-Mahdi," the anticipated rightly-guided leader within Islam who was to bring divine justice at the end of days. His message of religious renewal and a return to Islam's true origins was especially appealing to those who suffered economic hardships under Ottoman rule. Religious adherents, boatsmen, slave traders, and soldiers of fortune all united under the Mahdi's promise of an economic and political revival that would be made possible through military conquest and a strict interpretation of Islamic law. Ottoman officials recognized the threat of the Mahdi's philosophy and quickly sent a small force to capture him. They were easily defeated, as were subsequent expeditions dispatched over the next year. The victories of spears and clubs over the firearms and better training of British-led Egyptian troops lent credence to the claim that ibn Abdallah was in fact the expected Mahdi and that a religious revolution was near.

The rapid and unexpected military victories of the Mahdi drew the attention of the British, who had just settled into their offices in Cairo after putting down an Egyptian nationalist uprising in 1881. And though some strategists argued that the Mahdi posed just as much threat to regional stability as the Egyptian nationalists, Great Britain had neither the military resources nor the diplomatic support to deploy a full set of troops to quell what should have been no more than minor tribal skirmishes. Instead, the government in London proffered a small evacuation force under the command of British hero Major-General Charles George Gordon. "Chinese" Gordon had risen to military prominence in the 1860s, when he led Chinese forces in defeating the Taiping Rebellion and distinguished himself as a man who could work his way out of difficult situations. He was also no stranger to Sudan. From 1874 to 1880, in the joint service of the British army and the Egyptian Khedive, Gordon traveled throughout Sudan suppressing local revolts and attempting to halt the lucrative slave trade that shipped captured Africans up the White Nile to Khartoum and then on to Egypt. Although he had resigned from his Sudan post due to exhaustion, in 1884 Gordon answered his government's call to return to the volatile region and avert a potential military crisis.

When Gordon arrived in Sudan in February 1884, he carried two conflicting sets of orders. One, to evacuate the Anglo-Egyptian troops and civilians remaining in Khartoum; and the other, to restore good government—meaning one that would acquiesce to Ottoman control and thus, indirectly, to British interests. By mistake or for reasons known only to him, while on his way to Khartoum Gordon published the set of orders announcing the evacuation. From these documents, it seemed clear to the Mahdi and his supporters that Egypt was ready to abdicate its authority in Sudan. Gordon had lost all diplomatic leverage. Once in Khartoum, the seasoned general surprised onlookers yet again when he refused to abandon the city and dug in for a long siege. Over the next year, Gordon's increasingly desperate entreaties to Cairo and London to send reinforcements and supplies were ignored, refused, and then finally, reluctantly met. When the relief column reached Khartoum on January 28, 1885, they were too late. Just two days earlier, Gordon had been killed and the city had fallen.

The capture of Khartoum and the death of Gordon secured Mahdist control of central riverain Sudan. The Mahdi himself unexpectedly died six months later, leaving an infant son, Sayyid Abd al-Rahman, who would carry his father's religious and political clout into the twentieth century. The Mahdi's immediate successor, Abdallahi ibn Muhammad, worked tirelessly to strengthen the new state and insulate it from Ottoman, Egyptian, or British control. He relocated Sudan's capital from Khartoum to Omdurman and called on all true believers to join him in the Mahdi's chosen city. Khartoum's grandest houses were dismantled and bricks, doors, balconies, windows, and ironworks were shipped eight miles west across the White Nile to Omdurman. There, the new government constructed storehouses, a hospital, a treasury, a soap factory, a prison, and an impressive tomb for their fallen leader.[3] With independence secured, the new state turned to the task of implementing the messianic vision of the Mahdi, but was weakened by political rivalries, a severe famine, and economic downturns. Lacking the charisma of the Mahdi, for the next fifteen years Abdallahi ruled through a combination of religious invectives and fear.

More than building materials flooded into Omdurman. Tens of thousands heeded Abdallahi's call to come to the new capital, abandoning their tribal homelands for life in the city for the first time. Omdurman's population exploded to at least a quarter of a million people, three-quarters of whom were women.[4] Wives followed their soldiering husbands to the city, widows sought compensation or new husbands, and still other women labored as camp followers, providing domestic comforts to married and unmarried men. Large numbers of female slaves were also imported to provide sexual services or be traded as political bargaining chips. The sheer number of women upset economic and power relations. Masters who had once profited from the earnings of their female slaves in market stalls and *merissa* (beer) shops now faced a rapidly dwindling market share. Many forced their slaves to seek their own means of shelter and income. And though slave women were expected to remit a portion of their earnings to their masters, a good number took advantage of the economic crisis to distance themselves from their masters' control.[5]

The challenge of governing this diverse, newly urban population was one of the lasting legacies of the Mahdist period. The Mahdi's conquest of Sudan had been a cultural as well as military campaign. As the herald of the end of days, the Mahdi's religious directive was to guide his followers, known as the Ansar, away from the sinful tendencies that had corrupted the population. He issued emergency laws prohibiting long-standing practices such as the sale and use of wine and tobacco and loud, excessive mourning for the dead. A further set of laws addressed women's public appearance and behavior. Women were to cover their heads and bodies, and anyone who went about bareheaded was subject to being beaten. Women were also forbidden from entering the marketplace or looking after their cattle herds alongside men. Similarly, a man who was found speaking to a woman who was not his relative was punished with two months of fasting and one hundred lashes.[6] The heavily female, overgrown city of Omdurman presented its own problems. A special corner of the marketplace, prohibited to men, was reserved for women traders and women-specific products. War widows also had to be provided for. In his lifetime, the Mahdi had prohibited excessive bride-prices and instructed the Ansar to marry the Islamic legal limit of four wives. Abdallahi continued to enforce these directives, so much so that one observer noted that Omdurman was "continuously occupied in marriage ceremonies."[7] Historian P. M. Holt explains that the severity of these social rules "should not be dismissed as mere blind conservatism."[8] Years of violence had uprooted the existing social order. Strict guidelines governing behavior and the relationships between men and women were necessary to maintain control over the disparate populations that formed the Mahdist state.

Fostering a sense of unity was critical for the Mahdist narrative of redemption. The Mahdi discouraged the use of foreign imports and forbade the Ansar from dressing like the "infidel Turks." To demonstrate their allegiance and communal identity, men chose a new type of dress, consisting of a turban, knee-length cotton pants, and a variation of the local *jallabiyya* (robe) known as the *jibba*. The jibba had wide sleeves, pockets, and a neck scooped on both sides so that it could be worn back to front.[9] Its most notable feature was the colorful patches sewn onto the garment, which were meant to represent a life of humbleness and poverty as espoused by the Mahdi. Notably, women's tobes, though almost always an imported product, did not fall under the Mahdi's edict against foreign goods. After a century of consistent use among the upper classes, the tobe had gained an air of local authenticity in spite of its foreign origins. More practically, as religious fervor increased under the Mahdi, the tobe aptly satisfied women's need for chaste clothing. Together, strict legislation and changing forms of dress cemented a new identity characterized by a conservative, participatory version of Islam and resistance to foreign intervention. Faith and belonging were not simply spoken of, but acted upon. Thus, though relatively brief, the nearly two decades of Mahdist rule established a common set of values and behaviors that formed a cultural baseline for northern Sudanese nationalists generations later.

Back in England, the tragic death of General Charles Gordon brought a personal *raison d'être* to Britain's continued involvement in Sudan that was unparalleled in other parts of the empire. Popular opinion held that Sudan was to be reclaimed and redeemed for Gordon, not because of its geographic positioning or economic resources, but for its as yet unrealized potential of which only their fallen hero seemed fully aware. But it would be fourteen more years before Great Britain reentered Sudan, this time as part of the larger European "Scramble for Africa." In the spring of 1896, Great Britain, France, Belgium, and Germany were jockeying for control of the Upper Nile basin in central Africa. When Italian forces were defeated by the Abyssinian king, Sir Herbert Kitchener moved his troop of Anglo-Egyptian forces south from Egypt into northern Sudan. The intent was to offer indirect support to the Italians while also asserting British authority in the region. An astute tactician, Kitchener constructed a system of railroads that allowed him to rapidly move and resupply his soldiers across the inhospitable desert. This time, the Mahdist forces were no match for the Anglo-Egyptian troops. The Ansar were weakened by starvation and infighting among their commanders. Towns and outposts systematically fell. Over the course of two years, what had begun as a feint or series of maneuvers transformed into a concentrated campaign to win back Sudan.

The battle that claimed Sudan for England began on the morning of September 2, 1898, and was over by that afternoon. On the plains outside of Omdurman, eleven thousand Mahdist soldiers were killed; the number of wounded cannot be estimated. In painful contrast, the Anglo-Egyptian forces lost only 48 men, with another 352 wounded. On September 4, a flag-raising ceremony hoisted the Union Jack and, a carefully measured instant later, the Egyptian flag above the ruined governor's palace in Khartoum. The ceremony ended with a eulogy to General Gordon as a Roman Catholic priest entreated God to "look down ... with eyes of pity and compassion on this land so loved by that heroic soul."[10] Anglo-Egyptian rule in Sudan had begun.

We have no direct evidence of how Sudanese women responded to the Anglo-Egyptian conquest, but they almost certainly felt fear and profound loss. The violence was not confined to the battlefield. Three days of looting followed the loss at Omdurman. Sheikh Babikr Bedri, who would go on to open the girls' school at Rufa'a, reported that Anglo-Egyptian soldiers "entered our homes and took and ate everything within reach of their eyes and hands."[11] The town's residents broke into the grain stores. Remaining able-bodied Mahdist soldiers were impressed into labor gangs. Most infamously,

Kitchener's troops destroyed the Mahdi's tomb and threw his body into the Nile. Taking advantage of the chaos, slaves fled their owners or in some cases killed them. Bedri wrote, "On the day after the fall of Omdurman we saw corpses lying in al-Hijra street, and no one knew who they were or who had killed them."[12] Women of Khartoum and Omdurman were witness and victim to violence and looting. And in the aftermath of the conquest it is likely that they were far more concerned with protecting and providing for their families than with the persons and politics of the new foreign government.

Just five days after the ceremony at the governor's palace, news reached Omdurman that shots had been exchanged between English and French troops at Fashoda, a small town in southern Sudan. The town itself was of little importance, but France's control of the territory would thwart British plans for north-south dominance in Africa, from "Cape Town to Cairo." Kitchener, newly installed as Governor-General of Sudan, quickly sailed south to secure British interests in Sudan and, more generally, Africa. Kitchener was a man of action, better suited for the battlefield than administration. Thus, his governing role was short-lived. But as for the hundreds of British men and women who came in Kitchener's wake, like their hero Gordon who had refused to abandon Khartoum fifteen years earlier, once in Sudan, they clung on with a sentimental ferocity.

AN IMPERIAL ADVENTURE

The acquisition of nearly a million square miles of Sudanese territory raised a host of legal and political difficulties for the British Government. Although Sudan was conquered in the name of the Khedive of Egypt (who himself was under the *de jure* but not *de facto* authority of the Ottoman sultan), the campaign had been won with British finances and military acumen. Thus the government in London would not allow "Gordon's Sudan" to revert to solely Egyptian control. At the same time, neither Egypt nor France nor Belgium would allow for Sudan to become an outright British colony. In Cairo, British Counsel-General Lord Cromer proposed the creation of a new political entity: a condominium in which both Egypt and

Great Britain would hold co-dominion status. In 1899, the Anglo-Egyptian Agreement for the Administration of the Sudan established joint governance between the two states. Because Sudan was not to be a formal colony, the rather murky directive for these two powers was to oversee a period of political tutelage until such time as it was determined that the Sudanese were capable of self-rule.

It is noteworthy that in both British and Sudanese rhetoric the establishment of the Condominium was perceived as something of a second act rather than a new beginning. The British recalled their role in governing Sudan alongside Ottoman troops at the beginning of the nineteenth century and spoke of "reconquering" Sudan after it had been temporarily lost to the Mahdi. Likewise, many Sudanese labeled the onset of Anglo-Egyptian rule as the "Second Turkiyya," a new chapter of foreign rule first begun by the Ottoman Empire. Yet it was soon clear that this second period of occupation would be quite different than the first.

Even before the Anglo-Egyptian Agreement was signed, there were questions of its legality. Tellingly, sovereignty was not directly mentioned anywhere in the document. The British claim to the occupation and development of Sudan was based on the right of conquest. Egyptian sovereignty was ignored altogether; and there was no mention of the Ottoman sultan, who had a legal claim to the territories of both Egypt and Sudan. The term *condominium*, and the joint governance it implied, was a misnomer. The Governor-General of Sudan, the country's supreme military and civil commander, was to be an official of Egypt, appointed by Khedival decree— but only on the recommendation of the British Government. Thus it was the powers in London, rather than Cairo, that held real authority over the administration of Sudan. Egypt's role was confined to supplying middle managers and, most importantly, finances. Further legal nuances separated Sudan from the rest of the British Empire. Because Sudan was not a colony, its administrators reported to the Foreign, rather than Colonial, Office. With this bureaucratic sleight of hand, the British Government was able to assure critics that its purpose in Sudan was altruistic and not imperial. The imbalance of *de facto* power appeared unsustainable even to those who had proposed the guidelines for dual control. Cromer wrote, "Should it [the Condominium] eventually die and make place for some more robust, because more real, political creation, its authors need not bewail its fate."[13] Instead, the ungainly Condominium remained in place for the next fifty years.

The men charged with administering the empire's newest territory were an elite, athletic, and spirited group especially well suited to the geographic and diplomatic challenges of the region. Lord Cromer hoped the Sudan Political Service (SPS) men might be "endowed with good health, high character . . . not the mediocre by-products of the race, but the flower of those who are turned out from our schools and colleges."[14] These idealized guidelines resulted in a class of servicemen with nearly identical academic and social backgrounds. Of the nearly four hundred men who joined the SPS between 1899 and 1956, 285 graduated from either Oxford or Cambridge with honors.[15] Academics were to be complemented by athleticism. A common joke stated that Sudan was "a land of blacks ruled by Blues," a reference to the Oxford or Cambridge distinction of "Blue" given to those who had represented their school in the annual sporting matches between the two universities. In fact, it was no secret that physical hardiness was prized by the Sudan Government, as it was generally understood that athleticism inclined a new recruit to sports and game-hunting, which made the long lonely treks of the Assistant District Commissioner easier to bear.[16]

Even with these high standards, a thread of informality and camaraderie ran through the SPS. Unlike the Indian Civil Service, the most selective branch of the civil service, there was no written examination for employment in Sudan. The recruitment of Sir Harold MacMichael (who went on to hold the highly respected post of Civil Secretary) is comical but not uncommon. Having received a gift of a brass seal from a friend in Delhi, MacMichael sought out orientalist professor E. G. Browne to decipher the seal's inscription. Professor Browne greeted MacMichael with a *non sequitur*, asking "Have you come about the Egypt and Sudan Civil Service?" After an hour of talking about the East, young MacMichael decided to apply. And, in spite of having seen a picture of an imposing sandstorm, chose to be posted to Sudan.[17] Collegial interviews combined with good pay and excellent leave (ninety days, beginning only once one had exited the country) to make service in Sudan very attractive to ambitious young men looking for excitement and adventure.

It was adventure tempered with a sense of purpose. Almost to a man from country families, SPS officers "were imbued from birth with a sense of the duties, responsibilities, and privileges of the gentry. The devotion to duty, the love of the out-of-doors, the paternal feelings of responsibility toward the lower classes within the village community, and even the enthusiasm for village cricket shaped those attitudes of mind and created that confidence to rule."[18] Dutch satirical author Odette Keun echoed these sentiments. Writing that although she generally considered British men abroad to be rowdy and obnoxious and "thank[ed] the Lord God of Nations" that she was not one of them, upon visiting Sudan she found "this same vacuous, noisy, deadly dull, inconsiderate English graduate is governing men . . . [and] has to become one of an order of Samurai."[19]

Both portraits are overly flattering. The privilege of the white Englishman easily and often slipped into entitlement and prejudice. And yet with their shared middle-class, paternal background, many of the SPS believed that they were embarking on something quite different and worthwhile. In a survey of former Political Service officers, John Phillips, who was married to none other than Charles Gordon's niece, explained, "The nature of my mission (when I thought about it amid all the new and exciting distractions of the journey) I envisioned as combining the pleasure of meeting the physical and mental challenge posed by the Sudan and its climate . . . with the opportunity of carrying on what others had begun, in bringing orderly administration and a better life for peoples whom I believed to need more of both." Another respondent was even more ardent in his claims of exceptionalism: "Before answering any questions, I would point out that the word 'colonialism' is incorrectly used in connection with the Sudan. . . . The whole object of British recruitment to the Sudan Government was to lead the country to independence. . . . The words 'colony' and 'colonial', as defined by the Oxford English Dictionary, do not apply to the Sudan and I don't think they should be used." Even a number of Sudanese viewed

British rule as a project that focused on guidance, rather than submission. One southerner noted, "When they [the British] tie your hands, they tie you with silk, not with iron chains."[20]

Regardless of these romantic colorings, the British conquest of Sudan was part of an imperial program. The territory was held to secure British interests in Egypt and the Suez Canal and as a bulwark against French encroachment across the rest of Africa. Local subsistence farming was overturned in favor of large-scale cotton crop production to supply Lancashire mills. And imported cultural standards of Victorian morality and civility were used as measures of whether Sudan was politically ready for modern statehood. Most critically, the intentionally divisive policies employed by British administrators in northern and southern Sudan laid the groundwork for fifty years of civil war after the country's independence and the eventual secession of South Sudan in 2011. For the historian, there is no question that Sudan was a subjugated territory (if not a legal colony) in the British Empire. Nevertheless, Britons' belief that they governed with ties of silk and not chains granted a strong sense of mission to their imperial adventure.

WHY DON'T YOU BRING OUT YOUR WIVES?

The scene that greeted these adventurers was not promising. An 1884 British intelligence report described the "very mixed character" of Khartoum's people and neighborhoods. At the center of town stood a mosque and marketplace with coffee houses and brandy shops. A Coptic school, barracks, and hospital were nearby. The main east-west street boasted the governor's residence, offices, and large mansions. Aside from these, the majority of the homes were "of a miserable description, consisting of sun-dried clay, cemented with cow-dung and slime."[21] Under Mahdist rule, whatever quality structures Khartoum had possessed were disassembled for the new construction in Omdurman. Reflecting on the decline of the old capital, long-serving SPS man Edwin Sarsfield-Hall wrote, "Thus did the old Khartoum pass out of existence with its stenches and its unsavory reputation for vice and ill-health. . . . Now it was to lie abandoned forlorn and in ruins for 12 long years until its destructors were themselves destroyed."[22] Khartoum's empty ruins contrasted with the crowds of the Mahdist capital. War correspondent G. W. Steevens described Omdurman as a "rabbit-warren," filled with houses "too flimsy for the name of sheds" and throngs of people who "tumbled over each other like ants." As he saw it, "oppression, stagnation, degradation, were stamped on every yard of miserable Omdurman."[23]

The conquerors reestablished Khartoum as Sudan's economic and political center, but raised concerns about whether the city was fit for European habitation. Even the War Office was reluctant to keep British troops in Khartoum for any length of time outside the milder months of December through March. Posting soldiers for longer periods would result in diminished health and efficiency and a "considerable loss of life." In no uncertain terms, the War Office warned, "All the ground about Omdurman and Khartoum has been fouled by the bestial habits of a filthy race, and so sure as we put Europeans there, so sure will they contract and die of fever." It seemed that Sudan itself might prove more deadly than the Mahdist soldiers. It was Lord Cromer, eager to settle the question of Sudan's administration, who put an end to these loud protests. He reasoned that Egyptian forces were already stationed in Sudan and the only question that remained was whether "our flag would be supported by British troops."[24] The troops stayed on.

Sudanese women appeared no better under the imperialist gaze. A far cry from imagined harem beauties of the Arab world or the exotic women of the African jungles, early glimpses of northern women fell far short of imperial expectations. One administrator warned that all Sudanese women were potential prostitutes.[25] Another countered that women of certain tribes were too "dirty" and "shy" to pose much of a sexual threat.[26] Odette Keun, put off by the racial mixing and relative undress she perceived in Sudanese women, reported, "I do not know what ethnologists make of the various strains of this population, but one thing is certain: the blend has produced an appallingly ugly type.... The men are clothed, and the women enwrapped in stuffs from their waist downward, but their bust is ordinarily exposed, and never in my life did I see such unredeemably hideous breasts."[27] Steevens devoted an entire paragraph to the variety of women he saw in Omdurman: "Black women from Equatoria and almost white

women from Egypt, plum-skinned Arabs and a strange yellow type with
square bony faces and tightly-ringleted black hair; . . . the whole city was
a huge harem, a museum of African races, a monstrosity of African lust."[28]

It is hard to know how to interpret these highly prejudicial descriptions
of Sudan and its people. M. W. Daly suggests that Britons exaggerated
the negative qualities of the country so as to underscore the benevolence
of their roles as reformers rather than conquerors.[29] This is certainly plau-
sible. There is also no denying that recent events had left visible scars on
the two cities. Khartoum was dismantled and abandoned. Omdurman, in
turn, overgrown with migrants and recovering from famine, was now home
to thousands of war widows and wounded veterans. But the foulness that
imperialists observed does not have to be taken literally. Dirt is metaphorical as well as physical. It should be understood as a "situational, rather than
substantive, category" that defines one's relationship to existing social and
political order.[30] Viewed this way, filth, pollution, and ugliness served as
rhetorical shorthands for difference.

In imperial contexts, women's bodies carried the burden of perceived
dirt and deviance; and Sudan was no exception. Brown skin, unfamiliar hair
styles, and immodest dress demarcated the boundary between Europeans
and natives, Self and Other, civilized and uncivilized. For women especially,
dirt was elided with sexual impropriety to give a doubled sense of impurity.
What early administrators may not have realized, however, is that they were
seeing only a particular portion of Sudan's female population. Like its Middle Eastern neighbors, northern Sudan adhered to a strict harem culture
within its middle and upper classes. Adult women and girls past the age of
puberty stayed shielded in their homes, only venturing out for visits to family and neighbors or community events. In contrast, the women who were
regularly seen in public worked for a living: selling goods in the market,
brewing tea or beer, or serving in foreign or upper-class Sudanese homes.

The two classes of women were easily distinguished by the color and
quality of their clothes. Middle- and upper-class women wore white tobes,
a rectangular garment that wrapped twice around a woman's body, draped
over her head, and crossed again over her chest before coming to rest on her

left shoulder. For those desiring more modesty, the lower half of a woman's face could also be covered by pulling the last piece across the mouth and tucking the corner into the folds around the head. With no ties or fastenings, this complex system of wrapping was "particularly difficult for the uninitiated to manage" and was therefore best suited for the sedate, minimal movements of the elite.[31] These shrouded women, however, were hidden from imperialists' eyes. In contrast, laboring women in public view wore simpler, less voluminous tobes of roughspun cotton, dyed indigo blue or black. Their means of wrapping was far less elaborate, leaving more of their bodies exposed and their hands free to work. An SPS man's first encounters would have been with these working women in blue, those who were most vulnerable to the ravages of war and the upset of imperialism. Therefore, the profuse descriptions of filthy streets and wretched bodies say less about the actual conditions in Sudan and more about the sense of utter foreignness and displacement that Britons experienced upon arrival.

The stark gender imbalance of the imperial administration further contributed to the misrepresentations of Sudanese women. It was a man's world for the first decades of the Condominium. Sudan was considered a hardship post, which accounted for the generous leave and pay, but that meant it was not a suitable place for British women. The harsh climate, relative isolation, and spartan living quarters were manageable, and perhaps even appealing, for an ambitious young man, but the lack of roads, medical facilities, and other reliable infrastructure made the country much too dangerous for the fairer sex. In those early years, no Sudan Political Service member was allowed to marry or bring his wife to Sudan until he had reached twenty-eight years of age or completed four years of service. After WWI, the restrictions were lowered to two years of service or twenty-seven years of age.[32] Still, it was not until the late 1930s, when hospitals were established and transportation improved, that significant numbers wives and children traveled out to Sudan, and then for only the mildest months of the year.[33]

Tellingly, when British women began to spend considerable amounts of time in country, descriptions of Sudanese women changed dramatically. This was partially due to the fact that by the 1930s a small but growing number

of Sudanese women and girls benefited from imperial education programs.
Even more important, British and Sudanese women forged relationships in
the intimate domains of domesticity and caregiving that were inaccessible
to male civil servants. Elizabeth Blackley recalled the headmistress of a
local school as a "gentle beauty . . . [who] kept perfect discipline and maintained a high standard of education."[34] Evelyn Simpson described Gameila,
the longtime nanny for her children, as "completely uneducated and very
black, nevertheless she was spotlessly clean and utterly loyal."[35] And trained
nurse Peggy Vidler admired the skills of nurses in Omdurman, who were
especially adept at taking blood samples with a syringe, which even the
nurses in London's St. Bartholomew's Hospital were not yet trained to do.[36]
Even the most unsavory characters could be redeemed through sewing and
friendship. Mary Oakley carried fond memories of teaching knitting and
sewing to the female inmates in the Khartoum North Prison. "My final
farewell to them in the prison was a very weepy occasion. The Wardenesses
[*sic*] wept, I wept, the eight prisoners all wept too. I think I should have
a place in the Guinness book of records as the only person who has been
kissed by eight murderesses in one afternoon."[37]

Nurses, nannies, and murderesses aside, the still-limited number of
English women and the seclusion of Sudanese women made it difficult
for their male counterparts to forge personal relationships. Cross-cultural
visits to one another's houses were rife with potential *faux pas* and etiquette
missteps. Administrators dreaded the interminable thirteen-course meals
(evocative of the "English Regency Period") served in upper-class Sudanese homes.[38] When it was their turn to host, Britons decided that tea was
the most appropriate meal so that their guests did not have to struggle
with a knife and fork. Yet, even an afternoon tea could be imposing. One
Sudanese civil servant recalled his host trying to put him at ease by saying, "'Come in your shorts.' . . . At the time we thought it was just a way
to order us about. . . . We resented it. . . . One or two people used to go in
pairs of trousers, just to establish their personalities!"[39] The suggestion to
"come in your shorts" was intended to convey the informality and friendly
atmosphere of the gathering. And yet Sudanese men well understood that

to show up in short pants while their British superiors wore long trousers would only further underscore the divide between them. The personality displayed by Sudanese men who wore trousers was not about originality in fashion but a demonstration of independence and an insistence on equal treatment. Women, British or Sudanese, should have been the social lubricant to soothe such situations. But without their presence and hospitable interventions, men were at a loss as to how to relate to one another outside of official spaces.

Yet the presence of a woman was not always enough to bridge cultural distances. In 1933, a wealthy Sudanese merchant who had managed to form a close relationship with a government official asked why the British had not "brought your wives out to this country since the war [WWI]?" The official, confused, remarked that the merchant had been invited to tea at his house the previous week. The man replied, "And nobody could possibly ask for a more charming hostess. . . . But we know what an Englishman's wife looks like. She wears a blouse up to there and she wears a skirt down to there. Not one of them has been out here since 1914."[40] The merchant had mistaken the fashionable shorter skirts of the 1930s as the mark of an English mistress rather than a respectable wife. The amiable relationship between the two men that permitted such blunt questions no doubt allowed the moment to pass with good humor. But in other circumstances, such a misreading might have proved disastrous.

The point to be made here is not a restatement of the cultural divide between colonizer and colonized, but the ways in which the presence or absence of bodies signaled and shaped imperial rule. Rising hemlines and Sudanese men in shorts were not marginal curiosities, but vital markers of class, status, and identity that defined imperial relationships.

Paul Landau provocatively argues that the bodies of colonizer and colonized were in much closer contact than is usually admitted. He writes, "The 'boy' who removed the mistress's nightsoil had to be trusted in quite another way" than the rest of the colonized population.[41] Admitted into one of the most private parts of the home, the "boy"—who was often, in fact, a man—would know as much about his employer's health and well-being as she herself did, and probably more than her husband. The limitations of basic plumbing and the dependence on a servant's discretion reveal the precariousness of imperial rule. In Sudan, small wooden outhouses were attached to Europeans' homes. A "bucket man" traveled from house to house, removing and replacing filled latrine buckets through a hinged flap on the back of the outhouse. This unsavory task was not always kept out of sight. One SPS wife remembers, "Once when we were out to dinner and in the middle of our meal a bucket man marched straight through the dining room. I have never forgotten my utter amazement. Apparently there was no other way to the loo."[42] Bodily intimacy was an (often unspeakable) imperial reality. But exposed bodies are vulnerable bodies. And Britons turned a blind eye to the visibility of their own intimacies in precisely the same way that they ignored the bucket man who marched through the dining room.

In sharp contrast, the relative invisibility of upper-class Sudanese women's bodies caused a great deal of anxiety and, as result, shaped a great deal of imperial policy. As one officer reflected, "An Englishman in those days simply couldn't be taken into the heart of a Sudanese family, in the sense that he simply couldn't reach the stage at which he could ever meet the womenfolk."[43] The inaccessibility of the harem, and the secrecy it seemed to imply, convinced British administrators that they could never fully know the people they ruled. One further cultural point created a seemingly unbridgeable divide between the British and Sudanese: the ritual of female genital cutting. Technically known as infibulation, the practice consisted of cutting a woman's external genitalia (labia major, minor, and clitoris) and stitching it closed. Upon learning of the custom, Britons recoiled. One recalled, "The barbaric practice of female circumcision was always an insurmountable barrier to full social relations between British and Sudanese families throughout my whole service of twenty-six years in the Sudan."[44] Sudanese women's bodies were absent, but vividly imagined. And their most intimate scars became the measure of the distance between colonizer and colonized. Though couched in sympathetic terms, getting "to the heart" of the Sudanese was not about forming friendships. Imperialists' aim was to implement civilizing policies that would put an end to such oppressive and barbaric traditions. To reach women behind the harem walls would be to transform Sudan itself from the inside out.

THE RUFA'A EXPERIMENT

Administrators believed that a formal, European-style education was the first step in reforming, or getting to the heart, of Sudanese men and women. On the heels of his victory at Omdurman, Kitchener proposed a "Gordon Memorial College" for the city of Khartoum. In a grand act of civilizing showmanship, he quickly raised over £100,000 in a fund-raising drive across Great Britain. On January 3, 1899, just four months after the Anglo-Egyptian conquest and when construction on the college had barely begun, Kitchener informed local workers that Lord Cromer would be arriving in two days to inspect the building site. Trenches were dug at a record pace, Lord Cromer duly laid the cornerstone, and the ceremonial trowel was sent to Queen Victoria. A few days later, under the cover of darkness, the cornerstone was removed so that it could be repositioned once the building foundations had been properly sighted and planed.[45]

Despite the rush to found an institution in Gordon's name, uncertainty over the ultimate purpose of government-sponsored education reduced the transformative potential of the project. Prior to the Condominium, Sudanese boys and even a small number of girls attended *khalwas*, informal religious schools that taught reading, math, and the Quran through rote memorization. But khalwa graduates were ill-equipped to carry out the administrative duties of the new government. In need of a corps of low-level civil servants, Sir James Currie, the first Director of Education, proposed establishing two or three primary schools to prepare Sudanese boys for Gordon College and eventual government work. The schools' curriculum was narrow and targeted, asking that its graduates "understand the merest elements of the machinery of government." This was an intentionally conservative plan. Currie argued that given the poverty of the country, it would be imprudent to devote financial resources to any school that was not directly connected to the well-being of Sudan's administration and economy.

As a result, the remainder of the government's educational energies was aimed at *kuttab*s, vernacular elementary-level schools, which provided no more than a basic education in the "Three Rs" and religion.[46]

Thus the imperial curriculum was awash in contradictions. The comically rapid founding of Gordon Memorial College seemed to suggest that the Sudan Government, with the support of Britons back home, intended to educate Sudanese men at the very highest level. In practice, the limited construction of primary schools demonstrates administrators' reluctance to introduce a new educational system. As in other parts of the empire, many believed advanced education to be an expensive, and potentially incendiary, tool best left in the hands of a privileged few. From 1900 to 1920, only a handful of boys were groomed to be sublevel native administrators. The first primary school opened in Omdurman in 1900, and a year later another was established in Khartoum. In 1903, 600 boys were enrolled in primary schools; but by 1914 the number of students had only risen to 783. In keeping with Currie's plan, the Anglo-Egyptian administration purposely kept enrollment low and sought to educate no more boys than the government needed.[47]

The possibility of girls' education similarly fell victim to the practicalities of early imperial rule. Activist and educator Haga Kashif Badri is at her most ardent when speaking of the failure to provide opportunities for girls' education. She writes, "The British administrators tried their worst to obstruct the establishment of the first formal school for women. The policy was that delay in female education would mean the perpetuation of backwardness and prolongation of colonial rule."[48] Haga Kashif is right to note the link between women's low status and continued foreign intervention; however, she misinterprets British hesitancy to establish girls' schools as a conscious policy to maintain imperial control. There were clear practical concerns: building schoolhouses and locating and paying qualified female teachers would require no small expense. More significantly, residual political unrest gave even the most progressive administrators pause in proposing any reforms or programs that might upset existing social norms. Having just defeated the Mahdi and his heterodox form of Islam, and still fearful of a possible insurgency led by his son, the Sudan Government was eager to appease and ally itself with the country's conservative, orthodox Muslim clerics. A tacit gentlemen's agreement maintained that Sudan's local leaders would tolerate Anglo-Egyptian rule as long as the administration did not interfere with personal status (family) laws and left questions of religion alone. This uncharacteristic "hands-off" policy also extended to most aspects of women's culture and traditions. To push for girls' education seemed certain to invite criticism and perhaps even prompt a rebellion. Lacking funds and fearing political instability, the Sudan Government left the question of girls' education for another day.

Other organizations, spurred by a higher sense of purpose, did take on the risk of establishing schools for girls. International missionary organizations had followed Kitchener to Sudan in 1898 and were eager to begin working with local populations. Again due to the agreement that left issues of personal status and religion in the hands of the Sudanese, missionaries were not permitted to actively evangelize in northern Sudan.[49] However, they could provide social services. As part of this initiative, in 1900 the Catholic Verona Father's Mission opened two girls' schools, St. Anne's School and St. Joseph's School, in Khartoum and Omdurman, respectively. Enrollment was limited, and after four years the two schools had just over four hundred pupils combined. In 1903, the Anglican Church Missionary Society took over a failing Coptic school to open its own school for girls. The school took off quickly. After a year it had eighty girls enrolled, and in 1905 the school purchased an acre of land for further expansion. Across the river in Khartoum North, the American Presbyterian Mission established its own school in 1908; unlike its peers, it took in boarders and orphans with special needs. Theological differences notwithstanding, the curricula of the four schools were very similar and centered on reading and writing (in Arabic and English), needlework and embroidery, and Christian Scripture. A special "conscience clause" permitted Muslim girls to excuse themselves from religious lessons if they chose to.

The very existence of the conscience clause is evidence of the distance between the missionaries and the Sudanese populations they hoped to minister to. Missionaries could provide services, but they could not preach.

Young girls would learn domestic skills, but they would not hear the words of salvation. In fact, the majority of girls attending the mission schools were not Sudanese but Syrian, Egyptian, Abyssinian, Armenian, and European: daughters of businessmen and merchants who had come to Sudan for work.[50] Given the foreign, Christian foundations of these schools, it is perhaps surprising that any Sudanese girls enrolled at all. Those who did came from upper-class families, often with their own international ties. Thus, despite a healthy collection of schools in the capital region, missionaries across denominations failed in their attempts to reach a wide number of Sudanese girls. Instead, those who benefited from a missionary education were, by and large, elite outsiders.

It fell to an enterprising Sudanese man with thirteen daughters of his own to establish an educational program specifically for Sudanese girls. A veteran of the Mahdist Army and a merchant who had run into hard times, in 1903 Sheikh Babikr Bedri accepted the position of headmaster for a government-run boys' primary school in the village of Rufa'a, southeast of Khartoum along the Blue Nile. Though an educated man, Bedri was not trained in formal methods of teaching. Only a few days before he was to open the school, Bedri traveled to Khartoum to observe a government classroom in progress. There, his first lesson was identifying the blackboard and learning "what in Heaven's name it was for." He proved a quick study. Driven by passion and his own sense of mission, Bedri memorized calisthenics drills, taught himself exponents and square roots, and constructed a globe for his students out of a hollowed pumpkin.[51] A year later, Bedri began to petition the Anglo-Egyptian Government for permission and funds to open a school for Sudanese girls. He wrote, "I have eleven daughters at home at the right age for education. . . . Give me £10 and I'll build a classroom and open a girls' school. If it goes well it can continue in it; and if not, it can be a room for the [boys'] school watchman."[52]

More than the sheer number of his daughters inspired Bedri. In his memoirs he describes the value of a "modern education which would enable a girl to run her home in such a way as to attract educated young men of her own race, from among her relatives or fellow citizens." A man ahead of his time, Bedri recognized that the education of Sudanese boys and girls were complementary processes. Without a pool of eligible women, Bedri warned, the rising class of Sudanese intelligentsia would seek out foreign wives and, in effect, "bring to nought our efforts to educate them [Sudanese men]."[53] As he saw it, an educated man required an educated wife to ensure the social uplift of his family and community. Decades later, nationalists would repeat this same logic and argue that the education and progress of Sudanese women was integral to the strength and progress of the Sudanese state.

After two years of firm denials, James Currie granted Babikr Bedri permission to open a girls' school, on the condition that he use his own personal funds for construction, supplies, and salaries. Despite giving his blessing, Currie, along with many other officials, worried that the very concept of girls' education would be poorly received. Bedri assured them, "I'm a local man and I know my home town. . . . I have influence with the local people of my own town and I have their confidence."[54] A popular figure with plenty of local clout, Bedri was allowed to break the gentlemen's agreement of noninterference in matters of society and culture that imperial administrators could not. In 1907, the initial class opened with seventeen girls: nine from Bedri's own family and the rest from the leading families of Rufa'a.

Bedri's first and biggest challenge was locating an appropriate female teacher. It was more than a matter of academics; foremost in Bedri's mind was the need to find an instructor of unimpeachable character. He writes, "I set myself to find a woman skilled in embroidery, dressmaking and needlework. She must also be a citizen of Rufa'a for two reasons: first, because she would need less salary and second, because she would be an advertisement for the school . . . because local people would be aware of her good moral character and not make accusations against her."[55] Even with the confidence of his neighbors, Bedri could not afford to completely ignore Sudanese values. Far more than the content of the courses, the success of this very first girls' school rested on finding an instructor whose unimpeachable character would lend credence to the entire venture. Bedri's conscientiousness was rewarded. Attention to social mores, hard work, and good results won over most detractors, and the school proved a success.

Impressed and emboldened by Bedri's accomplishments, in 1911 the Sudan Government took over the Rufa'a school and opened the first state-run primary school for girls. The protests and revolts that administrators feared never materialized. Even so, growth was slow. Over the next decade, four more primary schools opened in the towns of Kamlin, Merowe, Dongola, and El Obeid. Notably during those years, no government schools for girls were established in the far more populous capital region, where missionary schools still provided limited instruction.

As Bedri had predicted, many Sudanese viewed girls' education as an asset in a world that was slowly, but surely, modernizing. Young women with just a few months of schooling became the most eligible matches on the marriage market. This enthusiasm prevailed even in rural areas where newly established "needlework homes," run by Egyptian or Syrian women, taught sewing and embroidery along with cooking, Arabic, and arithmetic. Like their urban peers, girls educated at the needlework homes were considered highly desirable wives, and many were married before completing their coursework. In light of this, needlework homes provided lessons on wedding rites. Upon the occasion of her marriage, a Sudanese bride performed the "pigeon dance," so called because, with arms straight at her sides and chest and buttocks arched out, the bride takes mincing steps much like a pigeon. Traditionally, married friends and relatives had taught her this special dance, but now, needlework homes took on the task of dance instruction as part of their curriculum. For these young women on the verge of adulthood, home economics and arithmetic were just as integral to their preparations for marriage as learning the steps of the pigeon dance. New lessons in reading and writing combined with traditional domestic skills to create a composite idealized type. She would embody the best of old and new and perform the pigeon dance with the same precision as she calculated sums. Sudanese fathers well understood the value of the doubled curriculum: they paid for their daughters' lessons in gold.[56]

Although the first experiment in girls' education proved successful, it would be another generation at least before Sudanese women would write and record their experiences with imperialism. This did not mean, however, that women were uninformed or uninterested in the workings of empire. In truth, women were keen and regular commentators on the changes brought by Anglo-Egyptian rule. They expressed themselves not on the page, but through their everyday form of dress: the tobe.

The tobe was introduced to Sudan in the late eighteenth century. By the twentieth century, each new style of tobe was differentiated by a name that ranged from a basic label identifying the origin of the cloth to a fanciful marketing gimmick. The lowly damuriyya tobes were made of locally manufactured roughspun cloth and named for al-Damer, a town in the northeast. The "Bengali," a midquality tobe edged with a blue stripe and favored by midwives and teachers, was imported from Bengal. At the other end of the spectrum, the "Tootal" tobe was a general term used for the highest-quality tobes manufactured by the Manchester company Tootal, Broadhurst, and Lee. In addition to these standard styles, creative and humorous names highlighted the novelty and desirability of new tobes. A fashionable 1915 tobe named "Son of the Steel Blade" does not sound luxurious, but brides reportedly "sulked" if they did not receive it as a gift from their soon-to-be husbands.[57]

There was no standardized or universal practice for naming tobes. Tobe fabrics arrived in Sudan on large bolts, bearing no more than the label of the manufacturer. It was up to local merchants to carefully consider what name to give each new batch of garments. Monikers that referenced contemporary issues or themes let a woman know that her chosen tobe was the very latest in fashion. Once named, new tobe styles were popularized orally, spreading from peer to peer via word of mouth. More formally, specially composed love songs and tunes sung at weddings to praise the bride also advertised new styles.[58] Merchants hoped that women who attended a wedding or heard a tobe described in a romantic ballad would then seek out the new fashion for their own. Identifying fresh styles took a keen eye. While poor and working-class women dressed in tobes dyed a dull indigo or black, the highest-quality garments were dazzling white. This means that the stylistic shifts that accompanied these fanciful names were slight—a difference in the thickness of the stripe, the density of the dots, or the weave of the material itself.

Behind these pleasurable fashion choices, an important collaborative process in social commentary was at work. Although male merchants selected names, women's preferences determined the success of any one style. Tobes whose designs or labels failed to resonate with women rarely became popular. For the historian, tobe names operate in much the same way as a headline or photograph: they do not tell the whole story, but provide invaluable clues to the interests, values, and experiences of Sudanese women. By way of illustration, another memorable tobe from 1915 named "The Post Office Pen" highlights a sense of connection and possibility in a modern age. As part of Khartoum's reconstruction, a new post office building dominated the city skyline just a few blocks from the Governor-General's palace. And yet, it was the pens on strings attached to the counters inside that captured women's imagination. It would have been rare for a woman to venture into the post office on her own, and so news of these special pens was likely gleaned from bits of information brought home by husbands or brothers. Nevertheless, to talk of such mundane instruments was to talk of empire. The pen on a chain in the Khartoum post office was not a gag or a novelty, but a very real indicator of imperial systems and progress. The presumably simple act of mailing a letter implied the establishment of a regular mail system with multiple offices, literacy on the part of the sender, and, most poignantly, the existence of a distant friend or relative who was eager for news. Far from being isolated or secluded, the woman who donned "The Post Office Pen" claimed a part of this exciting world for herself.

Yet such forms of political expression were illegible to British observers. The specter of seclusion, female genital cutting, and other body rites loomed large over the imperial mission. In the eyes of imperialists, these "barbaric practices" symbolized all that was backwards and in need of reform in the country. As eager Sudan Political Service men settled into their new posts, healing women's bodies and correcting women's culture would be a significant part of their task of reforming the country as a whole. A civilizing logic argued that only when women were brought out from under oppressive traditions would Sudan be deemed ready for its own independence. Education was a critical first step. For both Britons and Sudanese, it was far more than an intellectual exercise. The Rufa'a Girls' School and needlework homes put in motion a decades-long process of defining a new type of Sudanese woman: one who was adept at dressmaking, could balance household accounts, and might on occasion visit the post office to send a letter to a friend. Already the characteristics of what made a desirable wife were shifting. With imperial civilizing rhetoric backed by unexpected local support, by 1920 the stage was set for a determined increase in women's and girls' educational programs. And as girls moved from their homes into government classrooms, their relationship with empire—its demands, intrusions, and opportunities—grew ever more intimate.

℀ CHAPTER 2 ℀

"FORTY WHITE TOBES"

Enclosures and the Campaign for Pure Bodies

Mabel Wolff arrived in Omdurman in November 1920 armed with a baby doll and a deformed fetus preserved in formaldehyde. She had come to establish and serve as the first headmistress of the government-sponsored Midwifery Training School (MTS). Although her arrival was eagerly antici-pated by British administrators, initial accommodations were minimal and, until a well could be dug, the MTS staff depended on a neighboring prison gang to deliver water each day. Mabel was no stranger to hardship in the Middle East. She and her older sister, Gertrude, were born in Port Tawfiq, Egypt, where their father was a clerk in a shipping firm. After complet-ing their training as nurse-midwives in Britain, the two sisters returned to Egypt, where they managed dispensaries and a midwifery school in the oasis town of Fayoum. In 1925, Gertrude joined Mabel in Sudan and headed the nursing program at the Omdurman Civil Hospital. The two women's efforts to introduce modern medical practices into a society in which nursing and caregiving were deemed the responsibility of relatives or slaves was no small task. But their patience and no-nonsense approach soon won them many adherents. In just a few short years, the "Wolves," as they were affection-ately known, became such formidable characters that a government official remarked, "The male Sudanese of Omdurman feared less to be brought up on a criminal charge before [the] District Commissioner . . . than a private castigation from the Wolves, grim and eloquent, with the womenfolk all tittering in the background."[1]

If rumors can be believed, the cry for medically trained midwives was first heard at a dinner party. One evening in early 1920 Grace Mary Crowfoot, wife of the Director of Education, was seated next to Governor-General Stack at dinner and persisted in asking for his views on female genital cutting. Unfamiliar with the custom, the next day Stack asked his Director of Intelligence for details and, upon hearing them, vowed to eliminate the ritual.[2]

Popularly (though inaccurately) termed "pharaonic circumcision," the procedure was among the most drastic forms of female genital cutting in Africa or the Middle East. Practiced predominantly in northern Sudan on girls between the ages of five and ten, this form of genital cutting excised all of the external genitalia (the clitoris, labia major, and labia minor) and was followed by infibulation: the stitching together of the vaginal skin, leaving only a small opening for menses and urine to pass through. Adding to the perceived horrors of the ritual was the figure of the *daya*, the traditional Sudanese midwife who carried out the procedure. British descriptions painted these women as dirty, nearly blind crones who operated with a rusty straight razor wrapped in soiled rags.[3] Once a young girl overcame the very real risks of infection, sepsis, and puerperal fever and married and became pregnant, the daya was called in again. This time she aided in the act of childbirth by cutting through the scar tissue to remove the infant and then re-infibulating or restitching the mother's body closed again.

Imperialists recoiled from the vision of delicate surgeries carried out with blunt instruments in unhygienic conditions. They condemned female genital cutting as a barbaric means of preserving a girl's chastity by decreasing her sexual desires while at the same time accommodating Sudanese men's "sadistic pleasures."[4] There seemed to be no greater sign of Sudan's primitivism than this savage, sexual ritual.

The focus on sexuality, however, was misplaced. For the northern Sudanese, the primary purpose of genital cutting was not to regulate sexual behavior but to ensure fertility. Today, culturally attuned reformers understand that abandoning the practice of female genital cutting requires instilling a new definition of healthy and reproductively ready bodies into Sudanese society. In the first half of the twentieth century, imperialists sought a more direct route: to put an end to the horrifying rite by reeducating its perpetrators, the dayas. The goal of the Midwifery Training School would be to rival and replace the dirty, unschooled dayas with a new class of midwives trained in the medical basics of obstetrics and gynecology. Dayas were the gatekeepers of women's sexual and reproductive worlds. Because of the practice of infibulation, no birth in Sudan could go unattended. It made sense, then, to focus reformist energies and limited government resources on this special class of women and hope that change would flow outward.

For administrators like Governor-General Stack, Sudan's entire welfare was at stake. The country was suffering from significant underpopulation. Famine in 1913–14 weakened a population still recovering from the violence of conquest; four years later, the influenza outbreak of 1918–19 brought further loss of life. By 1921, released from wartime austerity measures, Stack was in the midst of planning a massive irrigation and agricultural scheme set to open in the mid-1920s. Increased agricultural production demanded a host of healthy laborers. Healthy laborers descended from healthy mothers. And so, the call was put out for the Wolves to come to Sudan.

The beginning of the MTS and its directive to reform women's bodies and culture coincided with a temporary loss of government control over Sudanese men. In 1922, after failing to suppress three years of sustained nationalist protests in Cairo and Alexandria, Great Britain unilaterally declared Egypt an independent state. Immediately, the Egyptian Khedive, Ahmad Fuad, took the title of "King of Egypt and Sudan" and called for the political unity of the Nile Valley. The British Government refused to recognize Fuad's extended claims but strongly feared that Egyptian nationalist fervor would sweep up the Nile and infect Sudan.

In 1924 the still Anglo-Egyptian Sudan witnessed an alarming series of demonstrations against British rule. Leading the protests was the

White Flag League, a political organization headed by Ali Abd al-Latif, a former army officer from a southern Dinka tribe. He was joined in his cause by clerks, army officers, and Gordon College graduates. The league's goal of political unity with Egypt was as straightforward as its banner: a white field with the full length of the Nile, running from Sudan to Egypt, traced in the upper left corner. Abd al-Latif and his peers presented a new face of opposition. For the first two decades of the Condominium, administrators had feared tribal and religious uprisings, especially a revival of the Mahdists. Instead this secular, urban movement caught the Sudan Government unawares. On paper and in public, British officials dismissed the White Flag League protests as simple mimicry carried out by half-educated civil servants who were being paid by the Egyptian Government to cause trouble.[5] Although the demonstrations were soon quelled, the league's displeasure with the British and desire for unity with Egypt threw the faultlines of the Condominium Agreement into stark relief. By refusing to acknowledge the authenticity—if not legitimacy—of Sudanese grievances, British administrators renewed their claim to Sudan's good governance and downplayed the beginnings of anti-imperialist sentiment. For its part, Egypt refused to give up its claims to Sudan. It looked as if the awkward Condominium was coming to an end.

Any hopes of an amicable settlement between the two imperial powers were lost on November 19, 1924, when Governor-General Stack was shot and mortally wounded while traveling through the streets of Cairo. His death the next day provided an opening for Great Britain to end Egyptian influence in Sudan. Without waiting for permission from London, British High Commissioner Lord Allenby ordered the immediate evacuation of Egyptian troops from Sudan. When Sudanese battalions, rightly confused over who was their commander-in-chief (the Egyptian king or the British governor-general), sought to join the departing Egyptians, they were fired upon, killed while hiding, and tried and executed for mutiny. Sudanese memory marks 1924 as a year of nationalist revolution. But in putting down the White Flag League and evacuating Egyptian forces, Britain had in fact made great gains in solidifying its own control of Sudan. The agreed-upon

dual control of the Condominium, never entirely clear, lost all of its meaning in 1924. Egypt's already secondary role in the Sudan Government was
reduced to little more than financial support—though Sudan would remain
a bargaining chip in Anglo-Egyptian affairs for the next thirty years.[6]

The forced removal of the Egyptian troops was rapidly followed by
an exodus of Egyptian civil servants. Teachers, at both government and
private schools, were among the first to be dismissed or urged to leave.
The lack of qualified instructors to fill the vacant positions was felt immediately, and a conflict between imperial politics and imperial praxis soon
arose. In the minds of British officials, the security of the country depended
upon shielding the Sudanese from foreign sparks of nationalist fervor. If
Egyptians were one source of trouble, education was the other. The problem was not unique to Sudan. Administrators across the empire warned
that too much education could lead to "effendyism," an undesirable state in
which colonized people misappropriated the behaviors and privileges of the
imperialists. The protests by the educated White Flag League had been a
disquieting case in point.

However, the government could not function without a trained class of
Sudanese civil servants. Faced with a drastically reduced teaching pool and
anxious over the potential mobilization of the intelligentsia class, administrators shifted their educational energies from kuttabs (elementary schools)
to the older, local form of instruction, the khalwa. While a select group of
students would continue to attend government schools in order to prepare
for low-level government positions, far greater numbers of Sudanese boys
attended hastily established khalwas and received no more than the most
rudimentary instruction. For the moment, the government made no real attempts to hire or train qualified teachers to replace the departed Egyptians.
Khalwas did teach arithmetic and writing, but most administrators agreed
that more advanced subjects could be avoided in favor of lessons on local
history and tribal customs. From 1924 to 1930, the number of elementary
schools for boys was reduced from 95 to 87. During the same period the
number of government-subsidized khalwas increased from 78 to an incredible 768. This was a significant tightening of an already conservative policy.

Twenty years earlier, Currie had purposefully designed his educational program to keep the class of Sudanese intellectual elites small. After the events
of 1924, the political risks that accompanied higher education seemed too
great and the now entirely British-led government privileged security at the
expense of progress.[7]

While education for boys stagnated, programs and opportunities for
Sudanese women and girls, of which the Midwifery Training School was
a large part, grew. From 1921 to 1931, the same years in which boys' schools
declined, the number of primary schools for girls increased from five to
twenty-three, with 2,095 students.[8] These seemingly contradictory ap-
proaches to education can be explained by the gendered assumptions and
aspirations of imperialism. Unlike their male counterparts, educated Sudanese women did not appear to pose a political threat to the imperial order.
In fact, the philosophy of imperialism maintained that educated women
were a critical sign of social progress. However, the purpose of instruction
was quite different. Instead of training civil servants, girls' schools would
produce better-informed wives and mothers. In this way, imperial education for Sudanese women and girls did not necessarily seek to bring women
out of their homes, but rather sought to refine their roles within it. Here
again, the dismissal of Egyptian officials and their families proved significant. It fell to British women, like Mabel and Gertrude Wolff, to model
progressive forms of femininity and womanhood for the next generation. If
educated Sudanese men were too unpredictable, Sudanese women's bodies
and minds were the hoped-for sites of measured progress and reform.

INSIDE THE HAREM

Reaching those bodies and minds meant breaching the walls of the harem.
Then as now, in Western imaginations the word *harem* evoked visions of
elaborate, secluded rooms housing beautiful women who did little more
than engage in sensory and sexual pleasures. In fact, the harem is a system of personal and spatial organization that separates public from private.
Critically, both men and women police the harem's boundaries. Thus, within
this system, gender segregation is not inherently oppressive but rather "an

acknowledgement that each sex has the right to a collective social world that the other sex must accept, respect, and protect."⁹ Social values and relationships followed the physical lines of the harem. Imperial reform required navigating both.

For northern Sudanese women in the first half of the nineteenth century, their collective social world focused almost exclusively on productive households and reproductive partnerships. Marriage was a union of economic resources as well as the joining of a man and woman. Wedding rites were entirely funded by the groom and his family and lasted anywhere from seven to forty days, during which the bride and groom progressively spent more time together in a series of orchestrated ceremonies. Even the most modest wedding demanded a significant outpouring of cash and gifts. The groom was responsible for paying a brideprice, providing food and drink for the days-long festivities, and, most importantly, furnishing a new home. Typical furnishings might include "two anqaribs or a double bed with brass knobs and rails, mattresses, long flat cushions, a copper tisht or tub, a big round saucepan for the mulah, large red wooden boxes for spices (huqq), and coffee- and tea-glasses and cups."¹⁰ Like the items in the new home, a sizable bridewealth of new tobes, underwear, dresses, and shoes outfitted the bride for the next stage in her life.

This was an intimate economy. Sexual penetration was neither the object nor the climax of the marriage ceremony. In fact, depending on the extent of a woman's genital cutting, full penile penetration and sexual intercourse may not have been possible for months. Thus, Sudanese men asserted their masculinity and preparedness for marriage not by performing sexually, but by providing for their new wives materially. The enormous collection of wedding gifts was often called a "burden" (*shayla*) or "suitcase" (*shanta*). A man's ability to mobilize such resources attested to his worth. The bride's acceptance of these gifts materially indicated her move from the house of her father to the care and protection of her husband. It was her responsibility to maintain and make use of these goods, so as to show her husband's prosperity to the best advantage. In anthropological terms, the wedding gifts "set in motion" a reciprocal relationship between husband and wife, "inaugurating his role as producer-provider and her complementary one as consumer and, ultimately, reproducer."[11] Marriage was a partnership of economic and reproductive exchange. A well-appointed home filled with children was living evidence of a mutually productive union.

A woman's body also carried the marks of these intimate exchanges. Leading up to the wedding celebrations, a young bride had her lips tattooed, ears pierced, body hair removed, and henna applied—all highly visible adornments reserved for sexually active women. Unseen, the scars of female genital cutting had prepared a girl's body for the responsibilities of marriage long before her wedding day. As northern Sudanese women understood it, the purpose of the operation was not to diminish sexual desire but to construct a fertile purity. This was a rite of preparation, not destruction. Infibulation physically enclosed the womb and thus guaranteed the birth of pure children. Labor for an infibulated woman was painful and carried considerable medical risks. Yet the ritual persisted in spite of these difficulties because the process of enclosing the womb confirmed women's social importance, not as servants or sexual submissives, "but as mothers of men" and "co-founders" of esteemed lineages.[12] Peggy Vidler, who supervised Sudanese nurses at the Khartoum Civil Hospital in the 1940s and 1950s, well understood the importance of producing children—if not the larger cultural meanings. Recalling her work with women at the hospital, she wrote, "One might have expected these poor, oppressed women to dread child birth with the complications of circumcision, but it was the one thing that gave meaning to their lives, and infertility was a disaster—only a little less so was a family of daughters!"[13]

The centrality of motherhood to women's gender identity was impressed upon Sudanese girls from the earliest age. In Western societies, gender is, by and large, determined by one's biological sex: a child born with male genitalia is raised and socialized to be a "man." In contrast, in northern Sudan, gender—an awareness and understanding of one's role in society—determines sex. As anthropologist Janice Boddy explains, "Anatomical sex dictates nothing; rather, it indicates a *potential* that needs to be socially clarified and refined. Genital cutting makes it possible for persons to embody their envisioned moral gender."[14] Genital cutting clarified or reified one's sex by removing the masculine clitoris and inner labia from the vagina and the feminine foreskin from the penis.

The act of circumcision was the culmination of years of instruction on gender roles and social values. In fact, female genital cutting was only one part of a sophisticated system that guarded and guided women's bodies. Within Sudan's harem culture, themes of enclosure and protection were repeatedly found in the everyday practices of women's lives: in the concentric circles of decreasing safety as one moved from the home outward beyond the boundaries of the village; in the preference for "close" marriage with cousins from the paternal line; and in the round, impervious symbols of fertility and purity such as ostrich eggs or even, as the twentieth century progressed, tinned cans of food. Only when a girl understood the meanings behind these signs and symbols would infibulation physically close her own fertile body, making it ready for marriage and motherhood. Thus, for Sudanese women and girls, enclosure and purity were not metaphors, but real and determining facts of their lives.[15]

Yet it would be a mistake to conclude that the harem was entirely enclosed, or that wives alone were responsible for their fertility. A host of service women such as hairdressers, dayas, and slaves were key players in the successful execution of marriage rites and childbirth. The intimate nature of their work connected these service women to families as if they were kin. Equally important, the regularity of their visits fostered a valuable circuit of information about sex, reproduction, and family that moved between homes.

In the nineteenth and early twentieth centuries, one of the most defining aspects of a Sudanese woman's appearance was the *mushat*, a rigidly braided hair style that divided the head into quadrants. As fashion statements, the tobe and the mushat went hand in hand. When the tobe slipped back off a woman's head, the mushat could be glimpsed. Especially coy women might fold their tobes in certain ways to reveal a beautiful mushat. The intricacy of the style meant that women could not fashion their hair themselves. Instead, specialized hairdressers, called *mushatas*, would be invited to a woman's home to style her hair. Fine plaits were restyled every three months, while thick plaits required monthly maintenance.[16] Because the braids took days to execute properly, a visit from the mushata was an extended opportunity to catch up on neighborhood gossip and reaffirm community connections. Plaiting hair was a tactile, personal act. The fingers of the stylist rhythmically moved across the scalp, parting and weaving strands of hair. A woman did her best to hold still as practiced hands pulled her hair taut.

The intimacy of hair dressing matched the intimacy of conversations between women. Through the long hours of styling, kinswomen and mushatas exchanged personal stories, tips, and local news. Because she often served women from all classes, the mushata was a "cultural broker, bridging the gaps between differing social groups and circulating information in a very personal way."[17] In addition to regular maintenance, mushatas were summoned to create special styles for weddings, births, and other holidays. Collectively, these visits created a pattern of meetings, a calendar of sorts, in which acts of beauty, sexuality, and fertility were marked and celebrated.

A mushata's compensation reflected her importance in productive households. While in her client's home the mushata was treated as family: passing time in the women's quarters and, as Mabel Wolff noted, being "well fed."[18] The presence of good food is evidence of the hairdresser's elevated status. Under regular circumstances, a Sudanese woman ate sparingly from the food that was left over from her husband's or father's meal. But when women gathered together for special events, a spirit of exaggerated hospitality prevailed as they cooked and consumed meals that they would not normally prepare for themselves.[19] Weddings inspired even greater generosity: mushatas received perfumed oils and, on occasion, new tobes as forms of payment.[20] Such gifts were expensive and rewarded more than just beautiful braids. The choice food, tobes, and scented oils affirmed the mushata's service to the reproductive well-being of the family.

The payments that a daya received even more explicitly acknowledged her care for the fertility of the families she served. Upon the successful delivery of a child, a daya was typically paid in millet or wheat, scented oils, and a portion of goat meat. More well-off families might also include payments of white flour, soap, cash, and a tobe.[21] These were not luxury goods, but they carried a notable symbolic weight. In return for her care for mother and child, a daya received nourishing items that enabled her own care.

Throughout their careers, the Wolves kept detailed accounts of the expenses associated with childbirth. One entry, titled "Sitt Batul's Own Confinement Expenses," provides unusual insight into how a family would have considered and processed such costs.[22] In addition to a long list of foodstuffs, oils, and scents purchased by her father, Sitt Batul received "1 tirka zanga, 1 tirka red, 1 tobe 'Abu Shanta' (for gift for midwife), 1 [tobe] 'Al Semaya' (having day of baby)."[23] No other items on the list are marked for the midwife, but it is certain that she received further compensation. What is noteworthy is the inclusion of the midwife's tobe in the list of gifts of clothing for the mother, Sitt Batul. Here, the costs of labor for both mothers and midwives are united in the family accounting. The dual gifts of tobes to Sitt Batul and her midwife are indicative of the cooperative birthing process in northern Sudan. Indeed, the parallel compensations to new mothers, mushatas, and dayas made explicit each service woman's worth in the marital cycle of production, consumption, and reproduction.

Household slaves were also witnesses to and participants in these important domestic rites. In 1925, just four years after the MTS opened, a law declared that all persons born after the Anglo-Egyptian conquest in 1898 could no longer be held in a state of bondage. Notably, the law did not make the emancipation of existing slaves compulsory, but instead provided a means to manumission for those slaves who wanted it. But legal codes did not translate easily to domestic realities, especially for the women who made up the majority of the enslaved population. Because slave women performed domestic service, British administrators had made a practice of deeming conflicts between a slave woman and her master to be domestic affairs and thus a matter for the Islamic, not civil, courts.[24] Owners took advantage of this legal distinction and when confronted with requests for manumission often produced false marriage certificates, which claimed a different kind of ownership that nevertheless bound an enslaved woman to her master's home.

Children further complicated the relationship between master and slave. Islamic law allowed for owners to recognize and claim as their heirs any offspring sired on slave women. But under the new civil code, a woman who applied for manumission risked declaring her children as illegitimate: unrecognized by both master and the legal system. As a result many slave women remained in or near their master's house in order to raise their children. With these legal and personal limits on an enslaved woman's freedom, it is hardly surprising that significantly fewer women than men sought and received manumission.[25]

Well into the mid-twentieth century, there persisted a class of women within upper- and middle-class households who were neither legally enslaved nor entirely free. The particulars of their experiences are lost to us. But their labor and service connected them to the rhythms of domestic life. Such women would have prepared and served the food that celebrated the arrival of the daya or mushata and stood in attendance during the pains of birth or pleasures of hairbraiding.

When fertility was threatened or domestic order disrupted, Sudanese women again turned to tobes, toiletries, and adornment. Those who suffered from recurring headaches, bleeding, miscarriages, infertility, depression, or anxiety often claimed that their bodies were possessed by *zar* spirits. Dating back to the mid-nineteenth century, the vibrant zar spirit possession cult describes a complex family of socially and ethnically diverse personalities who inhabit the bodies of women. Unlike other spirit possessions, the zar cannot be exorcised. Once possessed, a woman and her spirit enter into a contractual relationship: as long as a woman's body is cared for, the zar is satisfied. But abuse and neglect, especially on the part of a woman's husband, prompt the zar to induce prolonged illnesses, trouble conceiving, or miscarriages. Once angered, the spirit can only be appeased through the celebration of a zar drumming, an intense ceremony in which women and spirits interact with one another. Much like wedding ceremonies, zar drummings require large quantities of food and drink for guests, incense and perfume, as well as special dresses, jewelry, and tobes for the afflicted women. In this way, zar spirits "hold for ransom her husband's most valuable asset. . . . [They] want their host to be clean and attractive . . . [and] obliquely call upon a man to recognize his wife's value, implying that neither she nor her fertility should be taken for granted."[26] In the first half of the twentieth century, the spirits expressed what a Sudanese wife dared not: that she was unhappy and poorly provided for. Zar was a means for a woman (in full sight of her entire community) to attract the notice of her husband and compel gifts of food, new tobes, and perfume—all of which were instrumental in maintaining the health of the household. A husband could ill-afford not to comply.

The zar, visits from the mushata, and a daya's preparations for birth were collective moments in which women gathered to discuss their sexual and reproductive concerns and accomplishments. Although the rules of the harem appear to stress absolute enclosure, a regular culture of visiting placed Sudanese women in direct contact with their neighbors' most intimate concerns. Even as formal education for girls increased, these harem lessons remained vital. Through sight, smell, touch, and zar drummings, women and girls shared in a circuit of fertility. From 1921 onward, a new class of medically trained midwives would also make these rounds, bringing imperial messages of health and reform into the protected space of the harem.

SEEDS OF REVOLUTION

The initial search for midwifery students was not promising. Whatever the hopes of high-level officials, Mabel and Gertrude recognized the need to work as much as possible within existing midwifery practices, rather than against them. Thus Mabel looked for her first students among practicing dayas and their daughters. An administrator cautioned that successful dayas, already schooled in their own methods of birth, would be reluctant to submit to months of full-time training. He thought, however, "they might agree to 4 or 6 weeks and get anyhow knowledge of cleanliness and have this thoroughly explained and drummed into them, so that though they would be in no way trained, they would probably be very greatly improved in their work."[27] The first term in January 1921 began inauspiciously with just two pupils: Nura bint Omar, a daya aged seventy; and the doorman's wife, a woman with no experience who disappeared with her husband as soon as her training was finished. Less than a month into the term, two more women joined the school. They were Aziza Bercy, a sixty-eight-year-old daya, and Mastura Khidr, another woman with no previous experience.[28] In her first annual report, Mabel conceded, "Most of the Diayas [*sic*] were unwilling to live in the School and suspicious of what the training would mean to their work and very doubtful as to my capability or knowledge of Sudany deliveries. The patients likewise shared their view, dreading any interference with their customs."[29]

It was not just Mabel's capabilities, but her character that raised doubts. Mabel and Gertrude were unmarried and childless. Dayas could not imagine how the two women, with no reproductive experience of their own, could possess any useful information about the delicacies of birth. But the Wolves' characteristic patience and determination soon won the day. Six pupils enrolled for the second term, and by the year's end ten women had trained at the MTS and a new session was beginning with a further eight.[30]

The program that Mabel envisioned was rigorous, comprehensive, and above all, practical. Students boarded at the MTS for the duration of the six-month certification course. It was the first time these women had lived away from their families, and in light of this the MTS paid particular attention to students' domestic needs. The school provided transportation from a woman's village to Omdurman, lodging, fuel, water, a bed, two blankets, a uniform, and a small monthly stipend for the trainee's personal use. The students also received rations of milk, bread, and beans daily and small amounts of coffee, tea, sugar, soap, and washing blue each week.[31] On their own initiative, the women often pooled their resources: combining their rations of sugar and tea and sharing in the extracurricular responsibilities of cooking, cleaning, and childcare.

Inside the classroom, trainees followed a curriculum of basic hygiene, temperature reading, suturing, administering drugs, and pre- and postnatal care. Notably absent were lessons on reading and writing. Like women enrolled in nursing and midwifery programs in other parts of the British Empire, the majority of the MTS students were illiterate. Yet unlike other health programs, literacy was neither a requirement nor a part of midwifery training in Sudan. Instead, the MTS promoted a hands-on, praxis curriculum that stressed repetition and memorization. Medicines were identified by sight, taste, and smell. Suturing was practiced on old tires. And baby dolls imported from Europe served as training models. To be certified, a pupil midwife needed to have observed twenty cases, delivered twenty more, and have passed both oral and practical examinations administered by British doctors.[32]

These inventive methods obscured the trouble Mabel had in training and sustaining midwives according to her standards. Ideally, she had hoped to teach young, single women who could go on to become career midwives. But the close cultural associations between sexuality and midwifery discouraged unmarried women's participation. As a result, MTS midwives were usually married or widowed and, on average, in their late thirties. More important than age or marital status, Mabel sought to recruit women of good character who were popular in their villages.

Even these general guidelines proved hard to meet. A glance at the school's Midwives Register reveals the difficulties in cultivating both character and skill. The earliest entries are succinct in their judgments: "A good methodical worker—can read the thermometer at times" and "Very good and methodical at her work but slow and inclined to sulk. Reads temp." And finally, "Not wicked but too old." Even women who initially showed promise could turn into disappointments. A pupil in 1926 was described as "Not quarrelsome, rather slow and heavy but quite good and reliable." A cryptic note was added in 1930: "Her morals went to pieces" and her license was canceled. Another midwife in 1928 had a similar story. She was initially described as "nice natured and has greatly improved with the training—she will probably endeavor to carry out her training and work well." But by 1935, Mabel had concluded that the same midwife was "far too bulky for her to be even able to work efficiently." Outside the classroom, disciplining students could take considerable effort. Mabel characterized one particularly troublesome pupil as an "extraordinarily nice sweet tempered woman," who managed to keep sober for the duration of the six-month program "but had to be given quite a lot of sugar to make up for lack of spirits!!!"[33]

It is noteworthy that Mabel's critiques of poor performance were associated with bodies that were heavy, sullen, and slow. Except in extreme cases, a midwife's size shouldn't preclude her from performing her work. What Mabel was likely responding to, and attempting to describe, was a difference in attitude and approach to work. Nursing was not a familiar occupation in Sudan. Care for the sick traditionally fell to relatives or servants. The women enrolled at the MTS were learning not only new skills but also an ideology of caregiving. Elaine Hills-Young, an instructor at the nurses' training college and eventual successor to the Wolves, explained, "It is difficult to instil into these girls the true spirit of service for others. Very few of the trained or untrained are nurses in the real sense of the word, although some can do excellent work."[34] Good work was to be accompanied by good spirits. And while MTS midwives might learn the techniques of modern medicine, not all had adopted the iconic brisk and cheerful attitudes of British nurses. For Mabel, bodies reflected intangible differences of temperament, in which bulk and slowness signaled an absence of spirit and not necessarily a lack of talent.

Spirit, sobriety, and strong morals were imperative in a profession whose intimate nature already raised doubts about the character of the women willing to perform the work. A midwife's movement from house to house and her long and irregular hours challenged the established boundaries of enclosure. This, combined with her close contact with fertile and reproductive bodies, raised anxieties about a midwife's own sexuality.[35] Such concerns help to explain Sudanese women's preferences to secure the services of an older daya. In addition to a presumed greater expertise, older women past childbearing years brought no sexual threat of their own into the intimate moments of birthing. In fact, youth and enthusiasm seemed to work against potential midwives. Mabel found that young midwives who were "athletic" in their movements and "sufficiently interested in [their] work to refuse men's advances" risked being labeled sexual perverts or lesbians. These insults may have been more than a commentary on the sexual nature of a midwife's work, but also evidence of a generational conflict in which older Sudanese women feared losing their control over female fertility and sexuality.[36] Indeed, the comparatively younger MTS midwives not only introduced alternate methods into birth rooms, but claimed a new type of authority over women's bodies as well.

If Mabel and Gertrude could not always immediately identify weak characters, they routinely turned away "Sudany" women, those whose ethnic background linked them to southern Sudan and slavery. During the imperial period, the term *Sudany*, literally translated as "Sudanese," carried multiple meanings. Outside of a few progressive nationalists, in the 1920s and 1930s people in Sudan did not use *Sudany* to characterize or define a unified national identity. Instead, derived from the Arabic word for "black," *Sudany* denoted low social status and was most commonly used in reference to people in the south or the population of former slaves and their descendants living in the north. Depending on the context, imperialists and northern Sudanese used the terms *Sudany, black,* and *slave* interchangeably.[37] For the Wolves and the northern women they served, the intimate tasks of midwifery were no place for those with a questionable background. During the acts of genital cutting and childbirth a woman's body was exposed and vulnerable to unclean and harmful spirits carried by outsiders. The midwife's role as a gatekeeper was to guard against impurities at just such a time. A Sudany woman not only was a clear outsider, but she carried a potential threat herself. When searching for new students in the capital region or more populous cities, it was easy for Mabel and Gertrude to turn away interested Sudany women. Recruitment in rural areas was another matter. In letters to her sister, Mabel expressed her frustration that in the smaller towns the only women presented as possible candidates for MTS training were slave or Sudany "types." Rather than take on a low-status student, Mabel often left empty-handed.[38]

But Sudany women could not always be avoided. In November 1931, the District Commissioner of Khartoum North presented a young woman to be trained. Mabel reported, "When the bint [girl] did appear I discovered she was a common slave girl and not prepossessing at that, I told him frankly that we were not out for that type at all but as he said he would pay to have her trained. . . . I said I would take her over to Khartoum North

and see if they still required someone for the prisons."³⁹ Although Mabel
uses the word *slave*, the actual status of this young girl is unclear. Born after
1898, the girl could not legally be enslaved. Yet the stain of slavery endured
and she was condemned by her family's presumed past. Mabel asked that
in the future the District Commissioner ensure that the women he proposed for training were truly respectable, as the standards for the MTS
were "most particular." Not one to turn away a paying pupil, she assigned
the girl to the one location in which women's bodies and morality were
already compromised: the prison.

When Mabel declined to train Sudany girls, she affirmed local prejudices and also, increasingly, government policy. From the earliest days of
the Condominium, the south's rugged terrain and multitude of tribes made
indirect rule the most efficient and inexpensive administrative strategy. In
contrast to the densely bureaucratic north, a single British official was often
responsible for vast miles of territory in the south. Following the White
Flag League protest in 1924, the Sudan Government was determined to
prevent nationalist agitation from spreading southward. After much debate,
administrators developed a policy to "close" the three southern provinces,
Bahr al-Ghazal, Upper Nile, and Equatoria, to the sociopolitical influences
of the north. The "Southern Policy," adopted in 1929, drew an administrative
line across the bottom third of the country and, in effect, divided Sudan into
two distinct entities. Within the closed districts, new legislation eliminated
the office of the native district official; banned northern merchants; and
adopted English instead of Arabic as the lingua franca. Most importantly,
administrators argued, the closed districts would allow for the preservation,
or in some cases reintroduction, of indigenous customs that would prevent
people in the south from identifying with the anti-imperialist attitudes of
the Arab north.⁴⁰ The legacy of the Southern Policy far outlasted the imperial period. The artificial boundary created cultural and economic divisions
that solidified over the next two decades and set the stage for the outbreak
of civil war on the eve of Sudan's independence in 1955.

It was precisely the issue of local customs that delayed the development
of modern midwifery in the south. If administrators worried that north-

ern nationalist sentiments would infect the south, a parallel concern held that mixing between women might persuade naïve southerners to adopt the harmful northern practices of cheek scarring, lip tattooing, and female genital cutting. (This was a contradictory anxiety to the prejudices against the Sudany midwife whose presence threatened vulnerable northern bodies.) In an experiment in 1933, two women from the Upper Nile Province in the south came to train at the MTS. The two students were subject to even greater scrutiny than their northern peers. Mabel wrote, "In an unobtrusive way we keep a very vigilant eye on these blacks and try to keep them from being unduly influenced either by religion or harmful customs." There proved to be no danger of the southerners adopting northern practices. But the MTS staff struggled to keep the two women sober, plying them with sugar and sweets at the first "signs of their spirits weakening."[41] Despite this relative success, the experiment was not repeated. Of the 243 midwives certified at the MTS between 1921 and 1935, only three came from the Southern Provinces.[42]

But if harmful Arab customs deterred administrators from bringing southern women to train in the north, the lack of such traditions in the south discouraged the prospect of establishing a midwifery school there altogether. Because female genital cutting was not widely practiced in the south, concerns over southern birth rates and a population of healthy laborers, which had provided the rationale for establishing the MTS, were less acute. As a result, the government decided not to extend midwifery education to the closed districts. Instead, the government left issues of southern women's health firmly in the hands of foreign missionaries.

Back in Omdurman, the Wolves' firm selectivity in choosing their students bore fruit. Ten years after the opening of the Midwifery Training School, Mabel boasted to Gertrude that the 1931 class of midwives were doing so well that future students would only be accepted "with a signed letter from the sheikhs stating she is a woman of good morals and character and approved of by the villages and women especially."[43] This was a coup for the Wolves. In spite of numerous obstacles, the school had progressed from a desperate search for quality students to selecting candidates based on local leaders' recommendation and community consensus. Local approval signaled local investment. And the MTS seemed well poised to fulfill its mission of constructing a special class of women who would join new medical knowledge to vital bodily traditions.

∼

Perhaps nothing illustrates the imperial disruption of harem rituals so well as the repositioning of women's bodies as they gave birth. Until the 1920s, northern Sudanese women went into labor standing upright. A shallow hole was dug in the dirt floor and a rope suspended above it. The daya sat straddling the hole with her legs, while the expectant mother stood in the center of the hole, bracing herself with the rope. As she grew fatigued, relatives and friends stood alongside the laboring mother to support her weight and hold her up. The final stages of childbirth were managed by touch rather than sight, and a cloth was thrown over the lower half of the mother's body. Mabel remembers that during the very first delivery she witnessed in Sudan, "at the most critical moment, someone enveloped both the Diaya [sic] and my head in a tobe and for a few moments we were quite helpless, or at least I was, being unused to such an ordeal."[44]

Countering this taxing position, the Wolves introduced the supine birth, intended to relieve the strain on the woman's pelvic muscles and back. Popularly called the "Mackintosh birth" because the mother was laid on plastic or rubber sheeting, there is conflicting evidence on how this new position was received by Sudanese women. As early as 1926, Mabel reports that young mothers were boasting that their child was a "son or daughter of the Mackintosh." And in an unexpected bureaucratic benefit, a child's age could now be estimated based on whether she was birthed using the Mackintosh method.[45] Yet the switch to a supine position was not as smooth or easy as Mabel suggests. Eileen Kendall, headmistress of the MTS from 1946 to 1955, remembers that some Sudanese women were initially suspicious of the Mackintosh and worried that the rubber sheeting was in fact made of pig skin—an animal considered unclean in Islam.[46] Fears lessened and acceptance grew as elites took up the new position. Beginning in 1926, the wife of religious leader Sayyid Ali al-Mirghani had all three of her children delivered by Mabel Wolff and is credited with inspiring other women in the capital cities to do the same.[47] Yet others may have felt they didn't have a choice. Women who birthed children in both positions claimed that labor was easier and quicker "on the rope," but that midwives would only administer anesthesia to mothers who would lie down.[48]

The cultural violence that accompanied laboring women on their backs may not be immediately apparent. Fertility and reproduction were the hallmarks of Sudanese womanhood, and the Mackintosh birth quite literally upended how the most fundamental function of motherhood was to be carried out. We do not know how women interpreted or explained this new position with respect to their existing traditions. Observable, improved postpartum outcomes due to more rigorous hygienic standards may have been enough to convince some women that the Mackintosh birth was the better option (though in fact the two were in no way linked). In other instances, the line between choice and coercion blurred. One thing is clear, however: as women moved from the rope to the Mackintosh, they increasingly aligned their bodies to the standards of an outside authority.

Among those who were curious about the new birthing methods was Sitt Batul Muhammad Isa, a young woman from Rufa'a. In 1925, Sitt Batul watched as a local midwife, who had just recently completed her training at the MTS, successfully delivered a neighbor's baby. She was so impressed with the midwife's cleanliness, equipment, and methods that when her own sister went into labor, Batul ignored her family's protests and ran to fetch the MTS midwife. Soon after, Sitt Batul sent a letter to Mabel Wolff expressing her interest in the training program. In January 1926, again defying her family's objections, Batul enrolled in the Midwifery Training School.

Sitt Batul was an atypical MTS student. Unlike many of the early MTS pupils, Batul came from a well-off family and had even inherited some land and cattle of her own. Even more noteworthy, she had an elementary education, having attended Babikr Bedri's celebrated girls' school in Rufa'a. Despite all this, Sitt Batul's social status was uncertain. Her husband had abandoned her while she was pregnant; without his support, Batul and her newborn son were forced to return to her father's house.

In midwifery, Batul saw a path to independence and self-sufficiency. As she described it, the school was a "protected, clean place where one learnt to be useful."[49] However, things weren't altogether promising at the start. The Wolves found Batul "dull and difficult to train" and, after awarding her her midwifery certificate, transferred Batul to the less demanding nursing program at the Omdurman Civil Hospital. But Batul's determination and devotion to the Wolves didn't end. In 1930, after having proven herself at the hospital, Batul rejoined the MTS in the highly respected position of a Staff Midwife, where she was responsible for the instruction and recruitment of new students. From there, she began a noteworthy career that took her across northern Sudan, promoting and enforcing the MTS lessons of hygiene and obstetric care. In spite of her rocky beginning, Sitt Batul became a model of the MTS graduate, fully converted to the reformist teachings of Mabel and her sister. As Eileen Kendall affirmed, "No one can preach the gospel of anti–Pharaonic circumcision quite as [Sitt Batul] can."[50]

Kendall's reference to preaching is apt. The philosophy of the MTS wrapped the introduction of biomedicine in rhetoric of moral purity and responsibility. In her lessons, Mabel emphasized the spiritual significance of their work. "In midwifery there are two or more lives dependent on your skill and care, each baby you help from the darkness to the light of Day is a gift from God and you should be at all times worthy to receive it."[51] A midwife was expected to be in a constant state of readiness. This meant keeping her instruments sanitized and her hands, face, and clothes clean. Hygiene was not simply a professional responsibility, but a moral obligation. Only washed, skilled bodies could deliver healthy babies from the darkness into the light. This type of imagery had strong Christian overtones, but it matched Muslim sensibilities about cleanliness and purity as well. Because evangelism was prohibited in northern Sudan, preaching about clean bodies was carried out in classrooms rather than churches. In the newly established girls' schools, a guideline for a lesson about the dangers of female genital cutting stated: "It is imperative for a good girl to respect her body and keep it clean from dirt and defects as if it were a precious treasure, and [she] should endeavor to present it to her husband as a valuable prize which is a sound mind in a sound body."[52]

Though such lines were meant to argue against genital cutting, the rhetoric of bodily integrity and cleanliness inadvertently reinforced the symbolism of infibulation. A decade later, lessons against genital cutting would become decidedly more strident and reproachful. But for the moment, a peculiar overlap in language and concepts made it sometimes difficult to distinguish between new methods and old traditions. The word for circumcision, *tahur*, is derived from the same linguistic root as *tahir*, meaning clean, pure, and modest. In government classrooms, British and Sudanese vocabularies of cleanliness and purity swirled about one another and collided. And imperial descriptions of worthy and precious bodies felt familiar, not foreign. Janice Boddy speculates on how MTS trainees may have responded to Mabel's lectures on purity and preparedness: "Did students experience a shock of recognition? Or were their responses subdued, the wisdom so recognizable and banal, so matter-of-fact?"[53] Both imperialists and Sudanese women were committed to successful pregnancies. Both employed a language of purity, integrity, and preparedness. Where they differed was on the question of just what those pure bodies should look like.

Addressing female genital cutting directly proved far more delicate than administrators anticipated. Contrary to many of their colleagues, Mabel and Gertrude Wolff maintained that any attempts to unilaterally outlaw circumcision would drive the practice underground and do more harm than good. Instead, the sisters advocated for a gradualist approach based on popular support. Mabel expressed her hope that MTS graduates would serve as "minor missionaries," whose practice of modern medicine would curb, and eventually eliminate, genital cutting. "It may be many years before this custom can effactually be checked, but meanwhile the first seeds of silent revolution towards cleanliness and hygiene are being sown in the homes of the people."[54] Change would be delivered incrementally at the hands of midwives, in intimate moments and private spaces.

In the meantime, the Wolves taught their students to perform a modified form of infibulation that left most of the labia minor and clitoris intact. Performed under hygienic conditions with a sterile straight razor, the ritual had been tempered and medicalized—making it safer. But despite the "preaching" of accomplished midwives like Sitt Batul, genital cutting had not diminished in popularity or cultural significance. Indeed, the colloquial name for the modified procedure, "government circumcision," implied government *approval* of the practice. The term contrasted sharply with the full "pharaonic" (Egyptian) form of infibulation and came at a time when many Sudanese nationalists were deciding with which codominion power to ally themselves, Great Britain or Egypt. Boddy has argued that the rival forms of cutting mirror the "colonial imagery by the Sudanese, with Egypt as the source of harm and the British as guardians of local tradition, rationalized and scientifically improved."[55] These associations may have held meaning for some women. However, there is no evidence that a woman's politics led her to favor one procedure over the other. Full infibulation remained the preferred form of genital cutting for decades. Still, the association of the imperial government with the modified procedure is strong evidence that Sudanese women recognized increasing state intervention in what had once been women's private affairs.

GLIMPSES OF IMPERIAL ORDER

The term *government circumcision* was just one of a number of signs that publicized the changes taking place within the harem. Because of incomplete data, neither government administrators nor today's historians can quantify the efficacy of the MTS programs. We don't know how many women opted for the Mackintosh birth or whether infant mortality rates declined significantly. But we can trace the outward signs of imperial influence over these private practices. Counterintuitively perhaps, the strength of this intimate campaign to reshape women's bodies relied upon highly visible markers in which health, reform, and civility could be understood at a glance. At the center of these signs stood the midwife. Outside the harem and in full public view, she modeled and performed imperial lessons of progress.

Midwives wore the signs of change daily on their persons. While training at the MTS, students were issued one or two sets of tobes, one blue, one white, for their daily use. A receipt of items purchased at the Omdurman market shows that trainees' clothing accounted for a third of the MTS shopping budget. In one month, the school purchased fourteen bolts of cloth for shirts, another six for pants, and "24 blue tobes at p[iastre]10 each; 40 white tobes at p[iastre]19 each." The white tobes came at a significant cost: the only item on the shopping list that was more expensive was the school's supply of coffee for the month. But they were well worth the price. The common blue tobes were used for chores around the schoolyard, but it was the forty white tobes that separated MTS midwives from untrained dayas. Midwives wore the white tobes over their school uniform of a simple white dress "designed to be worn back to front or vice versa which allows evenness in the wearing out of them." For those who lived and worked in "more sophisticated places," uniforms were supplemented with white veils, coveralls, and aprons.[56] This distinguishing form of dress was intended as a sign of modern midwifery, and those who wore it were marked as practitioners of modern medicine. And yet many MTS students resisted the uniform at first, especially when asked to wear it outside the school grounds. They likely felt uncomfortable or ungainly in the unfamiliar cut of the shift dress or the multiple layers of coveralls and aprons. However, their bodies grew accustomed to the new shapes, and upon graduation most MTS midwives purchased dresses similar to their school uniforms.[57]

Some midwives, though, lapsed into old habits once they were no longer under the Wolves' watchful eyes. On an inspection tour in 1937, Mabel dismally noted of one MTS graduate that she "looks a poor specimen and underfed and white tobe borrowed from a neighbor."[58] Without the money to buy her own clothes or even enough food, the midwife was a meager advertisement for the advantages that supposedly came with modern medical training.

Even good work could be sullied by an unkempt appearance. In Sinkat, Mabel met a woman who had recently begun taking on cases as a midwife. She noted, "I was really so pleased, the only thing I hauled her badly over the coals for was her untidy and rather slovenly dress, but before I left Batul saw that she bought the necessary material for a complete new outfit and I think she will pull herself together."[59] Proper dress signaled the professionalization and rising standards of midwifery. And it was no accident that white tobes and uniforms required the same hygienic diligence as that which was needed to keep medical instruments sterile and ready for use. New forms of dress were a physical manifestation of new medical practices.

꙳

Photographs grant us some idea of the visual impact of the new corps of midwives in their bright white tobes. While on their inspection tours, Mabel and Gertrude frequently took pictures of trained midwives and dayas working throughout Sudan. The result is a large, detailed collection of photographs documenting the rapid changes in Sudanese midwifery throughout the 1920s and 1930s. Most of the subjects are posed, and thus the pictures should not be understood as candid shots of unscripted moments. Rather, the photographs narrate a consciously crafted story of the spreading success of MTS medical training. Indeed, the Wolves expected their friends and colleagues to be able to "read" these photographs and understand the larger imperial narrative of progress in Sudan. One picture from the 1930s (Fig. 2) seems to depict the pinnacle of MTS success: A trained midwife, dressed in a white tobe and smiling confidently into the camera, holds her medical box in one hand and her kettle for boiling water in the other. Behind her is a gate with a sign announcing her services. Even more than her tobe, the sign crucially marks this woman's training and distinction. Not only does she have the resources to commission a sign, but she anticipates that her clients will be able to identify her and her services through the written word. Remembering that even trained midwives were usually illiterate, the woman in this photograph embodies the hope of the campaigns of both medical midwifery and girls' education.

Contrast this model of progress with the photograph of a traditional daya in the Red Sea Province (Fig. 3), one of the most detailed images of the Wolves' collection. Unlike the upright and ready stance of her educated

FIGURE 2. Trained midwife with sign, midwifery box, and kettle, ca. 1930s, SAD 743/1/10 (M. E. and G. L. Wolff Collection). Reproduced by permission of Durham University Library.

FIGURE 3. *Daya* with striped tobe and jewelry, Sinkat, ca. 1923–1935, SAD 742/6/19 (M. E. and G. L. Wolff Collection). Reproduced by permission of Durham University Library.

counterpart, this daya sits casually and appears unprepared for the quick, decisive action required in obstetrics. Again, clothing and accessories help to tell the story. The daya's striped tobe and jewelry attest to the success of her practice. And yet to imperial eyes, the exaggerated nose ring and stacked bracelets cast an exotic air over the woman. There are no instruments in sight, and one anticipates that her long tapered fingers will be doing all the work.

Though body postures could change, variations in tobes provided a reliable visual shortcut for the differences in the women themselves. In a picture taken in the town of Wadi Halfa (Fig. 4), an MTS graduate, in a white tobe and holding her medical box, stands next to a daya, who wears a dark-colored tobe and is without any accompanying instruments. The women stand stick straight and squarely face the camera. More so than in many of the other photographs taken by the Wolves, the staging of these two midwives is highly evocative of the genre of nineteenth- and early-twentieth-century ethnographic photographs that purported to classify anthropometric "types" of people on the basis of stature, facial composition, and other physical attributes. These carefully composed images, which often featured a gridded backdrop or other instrument for measurement, were intended as scientific tools. Body measurements were critical for pseudosciences like physiognomy, which argued that a body's relative size and shape was indicative of specific character traits. But whereas such theories were usually applied to individuals, imperialists extrapolated for entire populations.[60] Cataloging people according to physique made sense of the unfamiliar cultures that Britons encountered and offered a means of assessing relative cultural and social civility. Crucially for the imperial civilizing mission, if the body was the outward manifestation of internal character, then as populations evolved their bodies would show signs of change. Photography was a means of documenting these transformations. In placing the two midwives side by side, Mabel, like an ethnographer, expected her audience to be able to recognize and interpret the differences between the certified midwife and her untrained peer. And yet the middle-distance framing of this particular photograph makes detailed comparisons impossible. Instead, the color and quality of the women's dress are the only real visual distinctions. Notably,

FIGURE 4. *Daya* and trained midwife, holding midwifery box, Wadi Halfa, ca. 1935, SAD 742/6/14 (M. E. and G. L. Wolff Collection). Reproduced by permission of Durham University Library.

the medical box, which contains the functional difference between these two midwives, is nearly lost against the sandy background.

The partially hidden medical box was no doubt unintentional. But its relative obscurity inadvertently reveals the true values of the dress and instruments associated with trained midwives. For the Wolves, the box with its drugs, thermometers, and sutures was the hallmark of their training program. When the school first opened, Mabel boasted that the MTS midwife was "intensely proud" of her medical box, "as it is the visible sign of her superiority over the untrained."[61] Yet in those early years, Mabel was more concerned with providing sound care to Sudanese women than with creating rigid class distinctions between trained and untrained midwives. In 1921, she wrote that many of the "old" dayas possess "a moth eaten tooth brush as nail brush and scissors that were never meant to cut" and suggested that new equipment could be provided to these women at cost.[62] A decade later, inspections revealed the unsatisfactory replacement of drugs and equipment on the part of trained midwives. Much of Mabel's correspondence in 1931 outlines a constant frustration with irregular stocking and dispersal of supplies. She suggested that drugs should be distributed freely to midwives and further wondered whether equipment could be renewed free of charge "in order to keep up the necessary standard." By then, however, Mabel would not tolerate dayas' access to MTS supplies. She urged, "Untrained midwives should not be allowed to have boxes and drugs and pose as trained midwives."[63] Anxieties over natives "passing" as someone above their station were common across the empire. In this case, Mabel feared that an old daya with a shiny pair of scissors and a supply of unfamiliar drugs might do irreparable harm and sully the name of modern medicine.

But Mabel was wrong: possession of medical instruments was not the primary, or even a reliable, sign of a trained midwife. Her own photo album showed otherwise. In the bustle of Khartoum, as in photographs, it was white tobes and uniforms, not thermometers and syringes, that marked the difference between an MTS midwife and the older generation of dayas.

While administrators worried over equipment, MTS pupils and graduates were realizing the social authority that came with their new uniforms.

Midwives' unpredictable movements, often late at night and unaccompanied, made them vulnerable to potential suspicions and criticisms about their character. Those who wore a good-quality white tobe benefited from increased urban mobility and ease of access to areas that had previously been closed to them. Reflecting on the difficult urban conditions in the 1920s, Sitt Batul remembers, "The streets were crooked and full of old wells, some of which had caved in—there were no street lamps, the pupils were never allowed out except in pairs and they had to carry a light at night or else they were liable to be arrested. By day they wore a distinguishing blue scarf on their white tobs [sic]."[64] The blue scarf further differentiated MTS midwives from other women. Matching the blue ribbon that SPS servicemen wore around their helmets, it identified Sitt Batul and her colleagues as imperial agents whose movements should not be questioned. The potholes in the street were just as dangerous to midwives as the social censure they risked by moving about unchaperoned. A flashlight and careful steps protected them from one, while walking in pairs dressed in distinguishing white tobes with a blue sash guarded them from the other.

Navigating pitted streets was only the beginning of expanded behaviors of mobility adopted by midwives and, later, other Sudanese women. In addition to performing circumcisions and attending births, midwives made frequent follow-up visits, staffed prenatal clinics, and visited area schools. Getting from one place to another required a thorough knowledge of the newly constructed boulevards of Khartoum and the twisting back alleys of Omdurman. Equally important was a certain degree of physical fitness. While most middle- and upper-class Sudanese women spent their days caring for the home or visiting with nearby neighbors and relatives, midwives walked. Enduring dust and the Sahara sun and careful not to sully their crisp white uniforms, midwives pushed their bodies to a level of physical exertion not shared by other Sudanese women.

More than most, Sitt Batul's position as a Staff Midwife meant that she was expected to travel even farther afield in order to inspect MTS graduates and recruit new students. She responded to this increase in physical demands by teaching her body to move in a new way. With the same determination that brought her to train as a midwife, Sitt Batul learned to ride a bicycle, with the Wolves as willing instructors. Once taught, she rode everywhere, from the Omdurman market to distant patients on the outskirts of the city. Batul had to overcome more than just the distance between her and her destination. Astride her bicycle, this courageous midwife challenged conventions surrounding a woman's body and its correct physical movements. In contrast to her measured, careful walk through the uneven streets, the bicycle carried Sitt Batul rapidly from place to place with no possibility for a chaperone.

A photograph of this new mode of transport shows a smiling Batul perched solidly on her bike's seat, her tobe tucked carefully around her (Fig. 5). The image is framed in such a way that Sitt Batul appears to be leaving the protection of the city's high walls for a journey through

FIGURE 5. Sitt Batul rides her bicycle, Omdurman ca. 1925–1935, SAD 742/6/1 (M. E. and G. L. Wolff Collection). Reproduced by permission of Durham University Library.

a lonely and unmarked landscape. The headlamp affixed to the front of her bike is further evidence of the dangers she would face as day turned to night. This vision of a midwife in motion persists in popular memory. Today, in addition to her medical work and mentorship, Sitt Batul is celebrated as the first Sudanese woman to ride a bicycle. It's a lighthearted legacy, but a meaningful one. The metaphorical and physical ground that Sitt Batul crossed on her bicycle was real evidence of the increasing social and physical mobility realized by Sudanese women in the first half of the twentieth century.

By the 1930s, two classes of professional women, midwives and school-teachers, were traveling ever farther from home. In addition to their movements around town, teachers and midwives frequently used trains and steamers to travel between the capital cities and outlying provinces. For both groups of women, their professional status allowed them to travel in better accommodations than the fourth-class coaches normally reserved for the Sudanese. However, the nature of their professions divided the women. Teachers were permitted to travel in second class, while midwives were required to stay in third. The discrimination against her charges infuriated Mabel, who exclaimed in a letter to her sister, "Really it makes my blood boil to think that our four staff women should not be granted 2nd Class warrants [seats] when they are doing such fine work and yet those blessed female school teachers who really are not worth any more than our women are allotted 2nd Class warrants. . . . I feel very strongly it is demeaning to our work and gives people a wrong impression of the social status of midwives in this country."[65]

The way in which a woman traveled was directly related to her social class, and third-class seats for staff midwives were an insult. Sudanese teachers and midwives came from similarly respected backgrounds and, in theory, should have been issued the same class of ticket. In fact, in comparison to other parts of the British Empire, Sudanese state-certified midwives were of a higher social status, belonging to the middle class and often related to village leaders. Yet in spite of the teachers and midwives' comparable backgrounds, separate travel warrants institutionalized imperial and

Sudanese prejudices against the intimate nature of midwifery and gave the (false) impression of two distinct classes of women.

More than social status and respect was at stake. The differences between second- and third-class travel took their toll on Sudanese women's bodies. In yet another letter on the subject of travel warrants, this time to the Director of the Sudan Medical Service, Mabel gives a detailed description of the physical toil of long journeys.

> It is not usual or customary for a Sudanese woman to travel unaccompanied or alone, especially the better type such as our staff. The accommodations provided for third class passengers on Nile steamers are very inadequate for women, where there is no privacy, little shelter, are [sic] amongst the men and on the Upper Nile boats even the cargo. On the trains too, when there is a change at any junction, all third class passengers are turned out on to the platforms to wait their connection irrespective of what time of day or night, or even the length of time they have to wait and during the months of November, December the nights can be bitterly cold; yet inspite [sic] of every discomfort and want of rest, as usually the third class passengers are packed like sardines, these poor unfortunate women on arrival at their destination are expected to be ready to start work immediately.[66]

This newfound mobility was a corporeal experience. A midwife's physical labor often started well before the real work of midwifery began. Traveling in cramped, cold quarters, exhausted female bodies that should have been protected were instead exposed to strange men and the nighttime air on the rail platform. Deference to their social class was a means to keep professional women safe. For Mabel, the second-class travel warrant operated in the same way as a white tobe with blue sash, by marking its bearer as belonging to an elite class of women whose authority was to be respected, mobility eased, and morality assured.

Classifying working women was part of a larger bureaucratic system that brought Sudanese women and their bodies under imperial control. Just three years after the opening of the Midwifery Training School, a government ordinance required that all practicing midwives in Khartoum and

Omdurman be registered and licensed. This marked the first real attempt by the Sudan Government to monitor women's sexual and reproductive health. In theory, licensing would bring independent dayas, who had not been trained by the MTS, under the careful surveillance of the state. Each midwife or daya was given a register in which she was to record the number of live and still births she attended each year. These registers were to be presented annually to a local doctor or medical officer, who would note the numbers and issue a license. In practice, however, the ordinance was woefully ineffectual. Registers were haphazardly kept; women denied practicing midwifery in order to avoid fines; and records held by government offices were frequently torn, lost, or misfiled. With poor bookkeeping and no means of preventing unlicensed midwives from working, the government could only guess at whether their efforts to improve maternal health and raise birth rates were working.

For her part, Mabel Wolff realized that the bureaucratic line between licensed and unlicensed did not reflect the realities of midwifery practice. The MTS inspection sheet for Fatima Ali Idris Karkarab, an elderly daya working in the village of Merowe, reveals the constant struggle over licensing. In March 1930, Fatima Ali was licensed but described as "too old and incompetent." In 1932, Fatima Ali's license had been canceled; even so, she attended seventy-two cases that year. Always practical, Mabel suggested that the daya's license be renewed, as "only death will prevent her from working." A year later, Fatima Ali paid five piastres for a new license, because her old one had been destroyed in the rain. At that point Mabel's register concedes that Fatima, now into her eighties, "has delivered 49 cases—is old but a great favorite."[67]

Fatima Ali's professional longevity (some might say obstinacy) is a testament to the limits of imperial control, but also demonstrates an awareness of new opportunities. For many expectant mothers, a paper license was in no way a measure of Fatima Ali's expertise as a daya. Instead, her authority derived from years of practical experience. Though medically untrained and living outside the capital, Fatima Ali was not unknown to the Wolves or the government. Moreover, she was monitored and judged according to their standards. However, the fluctuations within the school's records over how to respond to this elderly woman reveal the drawn-out negotiations between imposed state authority and local status quo. In the end, it was not Fatima Ali who backed down but Mabel who realized that it was preferable to waive the licensing standards for one daya than to lose even nominal oversight over unlicensed "favorites" who continued to attract clients. Perhaps Fatima Ali, too, found some benefit in the Wolves' approval and government sanctions. When her license was soaked by the rain, she paid for a new one. There was little legal or economic reason to do this. The government had proven willing to overlook her lapses, and her practice thrived with or without a license. It is possible, then, that even in those last years of her career, Fatima Ali saw a professional distinction in carrying a government license. Though not trained in the new methods, Fatima Ali gained prestige by making connections between her work and the expand-ing influence of the MTS.

In their movements, licenses, and clothing, midwives were vanguards of the new imperial order. A woman's tobe, once granted for reproductive labor, could now be earned through civic service. Just as a husband's gift of a tobe marked his wife's attainment of social adulthood, the tobe-as-uniform marked advanced training and professional membership. This was a new type of woman, whose identity was bound not only by her family but also by the government institutions she served. To be clear, white high-quality tobes remained the preferred fashion for elite Sudanese women. Yet in the hands of an emerging class of professional women, the basic white tobe became a symbol of new bodily behaviors and civic responsibility.

Such symbolism was not taken lightly. One of the more infamous an-ecdotes about an MTS pupil reveals the extent to which the connections between clothing, cleanliness, and imperial authority were made real. One day while making her rounds, Mabel decided to check on two new students attending to their first delivery. Upon her arrival, Mabel discovered, "To my horror one of them had only a loin cloth on squatting in front of the patient on an angareeb like a monkey. When I asked her the reason why she had discarded her clothes she said she was afraid of soiling the government uniform."[68] One can well understand the young woman's dilemma: having been told that the cleanliness of her clothes was of paramount importance, the aspiring midwife decided to take off her white uniform so that she could perform the dirtier aspects of her job. The humor of the situation only partially veils Mabel's great discomfort. Having removed both her tobe and uniform, the government-trained midwife had been reduced, in her supervisor's eyes, to little more than an animal. The practiced medical procedure she performed was outweighed by her primitive state of undress.

When examined carefully, this anecdote tells us much more about the significance of dress than about one woman's foolishness or disobedience. The earnest student fully understood the social and material value of her uniform, and it was with the intention of preserving its worth that she put the garment aside. Her mistake was in letting the symbolic form of her dress overwhelm its function. Working with the same sartorial understandings, Sitt Batul *put on* her uniform in order to move unhindered through town. She and her peers served as visible, highly mobile models of a new type of woman: one who was educated, of good character, and entrusted with the most intimate care of her community.

CHAPTER 3

THE SCHOOLMISTRESSES' RIBS

Dress, Discipline, and Progress

In early May 1944, over three hundred mothers, grandmothers, aunts, cousins, and sisters crowded the grounds of the El Nahud Girls' School to watch 142 schoolgirls demonstrate what they had learned that year. Only a handful of men were invited to the proceedings; among them were regional officials, the local judge, the headmasters from the two area boys' schools, and District Commissioner T. R. H. Owen. The attendees of the Mothers' Day celebration were fed tea and cakes and had "a hob-nob with the [school] mistresses" while the police band, seated behind a screen and kept in good humor with a steady supply of merissa, provided music. The students put on a variety of performances and theatrical sketches, including an Arabic version of the Pied Piper. Writing to his own mother after the event, Owen reflected, "We all enjoyed the show except perhaps [one of the attending officials] whose puritan soul is gravely suspicious of girls' education at all and sternly disapproves of dancing—he withdrew his daughter from the school 3 years ago on learning that the girls were taught calisthenics."[1]

More than just a good show, the Mothers' Day festivities signaled a new era of Sudanese women's lives beyond the confines of their home. For thirty years, the Sudan Government had struggled to establish and popularize formal girls' education. In spite of vocal support from Sudanese elites, government-run schooling for girls faced two significant obstacles: a lack

of qualified teachers and a strictly enforced harem culture that kept women
and girls out of public spaces. While teachers could (and would) be imported from abroad, it was a much more difficult task to draw women out of
seclusion. In this light, the 1944 celebrations in El Nahud marked not only
the intellectual accomplishments of its students but also significant social
change. The schoolgirls, singing songs and performing calisthenics, challenged conservative mores that held that a woman's body and voice should
be hidden. Equally noteworthy, the audience of three hundred mothers,
aunts, and cousins had also defied the practices of enclosure in order to
attend the celebration. Thus, women and girls benefited from more than
textbook lessons; they also took advantage of the opportunity to experiment
with new behaviors in new spaces.

PRODUCING SUITABLE WIVES AND MOTHERS

A generation after Babikr Bedri opened his school in Rufa'a with just seventeen students, securing a place in the limited number of girls' schools had
become highly desirable. In 1944, the country had sixty-two government-
run elementary schools for girls, an intermediate school, and a teacher
training college. A much-anticipated secondary school for girls was slated
to open the following year. Entry was determined by age, social standing,
and finally, merit. Eager parents occasionally lied about their daughter's
age—adjusting up or down according to the availability at different class
levels. Such deception was fairly easy, since a general lack of birth certificates meant that teachers and administrators used the presence of adult
teeth to try to determine a potential student's age.[2] In his frank and witty
memoir, T. R. H. Owen admits that belonging to a leading family was the
real key to gaining a place in school. "In a country where the privileges of
position and birth are traditional, the barren and mechanical justice of pure
competitive examination is neither thinkable nor desirable."[3] But Owen
perhaps overstates the case for nepotism. Officially, at least, preference was
given first to children who could produce birth certificates proving they
were at least seven years old (this carried the additional benefit of aiding the
Sudan Medical Service in its attempts to popularize the certificates); sec-

ond, to close relatives of teachers, nurses, and midwives; and finally, to "truly local children," those who didn't have the option to attend other schools in larger towns.[4] Through a combination of birth certificates, kinship, or sheer luck a girl might manage to secure one of the few thousand coveted spots in a government elementary school. Even more precious was one of the ninety seats at the only Girls' Training College, which prepared the most promising students to become teachers themselves.[5]

A graduate of the Training College or a mother with a daughter enrolled in school would have felt a particular affinity to one of the more fashionable tobes of the day known as "The Schoolmistresses' Ribs," whose stripes gave the garment a ribbed effect. This was not the first tobe to mark the country's progress in education. Another striped tobe, "The Doctors' Ribs," commemorated the first graduating class of the Kitchener School of Medicine in 1928.[6] Now, in a recognizable parallel, it was women's achievements that were being honored. The Schoolmistresses' Ribs left little doubt that girls' education was something to celebrate.

And yet there was far too little of it. In 1938, frustrated by the limits imposed on their own educational opportunities, over a thousand Sudanese men who had graduated from secondary school met in Omdurman to form the Graduates' General Congress. Their aim was to "promote the general welfare of the country" and work in a "spirit of friendly co-operation and obedience" with the government.[7] Despite assurances that the organization would not take any action contrary to existing policy, a year after its founding the Congress sent a letter to the Civil Secretary calling for a complete overhaul of the educational system. They condemned the government's existing program as "backwards" and cited a statistic in which only 6 percent of Sudanese boys ages six to twelve had received an education, whereas in Uganda over 33 percent of boys of the same age were educated. The unfavorable comparison to a black African colony was an embarrassment. The Graduates concluded, "Even if the present number of elementary and intermediate schools is doubled in a few years' time, it will still fall short of our aspirations, and—far from being compared with other Arab countries—it will not reach the stage achieved by neighboring countries." A clear racial hierarchy was at work. The northern Sudanese intelligentsia envisioned themselves as part of a distinguished Arab-Islamic heritage, and yet the quality of their educational system placed Sudan far below presumably less civilized African populations. As a solution, the Graduates proposed an expanded centralized program that would provide education for education's sake and grant a man the "qualities which make for success in his struggle for existence."[8]

As dismal as the prospects were for Sudanese boys, girls' education and the low status of Sudanese women were the main focus of the Graduates' reformist rhetoric. Their letter painfully stated, "Girls' education is so backward that it cannot be compared with any other country."[9] At the time, only 3,400 girls were enrolled in government schools across all of Sudan.[10] The Graduates directly linked these low numbers to the shortcomings of their nation. "To further the country's progress which is, to a great extent, retarded by the ignorance of Sudanese women, it is essential to provide as many schools for girls as there are for boys and to raise the standard of such schools to a level that ensures the production of suitable wives and mothers capable of making a happy home and taking proper care of their children."[11] Malnutrition, inadequate housing, and poor sanitation were also cited as obstacles to Sudan's progress; educated wives could redress many of these faults. By extension, modern, healthy households would translate into modern, healthy nation-states. Thus, for Sudan's new intellectual elites, the strength of a nation and its citizenry was a domestic affair.

However, the men disagreed over just how much schooling was appropriate. If girls' elementary education strengthened homes and contributed to the nation's progress, it was less clear what benefits further education might hold. An exchange in *Gordon College Magazine* presented the cases for and against advanced girls' education. In an unsigned essay titled "The Disadvantage of Higher Education for Girls," the author agreed that an elementary education was appropriate for Sudanese girls so that they might raise their children, comfort their husbands, and understand their religious duties, but cautioned that anything further threatened domestic order. According to the author, no more than 2 percent of the country had a secondary education, and "the rest of the country does not even know how to read or write." With such low levels of schooling among Sudanese men, providing a secondary education for girls would "create a problem which we shall never be able to solve. . . . Shall we be able to marry girls who have received higher education to these uneducated people? The answer is obviously 'No'. Then to whom shall we marry them?" Though the statistics don't bear him out, the author feared that advanced education for girls would outpace that of boys, resulting in a class of overeducated women who would be dissatisfied with their husbands or, even worse, entirely unfit for marriage. The essay concludes with fears of loose morals and social chaos. "Would [educated girls] be content with the same standard of living as their fathers who are mainly peasants? Of course not. Also, higher education will certainly affect their character and general behavior. Instead of going out modestly and decently, they will wish to attend public shows and even share the activities of men, and to such behavior we will never agree."[12]

These criticisms are countered by another student, Abd Alla Bashir, in an essay titled "The Advantages of Higher Education for Women." Bashir turns to broader human history to illustrate his point. "All the most valuable deeds and assistance rendered to humanity are the end of the thoughts of those men whose countries were the first lovers of education and the first to care for it." A well-educated woman could better share in her husband's sorrow and happiness, entertain him, and accompany him on trips. Bashir writes, "Life in the house of an educated mother is of course far happier than that of an uneducated one. What an unhappy man the husband of the latter is, and how miserable is the life he leads!" In contrast to his classmate who focused on women's behavior and dissatisfaction, Bashir emphasizes the happiness of husbands. He repeats the familiar argument that strong households build strong nations. With educated parents, "their children are well brought up and accustomed to be virtuous and not vicious, trustworthy, courteous and obedient. . . . In this way, they are indirectly greatly helping their country."[13]

For better or for worse, Sudanese men saw a direct relationship between girls' education and the sanctity of the home. Conservatives worried that education would overturn gender hierarchies. When questioned on the subject of girls' education, a group of men in-training to be teachers asked,

"Would she cook for me? Would she bring a man's dinner to him in the fields? Could I beat her, if she did not obey me?"[14] The much more prevalent anxiety, however, was that Sudanese men and women were no longer well matched. This apprehension was not limited to Sudan. Throughout the Middle East, men and women raised concerns that the public march to modernity and self-rule was matched by discord and disruption in the home.[15]

While education for Sudanese boys proceeded slowly, and often in fits and starts, it still far outpaced the offerings for girls. Formal schooling and government jobs had created a small but significant class of highly educated Sudanese men who were now looking for comparable and companionable partners. Dissatisfied with local offerings, Sudan's leaders turned to better-educated and more "modern" Egyptian, Syrian, or even European women for their brides. Babikr Bedri had warned of such a marital upset back in 1907 when he cautioned that there was little point in educating Sudanese boys if Sudanese girls could not keep pace. By 1937, the perceived intellectual distance between Sudanese men and their prospective wives was so great that even the Sudan Government acknowledged that strengthened marriages were a reason for expanding girls' education. That year the Lord De La Warr's Education Commission, charged with evaluating the state of education in Sudan, concluded, "With the educated Sudanese the gap is becoming unbridgeable between the two halves forming the pillars of home life."[16] On this the government and the Graduates' Congress could agree. Closing the unbridgeable gap and ensuring modern domestic partnerships would form the heart of girls' education.

The one who took up this vital task was Ina Beasley, a spirited British woman with past experience in imperial education, who tempered her idealism with practicality. She arrived in Khartoum in 1939 at the age of forty-one, having decided that "Sudan was not as far from England as Burma which I had just left." The salary was not quite as high as in her previous positions, but at the time secure employment, even for highly qualified women, was difficult to come by. Perhaps more importantly, generous annual leave made it possible for Beasley to spend her summers in England with her young daughter, whom she had left behind.[17]

Over the next decade, first as Superintendent and then Controller of Girls' Education, Beasley transformed girls' education from its modest beginnings into a centralized imperial institution that shaped young girls into civilized women. Under her leadership, curricula were diversified and standards strengthened. Instruction expanded beyond elementary levels to include three intermediate schools, a teacher training college, and an elite secondary school. Subjects included reading and writing in Arabic, mathematics, cooking and childcare, and even physical education. For married women, imperial education took form in housewife clubs and night schools. Like their more formal counterparts, these programs included instruction in reading, writing, and arithmetic as well as highly popular demonstrations in knitting and cooking.

Beasley's exhaustive work was driven by her firm belief in the reformative power of education. In a broadcast on Radio Omdurman, Beasley outlined the civic mission of girls' education and its purpose in developing "well-balanced individuals." She explained, "The women of the country may then be able to cooperate in the solving of some of the serious social problems, which according to Sudanese men, is retarded only by the stupidity of women."[18] The rhetoric of her speech mirrored that of the Graduates' Congress and other elites. But on closer examination, Beasley presented an ambitious vision that went far beyond educating girls to be better wives and mothers. Indeed, she suggested that with the proper education Sudanese women might actively engage in civic dialogue and "cooperate" in addressing national concerns. By the end of the 1940s, Sudanese women activists, largely educated in Ina Beasley's schools, would boldly put forth the same sentiment.

At all levels, imperial educational programs were structured to match the domestic fantasies of the educated male elite. A curriculum that balanced reading, writing, and arithmetic with cooking, sewing, and child-rearing ensured that a girl's education would be applied to her home. The educated woman would still cook for her husband, but now with healthier recipes and greater economy. Beasley willingly acknowledged that education could be "an aid to matrimony." She writes, "If the prevailing custom is to make the best match possible from a worldly standpoint, without regard to more

romantic claims, then on purely pragmatic grounds education should prove
a good investment." In light of future marital responsibilities, Beasley expected a girl who had completed her elementary education to be "a good
cook, a good needlewoman and have very firm ideas on matters of hygiene
and cleanliness."[19] Men recognized these assets. In the village of Kassala,
husbands responded enthusiastically to a proposed Ladies Club for their
wives, saying, "You could teach them to press European trousers!"[20]

Yet some were starting to hope for even more from their wives. From
the 1930s onward, novels, magazines, and movies imported from Europe,
America, and other areas of the Middle East began to influence Sudanese
views of marriage and standards of beauty. Mutual compatibility—if not
romantic love—was now to be expected. Additionally, more and more Sudanese men expressed a desire for a "modern"-looking woman, one whose
face was free from scars and whose circumcision "had not been of the
Pharaonic kind." In a short story published in a popular Sudanese newspaper, the protagonist eschews multiple marriage prospects in hopes of finding
a wife with "the allure of Clara Bow, the enchantment of Greta Garbo, and
the smile of Lillian Gish."[21] And although government schools could make
no guarantees of allure or enchantment, a strict doctrine of hygiene, sewing
lessons, and a vocal campaign against female genital cutting attempted to
alter the bodies of young girls to meet modern standards.

AN AFRICAN *SARTOR RESARTUS*

Domestic lessons were, in truth, bodily lessons. Instruction in nutrition,
cooking, sewing, and bathing was a very real strategy to reform and reshape
Sudanese bodies. As a tool of the imperial civilizing mission, education was
a physical experience that laid claim to hands, hair, mouths, and genitalia in
addition to hearts and minds. Clean, well-fed, and properly attired bodies
would be living testaments of a new social order.

One of first tasks facing both British and Sudanese advocates of girls' education was ensuring that schoolgirls were properly dressed. Across northern
Sudan, forms of dress for unmarried girls were minimal and irregular. Most
wore little more than a headscarf, called a *tarha*, and a plain cotton skirt tied

with string. Chests were often left bare. While such levels of exposure may have been acceptable in the privacy of the home or for lower-class laboring women, British and northern Sudanese standards of modesty required that girls cover their bodies more fully as they made their way to school. Although some schools did provide uniforms (in the form of simple cotton shifts) for their students, Ina Beasley found that the most effective means of combating immodest dress was simply to teach girls to sew. After four years of domestic science lessons, a girl was expected to have made herself a set of clothes from "plain, stout calico" provided by the Sudan Government and paid for in installments by her parents. Except in instances in which especially skilled schoolmistresses introduced smarter cuts and patterns, the school dresses were far from fashionable; but they served their function in covering students' bodies.[22]

These sewing lessons carried a larger social and psychological purpose. More so than many of her colleagues, Beasley was a firm believer in the transformative power of dress. Alongside teacher evaluations and the logistics of founding new schools, Beasley's personal papers are filled with observations on local sartorial practices and optimistic comments that new clothing could bring about new behaviors. At one point in her memoir she jokes, "A whole treatise could be written about the effects of clothes in schools in emergent countries but this is no place for an African *Sartor Resartus*." Written in 1836 by Thomas Carlye, *Sartor Resartus*, or "The Tailor Retailored," was a satirical work calling for modern society to cast off its fraying institutions and remake itself. Beasley, however, was sincere in her belief that well-kept, modest clothing would lift Sudanese women and girls out of the "squalor" and "apathy" in which they lived. Acknowledging the "stimulating effect of clothes" and the confidence that grew from them, Beasley took satisfaction in reporting that "it became more and more noticeable how the girls benefitted from this dressmaking and taking a reasonable pride in their appearance."[23]

Beasley wasn't alone; across the British Empire, administrators, civil servants, and missionaries treated sartorial practices as both "sign and instrument" of imperial rule.[24] Clothing was a mark of difference and a means of control. To imperial eyes, the relative nakedness and perceived state of un-dress of colonized populations stood as evidence of their primitiveness, of a state close to nature. This exposure of the body and seeming lack of shame or modesty was entirely out of step with European civilizational standards. However, raising a culture from primitiveness was not as simple as wrapping a body in a calico dress. Even as they attempted to civilize, imperialists took pains to maintain the distance between themselves and those they ruled. With contradictory imperial logic, this often meant pressuring elites away from European styles and back toward traditional forms of dress.

At the turn of the twentieth century, most Gordon Memorial Col-lege students had proudly worn Western suits and ties, topped with an Ottoman-style fez. But when British fears about incipient nationalism took hold in the 1920s, college officials enacted a policy that prohibited students from wearing Western dress and forced them to return to their "native" robes and turbans. Although some did not mind putting aside the trappings of their foreign occupiers, most men resented being barred from such valu-able signs of modernity and progress.[25] Outside the classroom, meanwhile, men were free to fashion themselves as they wanted. Novelist Magdalen King-Hall was struck by the sight of "westernised" Sudanese on bikes and wearing "purple socks with startlingly brown shoes."[26]

Anxieties over the political effects of clothing trickled down from the highest halls of education to the elementary schools. Yusuf Bedri, son of Babikr Bedri, carried keen memories of the time he challenged imperial dress codes. While on his way to school twelve-year-old Yusuf was stopped by District Commissioner J. N. Richardson, who asked why Yusuf was wearing European-style shoes and not the more basic locally produced "native shoes." Yusuf replied that the shoes were a gift from his brother, who had bought them in a shop. Richardson grew angry and "sent me back in a furious temper to change my shoes and put on my marcoub, the native shoes. By the time I got back to school, I found the whole school paraded and Mr. Richardson was inspecting the shoes of the pupils. Every boy wearing European shoes was sent home to change into Sudanese shoes."[27] The morning's instruction forgotten, a larger lesson on imperial power was brought painfully home.

The image of the young boys and their shoes lined up under the watchful eye of the District Commissioner provides poignant testimony for how bodies experienced imperial power. And the contradictory policies regarding dress for male and female students demonstrate how clothing was used to enforce multiple threads of dominance and control. Men in Western suits and boys in European shoes posed a political threat. In contrast, schoolgirls' exposed and underdressed bodies were taken as a sign of cultural backwardness. In response, administrators restricted clothing options for one while dressing the other in shifts, whose seams and straight lines were modeled on European forms. In the south, the rules changed again. In accordance with the Southern Policy, southern Sudanese men were prohibited from wearing turbans, robes, or even long shirts. As one administrator explained in a letter to a local tailor, "Shirts should be made short, with a collar and opening down the front in the European fashion. . . . No more 'Arab' clothing is to be made as from today."[28]

These contrasting policies were not the result of administrative confusion. Sumptuary rules were an exercise in control, a means of ordering bodies and minds. Depending on the gender, race, or class of the individual, British officials alternately used clothing to divide, civilize, preserve tradition, or check nationalist sentiment. We might wonder how Sudanese families responded to these multiple sets of rules. Did they question the hypocrisy that put their daughters in seamed dresses and their sons in robes and turbans? Or did they recognize that the battle over dress was a struggle for agency and power?

In fact, imperial authority over clothing was not absolute. In the privacy of their homes, many elite women experimented with European fashions, combining pieces, colors, and patterns in unlikely ways to create their own modern aesthetic. This, too, created anxiety. Indeed, Beasley's harshest criticisms (and some of her most vivid descriptions) were reserved for women who misused or misappropriated Western styles. In both her diary and memoir, Beasley records one particularly memorable afternoon with a well-respected schoolmistress in Rufa'a. "We had tea on the verandah sitting up to the table—a sensible tea with just biscuits and fruit. Afterwards, dressed in all her gold regalia and a pink satin frock, she danced the bride's dance—a revolting sight from European standards."[29] Beasley adds further details and a dose of wry humor in her memoir, remarking that the heavy gold jewelry might have looked pleasing with a tobe, but "made a slightly repellent contrast against a bright pink satin frock of European cut." The movements of the dance "resembled a 'League of Health and Beauty' exercise for a double chin, another which involved much arching the chest and various significant wriggling of the breasts and buttocks. . . . Danced under the moon without any clothes at all, it might have had significance; in that tight pink satin frock I found it vulgar."[30]

Beasley had caught a glimpse of a world in transition, and it made her nervous. Historically, Sudanese wedding dances were performed nude so that the groom could assess the health and fitness of his bride.[31] By the 1940s, imperial standards of modesty and a growing prestige of imported clothing had shifted fashion preferences, such that many modern-minded brides chose to wear European-style dresses for their wedding ceremonies. Yet it was this very pink satin dress that offended Beasley's sensibilities. Reading closely, it is clear that Beasley was not put off by the bride dance itself, but by the performance of highly sexualized gestures and movements while adorned in Western dress. Here, proper attire had not performed its intended civilizing function. Instead, the combination of dress and dance unabashedly revealed the limits of clothing's transformative power. After a "sensible tea" of biscuits and fruit on the veranda, Beasley was ill-prepared for a dance better performed nude under moonlight. Her response is to exoticize the dance and relegate it to another time and place, one in which the shortfalls of the civilizing mission were not so apparent. In such a setting, the unfamiliar movements would have carried ethnographic "significance"; closer to home, they were merely vulgar. As Beasley succinctly concludes, "This is the first time I had seen it [bride's dance] in its entirety and I could only decide that here the East and West were not well blended."[32]

Satin dresses could not simply be put on; they had to be accompanied by an understanding of proper form and function. During a visit to Sayyid Abd al-Rahman's homestead to celebrate the opening of a new girls' school, Beasley had the rare opportunity to meet with his youngest wife, who was usually "muffled up" and kept out of sight. Beasley describes the young woman as being prematurely fat, but with lovely skin. "Unfortunately, this comeliness was not set off by the graceful folds of the tobe, for she was wearing a frock of some checked material ill-cut and badly fitting with European shoes and stockings. What amazed me most was a sort of bandeau round her head made of cheap red and silver lamé and giving a sort of coronet effect."[33] To be sure, the wife of one of Sudan's most important political figures had selected her clothing for this meeting carefully. Like the suits and ties of Gordon College graduates, the young woman's bandeau, shoes, and stockings were meant to demonstrate a parity between herself and Ina Beasley. They also allowed her to explore her own sense of individuality and style.

In a departure from the simple forms of Sudanese dress, the multiple components of European styles provided increased opportunities for self-fashioning. As John and Jean Comaroff explain in another context, "Western dress . . . opened up a host of imaginative possibilities for the Africans. It made available an expansive, expressive, experimental language with which to conjure new social identities and senses of self, a language with which also to speak back to whites."[34] But this was a language that imperialists strongly resisted. No doubt, Sudanese women also found pleasure in experimentation. But the combination of checkered patterns, cheap lamé, and sagged stockings suggested that though elites might purchase European clothes, they did not have command of them. Without a proper understanding of how pieces did or did not coordinate, Sudanese women appeared to imperial eyes to be wearing little more than ill-fitting costumes, not modern fashions. The logic of European dress (its color, cut, fit, and accessories) was a lesson to be learned and a critical accompanying step in shaping Sudanese bodies for new clothes.

Desires for others' fashions did not solely move in one direction. In a moment of uncharacteristic frustration, even a sartorial reformer like Ina Beasley could appreciate the cool comfort of the tobe. Soon after her arrival in Sudan, Beasley shared dinner at the house of a local sheikh, when he invited her to meet his wife. Beasley did not yet know Arabic and thus had no way of conversing with the woman, but was curious to meet her just the same. Her host led Beasley to a back room, which he unlocked with a large key. "Reclining on an *angareeb* piled with cushions was a beautiful young woman, her coppery skin set off richly by the soft draperies of a pink, silk tobe." The two women did their best to communicate with small talk and gestures, and the wife provided a box of high quality chocolates. Beasley writes, "Mostly I remember the pleasurable sight of her grace and beauty as she lay on the *angareeb* in her soft draperies while I sat stiffly on a wooden chair dressed in a short cotton frock rumpled from a long, hot drive in the front of a lorry."[35]

Here again, East meets West. Yet this time, the ever-practical Beasley regrets her heavy, wrinkled dress and wishes for the "soft draperies" of her companion's silk tobe. Each woman's mode of sitting is also indicative of her station and level of comfort, as the beautiful young wife easily reclines on a traditional Sudanese bed, while Ina sits rigidly on a wooden chair. Imperial order had been upended. Beauty and ease within one's own skin belonged to the colonized, while Ina Beasley, the model of Victorian propriety, was hot, rumpled, and distressed. It is Ina's palpable discomfort that makes this scene so poignant. Exhausted and alone in a room with a woman with whom she has little means of conversing, Ina longs for a moment to herself: to let down her guard, to loosen her collar and be caressed by lush fabric. Hers is not a literal desire for the tobe, but for what it represents in that instance: a moment of rest, a moment of grace. After fifteen minutes, Beasley and her hostess "heard again the key in the lock . . . [and] I was led back to the outside world."[36]

Cotton clothing, such as Beasley's dress, carried its own particular set of rules and disciplines. Unlike many forms of African or Middle Eastern dress that required little or no laundering, imported European styles "needed to be washed and maintained, binding wives and mothers to an unrelenting regime of 'cleanliness.' . . . It was a form a discipline that [was] monitored closely, ensuring brisk sales of soap and other cleansing agents both personal and domestic."[37] Though favored for its durability and breathability in warm climates, cotton fabric showed dirt, oils, and sweat to a much greater degree than did leathers, grasses, or animal skins. As a result, the seemingly simple act of putting on a cotton dress or shirt committed the wearer to attendant behaviors of frequent washing of themselves and their clothes.

Imperialists expected the labor required for the proper upkeep of cotton clothing to inspire, if not compel, an overarching personal discipline. Beasley's diary reveals the ideological link between clean bodies and ordered minds. Observing one struggling teacher's lesson, she records, "Zenab's hygiene as disgraceful as her arithmetic. Gave demonstration of a blanket bath which consisted of washing patient's face with corner of dirty tarha. She seems to be thoroughly slack."[38] Beasley makes no attempt to differentiate between her observations of dirty clothes and her critique of substandard lessons. Both were the result of lax attitudes and both were problematic.

Zenab's questionable mathematics and soiled headscarf reveal the tension between imperial visions of reform and the obstacles to sociocultural change. In practice, a few years of sewing lessons could not solve the problems of the underdressed schoolgirl nor provide the complete "stimulating effect" that Beasley was hoping for. Her troubles with a girls' school in the small village of Shabarga in 1941 are telling. "The school must be a difficult one to run as the children are very poor and often have to stay at home for lack of clothes. This problem in rural districts must be faced. Some of the older girls wore knickers and just tobes. The clothes of Class I were frequently very disreputable. Class IV had frocks made in school but often not paid for."[39] Inadequate dress hindered progress. Girls with few clothing choices arrived in a tobe, with little on underneath. Those who did have dresses had not been able to pay for them, and there was little hope that they or their families would purchase more material to make a second set. Both instances meant that girls' attendance at school was irregular.

Recognizing the poverty of the district, Beasley suggested that the girls adopt the *rahat*, a skirt made of leather fringe or grass, which would be inexpensive and easy to keep clean. Outraged, the Shabarga mothers replied that the rahat was only suitable for "Arabs wandering in the desert."[40] An important cultural assertion was at work here: dress forms were not so easily transferable. While young girls in other regions wore the rahat, in

Shabarga it was a sign of nomadic backwardness. On the other hand, the diverse clothing options that were available to the Shabarga girls (knickers, tobes, dresses) were evidence of the wider social and cultural ruptures taking place throughout Sudan. Although rumblings of a nationalist movement had begun, a recognizably "Sudanese" mode of dress had not yet been standardized. Indeed, Beasley's willingness to introduce the rahat to girls in Shabarga speaks volumes on the ongoing negotiations between civility, economy, and the importance of girls' education. Likewise, the Shabarga mothers and daughters struggled to balance modest dress and school attendance with their true sartorial selves.

One form of clothing that the Shabarga girls did adopt, as did thousands of other schoolgirls across northern Sudan, was the tobe. The standard outerwear of their mothers and older sisters, the tobe was already present and available in the home as well as the marketplace. Conveniently, the garment was common enough to not be associated with any particular tribe, ethnic group, or social class and satisfied both British and Sudanese standards of propriety. But what may have been envisioned as a stopgap measure until a more fitting form of dress could be found, instead proved to be the ideal combination of modesty and mobility. With surprising cultural dexterity, the protection the tobe offered to married women was now extended to the bodies of their daughters, who put on the tobe as they walked to school. In ways that had not been predicted, the traditional tobe permitted bold, progressive steps toward a modern education.

But although the tobe safeguarded young girls in streets, inside the classroom it brought nothing but trouble and disruption. As a garment originally conceived for the elite, the beautiful long folds of the tobe were not designed for active bodies. Unfamiliar with the tucks and folds needed to hold the large quantities of fabric in place, students in their new tobes were in a constant state of adjustment and paid little attention to their lessons. Beasley observed two girls crossing school grounds: "The younger of the two was evidently not very much accustomed to the garment and was constantly tripping over it. As they wore nothing at all underneath . . . there was nothing to do but wait until she learned to manipulate it."[41] Teachers struggled too. Though more adept at holding the tobe in place, instructors were restricted from a full range of motion and found it difficult to write on the chalkboard or carry out a demonstration. The overall effect was an air of constant movement and distraction.

In contrast, classrooms in which the girls removed their coverings once inside received Beasley's highest praise. At the Gulli Girls' School she noted, "The girls all had their tobes off all the time, folded up on their desks. This gave a much brisker look to the whole proceedings. The school was well situated with plenty of light and air and looked delightfully clean." In the village of Merowe, a well-behaved classroom looked quite "businesslike . . . since tarhas were removed on arrival and the mistresses taught without their tobes. They may have lacked the grace of the falling draperies but there was no bother about constantly hitching up long yards of muslin in going about the ordinary affairs of the classroom."[42] Of course, one must assume that these girls all had something suitable to wear under their tobes—perhaps a skirt or shift crafted as part of the school's sewing curriculum.

By 1949, the practice of not allowing tobes or tarhas in the classroom had become standard. A note from the Ministry of Education to British staffwomen read, "Teachers should always be clean and neat in their personal appearance and children as clean as possible. It is the usual practice for children to wear white dresses in school but the lack of a white dress should not prevent a child from coming to school. Dresses can often be improved by a little mending and this can be done at school in the 3rd and 4th year classes. No tobes or tarhas should be worn in school by the children."[43] The graceful aesthetics of the tobe were sacrificed in the name of efficiency, white dresses, and bright businesslike classrooms. Without their coverings, the bodies of students and teachers were revealed, stilled, and ready to be transformed.

The overlaps between progress, proper dress, and imperial control played out on young Sudanese bodies. Lessons on reading or mathematics were placed side by side with a domestic curriculum of sewing, hygiene, cooking, and childcare. Yet in order to access any of this information, students had to ensure that they were properly dressed, in the eyes of both their communities and imperial administrators. In a gesture rich with symbolism, the Sudan Government provided girls with the material and patterns with which to clothe themselves. Instructors, too, were held to account and needed to present a neat appearance in order to be deemed competent teachers. Thus in a very real way, education in northern Sudan and the possibilities it afforded were only made available to those who fashioned themselves according to imperial standards.

THE CAMPAIGN AGAINST PHARAONIC CIRCUMCISION

Once young girls' bodies were arranged and composed in the classroom, they were subject to further lessons on civility and self-fashioning. Like her peers, Beasley was horrified when she learned about the ritual of female genital cutting and, along with Elaine Hills-Young, the new headmistress of the Midwifery Training School, tailored lectures on the subject to all levels of girls' education. Lessons highlighted health risks such as recurrent infections, painful sexual intercourse, infertility, and difficulties in childbirth. Also woven into these arguments were themes of national progress, motherhood, and morality. Beasley's guidelines for a lesson for fourth-year elementary girls chastise, "Do you know that the Sudanese can never rise to be a nation on the same footing as others while this custom persists? . . . Do you know that your sons and grandsons are lessened by it? Do you know how shocked and disgusted people are in other countries when they hear of the custom in your country?"[44] Unfavorable comparisons to other nations were expected to spur change. As another lesson stated, "It is vital that girls who are avid for learning should know that circumcision in any form is not known by and is non-existent in the majority of civilized nations—e.g. Europe and America." Civilized women were "chaste through moral force and not through any painful bodily one."[45] It was often (and erroneously) pointed out that even in Egypt pharaonic circumcision had ended because the "more educated people realised the harm it caused."[46] Notably, there was no corresponding curriculum in boys' schools on reproductive health or the dangers of genital cutting. Administrators placed the burden of reform entirely on the shoulders of schoolgirls. It was their barbaric customs, their scarred bodies, that were impeding Sudan's progress.

We can't know how Beasley's lectures were translated in classrooms or whether British and Sudanese schoolmistresses actually used words such as *shock* and *disgust*. Upon hearing these lessons, students likely experienced their own shock, horror, and confusion. Although historians are reluctant to psychoanalyze their subjects, anthropologists study emotions as a collective phenomenon—a culturally constructed set of responses to the world. Emotions are embodied ways of knowing; they are actions and reactions as well as passions.[47] When schoolgirls were confronted with the negative emotions of imperialists, they had to contend with other acts and other ways of knowing that were already expressed on their bodies. For the majority of girls learning about the harms of female genital cutting were already circumcised. There was no set age for the ritual; girls were cut when they had reached the "age of reason," generally before puberty. But even this was approximate. In 1945, near the end of Beasley's tenure in Sudan, schoolmistresses carried out a small survey of the incidence of genital cutting in a few of the Omdurman schools. In one elementary school a total of eighty girls in the first and fourth years were examined. In the first-year class, ten girls, around the age of six, were uncircumcised. Among the fourth-year students, five girls, aged ten, had not been cut—but there was little doubt that it would be done later. All of the young women at the Intermediate School and Training College were circumcised.[48]

How, then, were these young women and girls to respond to imperialists' harsh criticisms of their most intimate parts? Beasley notes that the students at the Teacher Training College had lost some of their shyness in discussing female genital cutting. "The tendency now seems to be that they feel that it is a pity that they have been circumcised. There is nothing that they can do to alter the opinions of old people but that they themselves will do their best in the future."[49] Certainly some felt shame and anger over their cut bodies. Others would go on to become vocal activists against genital cutting. But many must have struggled to reconcile the reality of their bodies with reformers' arguments. They understood, far better than the imperialists, that genital cutting was part of a complex system of gender relations, sexuality, and reproduction. And as much as students may have desired to be viewed as civilized in the eyes of the world, local values of enclosure and morality still governed their lives. More than opinions needed to change. To put an end to the procedure would require shifting the very boundaries of women's social worlds. Looking about at her teachers and peers, a young woman was caught between the intangible promises of progress and the sense of belonging and responsibility that was already impressed upon her body.

⌒

Beasley's fiery curriculum was in concert with the Sudan Government's intensified efforts to end female genital cutting. In 1937, ill and exhausted after sixteen years of trekking throughout Sudan to recruit nurses and midwives, Mabel and Gertrude Wolff retired to England. They left with little more than with which they had come, having bequeathed most of their household items, right down to pictures in their frames, to their staff.[50] The position of MTS principal was filled by Elaine Hills-Young, former matron of the Khartoum Hospital, who was chosen because of her intolerance for "backwards" traditions. Upon taking up her new role, Hills-Young observed an MTS midwife perform a modified circumcision, complete with a sterilized straight razor, iodine, and frequent hand-washing. Even so, the new principal found "the spectacle sufficiently revolting" and declared that going forward no MTS midwives would be permitted to perform genital cuttings in any form.[51] Hills-Young did teach her students the safest methods for opening the scars of circumcised mothers in labor, but she provided no instruction on how to perform the hygienic modified cutting advocated by her predecessors. Unwittingly, Hills-Young had created a third class of midwives: those who were trained in hygiene and bio-medicine but had no experience caring for circumcised bodies.

This sharp reversal in midwifery practice came at an opportune political moment. In 1936, a new Anglo-Egyptian treaty gave Great Britain diplomatic breathing room to pursue greater interventionist policies in Sudan without fear of reprisals from their co-dominion partner. And in 1939, Douglas Newbold, a popular administrator who had long concerned himself with issues of female genital cutting, was promoted to the position of Civil Secretary, where he could direct matters of policy. That same year, the *mufti* of Sudan, the country's leading religious authority, published a statement in *al-Nil* newspaper explaining that circumcision was "desirable" but not compulsory and that the operation should consist of no more than cutting off part of the clitoris.[52] After two decades of waiting for seeds of change from below, the campaign against female genital cutting was now also being waged from above.

Joining government reformers in their campaign were two of Sudan's most influential political and religious leaders: Sayyid Abd al-Rahman al-Mahdi and Sayyid Ali al-Mirghani. The posthumous son of the Mahdi and leader of the Ansar religious sect, Sayyid Abd al-Rahman had initially been perceived as a political threat to the imperial state. But when he came out against the nationalist uprisings in 1924 and advocated for a program of cooperation with the British in preparation for eventual independence, al-Rahman quickly became one of the government's most important allies in swaying Sudanese opinion. His rival for Sudanese and British attentions was the leader of the Khatmiyya religious sect, Sayyid Ali al-Mirghani, whose family had opposed the Mahdi in the nineteenth century. Recognizing new opportunities for influence, al-Mirghani refused to concede the leading role in Sudan's political awakening to al-Rahman and came out in favor of Sudan's union with Egypt. From the 1930s through the 1950s, imperial administrators played the two men's personal antagonisms and political ambitions off one another, effecting a delicate balance in which both leaders kept their supporters in line in hopes of future concessions.

In the matter of genital cutting, the two leaders lent invaluable political weight and sanction to the government's growing intervention. Putting aside (or perhaps acting on) their deep-seated rivalries, both men contributed forewords to a government-authored treatise on the medical and social injuries of infibulation. Sayyid Abd al-Rahman voiced his "care for the education and uplift of Sudanese women," which, with the end of infibulation, would improve the country as a whole. Judiciously, al-Mirghani allowed that all countries had positive and negative traditions and he had no "doubt that it [pharaonic circumcision] will, together with other bad customs, disappear through education and enlightenment."[53] These were familiar refrains; both men linked the condition of women's bodies to the strength of their nation.

With the backing of local leaders and the new tactics of the MTS, the time seemed right for direct government action. In May 1945, the government's Advisory Council, composed of Sudanese notables, merchants, and civil servants, met with a number of administrative officials, including Ina Beasley, and unanimously passed a resolution stating that pharaonic circumcision was a "cruel and barbarous" practice and a "relic of pre-Islamic pagan days." A second resolution asking for legislation outlawing pharaonic circumcision passed with a vote of eighteen to nine.[54] A year later, in February 1946, the Sudan Government amended the existing Penal Code to state, "Whoever voluntarily causes hurt to the external genital organs of a woman is said . . . to commit unlawful circumcision." It was legal, however, to "remove the free and projecting part of the clitoris."[55]

With that, two distinct types of genital cutting were codified. In their meetings, the Advisory Council had condemned only the most extreme form of circumcision, infibulation or pharaonic circumcision. Instead they prescribed a more moderate procedure, known as *sunna*, which excised some portion of the clitoris and labia minora but did not stitch the genitalia closed. This distinction was supported by the legal opinion of the mufti, who concluded that genital cutting as practiced in Sudan did not conform to the procedures of circumcision outlined in Islamic tradition. This was a compromise of British ideals, but it was as far as Sudan's leading men were willing to go. As written, the legislation did not end genital cutting, but rather criminalized its most familiar form and replaced it with another. Under the new law, practitioners of pharaonic circumcision were punished with fines of up to 50 Sudanese pounds and prison sentences of up to seven years. Anyone who knew of the operation in advance and failed to notify authorities or aided in carrying out the procedure faced a fine of 20 pounds and a prison term of six months.[56]

When the law was announced, it was immediately clear that reformers had misread the tone of the general Sudanese population, especially its women. Fearing reprisals owing to the impending legislation, many mothers rushed to infibulate their daughters, some of whom were as young as three years old. Midwives were complicit in this; both MTS graduates and dayas continued to provide pharaonic circumcisions in secret. Some, conscious of surveillance from an MTS staff member or other "Britisher," would perform a modified circumcision only to return a month or so later to carry out the full pharaonic operation.[57] One midwife who was caught infibulating a young girl was dragged in front of an audience and slapped in the face by a British health inspector.[58]

In their modest flat in England, Mabel and Gertrude Wolff received a letter from Mary Crowfoot (whose fateful inquiries at dinner had inspired the MTS) reporting that pharaonic circumcisions were now being conducted "en masse." With uncharacteristic bitterness, Mabel replied that she was not surprised that the new law had contributed to a rise in the practice. "It makes me feel what a raw deal we got from our Department at times, especially the last year or two . . . [when the Sudan Medical Service] seemed to take pleasure in hurting one[']s feelings and belittling our efforts and lauding to the skies their particular pet, I even remember saying . . . that whereas I had proved my worth, she, Miss H.Y. [Hills-Young] had yet to prove hers."[59] By 1946, however, Hills-Young was no longer in Sudan. And if her inexperience had spurred the move to legislation, she was not the only one to underestimate how difficult it would be to re-form women's bodies and culture.

Just six months after the law was put in place, events in Rufa'a transformed the debate over female genital cutting into a nationalist riot. In September 1946, a Rufa'a midwife told government authorities that a local mother had infibulated her own daughter. The mother was convicted and sentenced to four months' imprisonment, but protests over the severity of the sentence caused her to be sent home, pending a decision on her sentence. The courts ultimately upheld the conviction, and officials came at night to take the woman away and return her to jail. That Friday at the mosque, Rufa'a villagers made a plan to stage a demonstration the next day. Upon learning of the planned protests, village officials insisted that boat owners dock their boats on the other side of the river so that the demonstrators could not cross. Sometime during the night, a few men cut the ropes, setting the boats adrift and bringing them back over the river. On Saturday morning, a thousand Sudanese men, some armed with sticks, crossed the river and charged the police station, cutting the phone lines, breaking up the furniture, smashing windows, and threatening the District Commissioner along with the midwife who had reported the case. Local police were sympathetic to the crowd and therefore useless in stopping it. Troop reinforcements were called from Khartoum, and it was they who eventually freed the unfortunate mother and returned her to her family. The riots lasted most of the day, leaving five wounded from gunshots.[60]

The lines surrounding the violence in Rufaʻa were not clearly drawn. Some protesters believed in the moral importance of infibulation. Others saw the uprising as an opportunity to voice their discontent with imperial rule. Running through it all was a closely felt clash over the jurisdiction of Sudanese women's bodies. The Sudanese midwife who reported the illegal operation had usurped parental control and attempted to assert her medical authority (albeit belatedly) over the body of the young girl. In return she, as an agent of the state, was subject to attack by her neighbors. A more nuanced view was held by one of the protest leaders, Mahmoud Mohamed Taha, founder of the religious reform movement the Republican Brothers. Like the midwife, Taha was against the practice of pharaonic circumcision, but he roundly rejected British authority to legislate Sudanese women's bodies. As he saw it, cultural rights were akin to political rights. The prohibition of one of Sudan's most intimate rituals was tantamount to a violation of national sovereignty.[61] For nationalists like Taha, only the Sudanese had the right to set standards of civility, morality, and harm.

In the end it was women who refused to cede authority over their most private parts. Lectures on health and progress and admonishments by religious clerics had not been enough to convince Sudanese women that infibulation was an instrument of primitivism, much less a crime. And the legislation that was meant to free women from an oppressive tradition in actuality placed women's bodies under greater surveillance. Rejecting the invectives of state and local leaders, Sudanese women paid lip service to the new law while continuing their own traditions. Three years after the legislation was enacted, Muriel McBain, a teacher at the Wad Medani Girls Intermediate School, reported the following to Ina Beasley: "I have talked to the teachers about the progress of female circumcision in the light of what they know and have heard. The information they gave me is anything but cheering. . . . Agreement was unanimous that the town and village women were verbally in favor of the 'Sunna' type, when anyone talked to them about it, but they had no inclination or intention to change their type of circumcision. . . . No true progress [will] be made until the present educated girls became grandmothers."[62]

Of course, a small minority of women had accepted the lessons on the dangers of genital cutting, but for the majority of the population pharaonic circumcision continued with no significant signs of lessening. And aside from the cases above, there is little evidence that the legislation against infibulation was routinely enforced. Administrators were so frustrated over the ritual's intransigence that they considered expanding the definition of sanctioned sunna circumcisions. However, such legal maneuverings would likely have made little difference. In this instance, like almost no other, Sudanese women were in command of their own bodies. Women asserted their own cultural sovereignty—one that was at odds with the imperial state and Sudan's male leadership. This did not absolve men from responsibility for the continuation of the practice, but it did mean that any reforms would have to be constructed on women's terms and in women's language. In time, girls educated in government schools would grow up to advocate for more moderate forms of genital cutting or its abolition altogether. But for the moment, harsh schoolhouse lessons and legislation with all its threatened punishments held little power. Imperial authority over women's bodies had reached its limit.

BLUEBIRDS ALL OVER KHARTOUM

A final legacy of the first decades of women's and girls' education occurred outside the classroom in a new choreography of dress and public behaviors. As imperial educators worked to reform schoolgirls' behavior, their students used those same disciplined bodies to take concentrated first steps away from the protections of their home. Haga Kashif Badri, a young woman in the late 1940s, recalls, "The girl students could move about with their toobs [*sic*] on after 9 o'clock in the evening without fear and without anybody escorting."[63] Her simple statement belies the dramatic shifts taking place in women's and girls' lives. For those who mastered its tucks and folds, the tobe freed a young woman's movements from the strictures of space, time, and familial supervision. Educational programs had women and girls traveling farther and staying out later, away from the critical eyes of conservative chaperones. These were transgressive acts: traversing the boundaries of space and social networks. And yet with an often unremarked confidence and courage, women and girls crossed such boundaries again and again, adjusting their bodies and dress as necessary, to claim new ground.

In spite of significant achievements, women's and girls' education remained something apart, hidden behind high schoolhouse walls. In T. R. H. Owen's account of the Mothers' Day events that opened this chapter, only a select group of men, with high social status, were permitted to join the hundreds of celebrating women. In contrast, the raucous police band was kept behind a screen. For those in attendance, the event must have been memorable, not only for the students' achievements, but also for the inversion of convention, in which women and girls were the central visible actors while men were restricted and contained.

Under more ordinary circumstances, shielding female bodies in semi-public spaces took great effort. Elizabeth Paul described the fortified setting for the first meeting of her Ladies' Club this way: "The compound of the girls' school was an obvious meeting place: there was a ten foot wall round it, and Sudanese wives who might not be seen out in broad daylight could make their way there at dusk. A police guard was provided, I never quite fathomed why. They sat on top of the wall—presumably the better to pounce on would be intruders, and showed great interest in the proceedings."[64] The humor of the policemen-turned-voyeurs aside, their very presence was indicative of the disruption and vulnerability posed by the Ladies' Club. And if would-be intruders had to cross the police barrier, so too did the women of the club. For all involved, this physical line of protection was a sharp reminder of the social boundaries that women and girls were trying to breach.

Walls were metaphorical as well. Reflecting on the challenges of working in Sudan, Beasley wrote, "Encouraging education . . . means playing with the cards dealt to you. One of these was to demonstrate that girls' schools could carry on behind high walls and custom not much infringed. . . . Gradually the girls would find their own way out when they were ready."[65] Finding one's way out was a slow and deliberate process. After years of working closely with the women in her social welfare class, health investigator Geraldine Culwick welcomed the new relaxed attitude of her students at the start of the 1952 school year: "Two years ago, the women all refused to doff their tobes (enveloping outer garments), but now they lay them aside and sit around quite easily and un-self-consciously in ordinary dresses (their normal wear under the tobe) with a headcloth—it takes a very sophisticated woman here to be at ease with a bare head."[66]

What Culwick terms "sophistication" is perhaps more accurately viewed as agency or control. Dress granted women a personal mastery of space. Within Arab-Islamic culture, constructions of public and private are fluid, not fixed. The harem is a physical location, yes; but it is also a set of behaviors. For centuries, Muslim women have manipulated veils and screens, restrained movements, and averted gazes in order to manufacture nodes of privacy in public.[67] In the twentieth century, imperial programs introduced semipublic sites that required careful negotiation. School buildings were liminal spaces in which a woman was neither in public nor protected by the enclosures of her home. When Culwick's students removed their tobes, an action normally reserved for the home, they recalibrated privacy in public: repositioning their bodies in relation to the classroom. Although they retained a headscarf for some modesty, these not-quite-sophisticated students nevertheless signaled a critical comfort with their surroundings and a growing ownership over an imperial space.

Younger generations moved from behind physical and figurative walls of enclosure much more quickly to become noted bearers of social and cultural change. Newly established branches of the International Girl Guides brought schoolgirls and their lessons out of the classroom and into public view. The first troop, begun in Khartoum in 1947, comprised girls from eleven different nations, including Sudan, Egypt, Greece, Syria, and England. Lady Enid Cumings, the Commissioner of Girl Guides in Sudan, recalls the early enthusiasm for the group: "The younger children were anxious to join too, but the name 'Brownies' was, of course, not suitable for these Sudanese girls, so we adopted the Indian alternative of 'Bluebirds'. My daughter, Carol, and Helen Hankin's daughter, Sally, were soon enrolled in the 1st Khartoum Bluebirds, and the Greeks soon followed suit. The Omdurman children were not far behind and soon there were Bluebirds all over the place."[68]

Cumings's branch of the Khartoum Bluebirds was more diverse and well off than others. In some towns and provinces, Guide troops were divided along ethnic lines. In others, a lack of resources meant that school dresses performed double duty. Still, an effort was made to set the Guides apart from other girls. Working in the railway town of Atbara, Peggy Vidler remembers, "Uniform and equipment was a bit of a problem as most of the girls were poor, but their school uniform was a white dress. We made the [neck] ties ourselves and dyed them a cheerful cherry red."[69]

Guide activities further emphasized a sense of select community and belonging. Local culture and the harsh environment generally precluded the traditional outdoor guiding adventures such as hiking and camping that were common in Europe. Though in 1948, a large group of Khartoum and Omdurman Girl Guides with "wildly emancipated" parents did manage to go on a desert picnic. Coming home after dark, the troop made a memorable racket, singing endless rounds of "Itsy Bitsy Spider" as an old bus dropped each girl off at her door.[70] Most Guide meetings, however, were more restrained and consisted of simple ceremonies, games, practical lessons in dressmaking and childcare, and training for the prestigious Red Cross badge. After months of exercises and drills, the girls' exams would be sent to London, where they were graded at the Red Cross headquarters.[71]

The Guides' skills were soon put to the test. In 1952, as part of a wave of nationalist demonstrations, the entire nursing staff, both male and female, of the Khartoum Hospital went on strike, leaving the patients without any care. Cumings remembers, "We thought we had better do something about it. . . . We took over the hospital nursing for about a week. . . . I took charge of the harem section with my senior guides who were only too keen to put their recent training into practical use. The patients cried when we left!" Years after leaving Sudan, Cumings received a letter from the current Chief Commissioner of Girl Guides, "saying that they were still carrying on and had recently broken a hospital strike in Omdurman 'just like we had done in the old days.'"[72]

In the late 1940s, strikes were a frequent form of anti-imperialist protest. Railway and utility workers, schoolboys, and the police force all struck—some multiple times. Thus, the walkout at the hospital was not particularly unusual. But it *was* significant that female nurses joined their male colleagues in protest. This left female patients unattended and provided an opening for Cumings and her Girl Guides to step in. Yet Cumings's scheme put her charges in an uncomfortable position: caught between the rising nationalism of their neighbors and the authority of the imperial state, represented in this case by both the hospital and Lady Cumings herself. We do not know what significance the girls, or their parents, gave to their roles as replacements for the striking nurses. At a time when nursing remained undervalued, the Guides' efforts at the hospital may have been dismissed as a novelty rather than a political maneuver. (And certainly the tactic was successful enough to be repeated years later.) What is clear is that national unrest made real the textbook lessons on hygiene, first aid, and basic care. And in this act of volunteerism (even in the unlikely service to the state) Girl Guides caught a glimpse of new civic roles and responsibilities.

⌢

For those who looked carefully, social barriers were shifting and new bodies were coming into view. Schoolgirls walked home without fear or chaperones; others attended picnics or cared for patients at the Khartoum Hospital. Lady Cumings's remark about "Bluebirds all over the place" provides apt imagery. Students in tobes and Guides in their uniforms were as distinctive as a flash of blue in the trees as they crossed into public spaces. Collectively, these young women served as visual markers of a new generation, well versed in modern homemaking and undaunted in their movements outside of the home.

Participation in imperial education programs manifested a difference in Sudanese women's bodies and behaviors, though not entirely in ways that administrators had planned. Schooled in reading, writing, and arithmetic, and cleaned and clothed (though still circumcised), schoolgirls' bodies were tangible evidence of the empire's civilizing mission. The journey from home to the schoolhouse was as transformative as anything learned in the class-room. Freed from chaperones and enjoying a loosening of social strictures, well-dressed, disciplined bodies set out to take on new risks.

Two photographs capture the momentum and materiality of this process. The first, taken at a Sports Day celebration in 1959, shows a troop of Girl Guides proudly on parade across the school's athletic grounds (Fig. 6). Al-though Sudan had been independent for three years, the imperial influence

FIGURE 6. Parade of Girl Guides at a Sports Day celebration, 1959, SAD 302/9/14 (H. C. Jackson Collection). Sudan Government photograph: Crown copyright. Reproduced by permission of Durham University Library.

lingers in the two European women leading the procession, the uniforms and neckerchiefs, and the continued popularity of Guiding, itself. The oldest girls wear tobes rather than the Guide uniform, but all are outfitted in ankle socks and tennis shoes. The imperial regulations that had confined Yusuf Bedri and his classmates to native "marcoubs" were gone. Independence brought freedom in footwear. And yet shoes continued to send powerful messages about progress and place. The tennis shoes of the young Guides were intended for bodies in motion, whether parading across a schoolground or hurrying to attend patients in a hospital. The parade was Beasley's vision of an African *Sartor Resartus* come to life. Proper bodies had finally been brought into harmony with proper clothing. Marching in their pristine white uniforms, the line of girls educated in imperial standards of discipline, hygiene, and morality extends beyond the reach of the camera's lens.

The second image is much more candid, catching the arrival of a group of women to their social welfare class in 1954 (Fig. 7). The photograph is the

FIGURE 7. Arriving to a social welfare class in a Gezira village, ca. 1954, SAD 428/3/256 (G. M. Culwick Collection). Sudan Government photograph: Crown copyright. Reproduced by permission of Durham University Library.

first in a series taken by Geraldine Culwick of her class that day. The other pictures show women smiling, sewing, and chatting with one another. And yet Culwick found it equally meaningful to preserve this moment of arrival. To memorialize this scene of her students, in slingback shoes and with sewing kits in hand, hurrying toward the school. Culwick (whose astute observation about women's gradual willingness to remove their tobes appeared above) has sighted a new model of the Sudanese woman: one who participated in community groups and moved with increasing certainty across the local landscape. The photograph is an "action shot" in the truest sense, for it captures the physical movement of women's bodies as well as the beginnings of women's public presence within Sudanese society. The next chapter discusses the obstacles and violence that greeted women as such scenes of boundary crossing were repeated again and again. Yet today, over half a century later, the footsteps of the women captured in this moment of arrival still echo with purpose and anticipation.

CHAPTER 4

THE WOMAN'S VOICE

Claiming City Streets

In late October 1951, Fatima Ahmed Ibrahim and her classmates sent a letter to the editor of a local newspaper outlining the inadequacy of girls' education. The letter critiqued the disorganization of the Omdurman Girls' Secondary School as well as the prejudicial attitude of many of the teachers and their frequent absences from work. It was printed in both the Arabic and English language versions of the newspaper and garnered a highly public response. Fatima Ahmed was called into Headmistress Sylvia Clark's office where she was given the opportunity to disassociate herself from the letter and name the students responsible. When the young woman replied that she had fully and freely participated in writing the letter, Clark rebuked her, saying, "You have gone against the traditions of your family, your religion, and your country."[1] The next day, the ten fifth-year girls staged a strike and were soon joined by the younger third- and fourth-year girls. Sudanese schoolgirls had struck before, in sympathy with area boys' schools; but this protest was at their own initiative and on their own terms.[2] The Secondary School strike ended after just a few weeks, but something powerful had been set in motion.

Founded in 1945, the Omdurman Girls' Secondary School was the capstone of girls' education. It was the only government school for girls at the secondary level in all of Sudan and admitted only the most promising students. The elite status of the school was confirmed in its curriculum, which went far beyond the "Three Rs" and hygiene and instead sought to reproduce an English education. A glance at some of the subjects covered in four years of World History reveals the school's ambitions. In the first year, students learned ancient history from Mesopotamia to the fall of the Roman Empire. The second year covered the Islamic world, beginning with the life of the Prophet Muhammad and ending with the defeat of the Abbasid Caliphate. The third year introduced "revolutions," from the Renaissance and Protestant Reformation up to the French Revolution and the coming of the Industrial Age. In their final year, the girls focused on international relations in the twentieth century, including the two world wars, the decline of the Ottoman Empire, and the rise of Arab nationalism. The English syllabus was equally expansive and included lessons on *Jane Eyre*, *Northanger Abbey*, *The Merchant of Venice*, and *Twelfth Night*. Teacher Lilian Passmore admitted that the stories of Shakespeare and Bronte were "so far removed from the experience and background of Sudanese girls that they are entirely uninteresting and even incomprehensible to them." Instead, her girls much preferred Agatha Christie's "thrillers."[3] Notably, Domestic Science was entirely absent from the curriculum.

Despite the school's strengths on paper, poor leadership and a lack of suitable staff made for persistent problems. At the time of the strike, the Omdurman Secondary School lacked a permanent headmistress. For the past few months four different women, Sylvia Clark as Controller of Girls' Education and three headmistresses from surrounding schools, all issued contradictory orders on how the school should be run, leaving the students caught in the middle. Giving even more cause for complaint were the four vacant teaching positions, which meant that class periods were skipped and critical subjects dropped. The chaos and disorder that resulted from the lack of staff is reflected in Passmore's bleak evaluation of the school a few years later, when it faced similar problems. "Owing to the difficulty of recruiting staff it was not possible to open the school this year until September 1954. . . . History was reintroduced into the curriculum in August 1953 after a lapse of three years owing to the lack of suitable staff. . . . General Science is not being taken this year by 1st Year [girls] as no teacher was available between August 1954 and January 1955."[4]

The elite school's difficulties in 1951 were no secret. Observing the schoolgirls' strike from her position as headmistress of the Omdurman Intermediate School, Kathleen Wood noted that the "war clouds have been gathering for some time." Two days before the strike, Wood wrote home: "The place [the Secondary School] is really in a frightful mess and I am afraid S.C. [Sylvia Clark] is not able to pull it together." Upon reading the young women's complaints in the paper, Wood could not help but concede that "there is a hell of a lot of truth in what the girls say!"[5]

Wood, of course, was referring to the school's administrative problems, but the students were protesting the strains of imperial power that ran through their school. In stories of the strike and its aftermath, Sylvia Clark quickly emerged as the villain. She had served and taught in Sudan since 1938, and in 1949 succeeded Ina Beasley as the Controller of Girls' Education. Seeing her only as an interim headmistress, it's possible that Fatima Ahmed and the other strikers were not fully conscious of Clark's high office or the power she wielded. After the humiliating letter to the editor and the publicity of the strike, Clark issued new, strict guidelines and penalties for student behavior in and out of the classroom. Girls' visits home were limited to one trip every two weeks. Visitors to the school were only allowed on Thursdays and Fridays between 4 and 5:30 P.M. All letters would be posted through the headmistress, who could open and read them if she thought it necessary. Disturbances of any kind could lead to dismissal without warning, and a student who left the school without permission would not be allowed to return. Clark further enacted her "revenge" by insisting that the striking students kiss her hand upon their return and refusing to grant teaching appointments to girls who had completed their course of study—though there were a number of vacancies at elementary and intermediate schools waiting to be filled.[6] When they learned of the new rules, local papers likened life at the Secondary School to a military program.[7]

Years later, in the opening pages to her history of the Sudanese women's movement, Fatima Ahmed would write, "Imperialism was embodied in the conduct of the British Headmistress Miss Clark and in the regulations in our school."[8] The Omdurman students faulted the prejudices of imperialism for the failings in their education. Despite its claims to elite status, the school's chronic problems made a mockery of the government's commitment to advanced education for girls. At the same time, Clark's punitive attitude ensured that her students could not forget that even this less-than-satisfactory situation came at the forbearance of the state.

In their respective accounts of the strike, Fatima Ahmed and her classmate Haga Kashif Badri identify only one British woman, a Miss Muriel Reed, who supported the girls in their action. Sudanese newspapers described Reed as the only schoolmistress certified to teach at the secondary level. Papers later reported that as a result of her support for the striking students, Muriel Reed was sent back home to England.[9] This is an unlikely story. According to Government Staff Lists for the period 1948–1950, Reed worked as a headmistress at the Omdurman Intermediate School, where she likely met Fatima, Haga, and the other girls who would go on to the Secondary School. In 1951, Reed was briefly posted to a different school in the town of Atbara before getting married and resigning her post. At this point, she disappears from government staff roles. Reed (now Mrs. Lionel McNeil) may have returned to Omdurman in time to witness (and support) the strike in the fall of 1951. But there are no records of any disciplinary action. And when she departed for England soon after, it was almost certainly for personal, family reasons rather than because of a government sanction.

The misreading of Reed's departure as an act of political exile rather than personal choice was an important plot point in the development of Sudanese women's activism. Her presumed dismissal for supporting the very students she was hired to serve seemed to reveal the Janus-faced nature of the civilizing mission. Thus Reed, like the girls of the Omdurman Secondary School, was a victim of the prejudices of the imperial state. Reed's appearance in both Fatima Ahmed's and Haga Kashif's memoirs links the young women's imperial education with their further political development. After a childhood and adolescence spent in government schools, Fatima and Haga had gained the skills and civic awareness required to launch a political movement. But the apex of their education had also revealed the painful inequalities that the girls were living under. The strike brought these threads together and set the stage for broader women's activism.

A change in the atmosphere was palpable. A few months after the strike, Wood reflected, "Sooner or later the day of reclaiming will come, the Sudanese women themselves are getting vocal, the university students' union has had several meetings and lectures, deploring the present condition of Sudanese women, and suggesting practical measures for righting the position. They didn't mention the one thing that would set things moving, namely, the chucking out of S. Clark!"[10] The students recognized what Wood herself may have been reluctant to admit: the barriers to women's progress lay within an entire sociopolitical system, not a few bad administrators. But Wood was correct in noting that the day of reckoning was near. When the young women left the grounds of the Omdurman Girls' Secondary School in protest, they took the first steps toward claiming new ground for themselves as political activists.

On January 17, 1952, Aziza Mekki Osman Azraq, one of the student strikers, called nine of her friends to her father's house to discuss the idea of establishing a women's union.[11] The group decided to call for a general meeting later that month to explain their intentions and elect a provisional committee of officers. Newspapers again took an interest and announced the details for the general meeting. On January 31, 1952, over five hundred women and teenage girls gathered at the Omdurman Girls' Intermediate School to discuss the present status of Sudanese women. The aims of the proposed union were explained, and attendees spoke honestly about the difficulties that had led to the dissolution of women's associations in the past. On April 24, the first general conference of the Sudanese Women's Union (SWU)[12] took place: officers were elected, an executive committee of fifteen was formed, and a constitution established. Thus, with widespread support and notable publicity, arguably the most popular and enduring women's organization in Sudan was born.[13]

A NEW FIRE

The strikes and organizing of young Sudanese women paralleled the increasing political activism of their brothers, fathers, and husbands. When the Graduates' General Congress was founded in 1938, it made no claim to speak on behalf of the political interests of the entire country. But in 1942 the Graduates asserted their rights as spokesmen for a nascent Sudanese nationalism and sent a letter to the Civil Secretary asking to be granted the right of self-determination at the end of the war. This was not a bid for outright independence, but a claim for the right to chose how their country would be ruled, and by whom. Their demands were poorly timed: Italy occupied Eritrea on Sudan's border to the east and Germany threatened the Nile Valley in the north. Faced with wartime crises, Civil Secretary Douglas Newbold rejected the Graduates' authority to speak for Sudan as a whole and suggested that the Congress had forfeited the confidence of the Sudan Government.[14]

While much of the Congress was prepared to wait, a faction led by Ismail al-Azhari, a mathematics professor at Gordon Memorial College, turned to Egypt for support. In 1943, al-Azhari founded the first true political party in Sudan, the Ashiqqa Party. Echoing the demands of the White Flag League twenty years earlier, al-Azhari and the Ashiqqa called for the immediate unity of the Nile Valley. He was joined by Sayyid Ali al-Mirghani, the head of the Khatmiyya religious sect, whose dynastic power was bound up with Egypt's long influence in Sudan. Alarmed, more moderate nationalists formed the Umma Party under the patronage of Sayyid Abd al-Rahman al-Mahdi. With his father's same charisma and a keen understanding of the machinations of the Sudan Government, Sayyid Abd al-Rahman called for continued cooperation with Britain in order to prepare for a gradual move to a fully independent Sudanese state.

With that, Sudan's religious and dynastic rivalries, which had begun to diminish among the younger generation who spoke in secular political terms, were revived.[15] A myriad of political parties appeared during the 1940s and '50s. In spite of this, the political spectrum remained narrow and limited. Instead of defining themselves according to social or economic interests, parties were built around sectarian leaders, such as the two Sayyids, who could be counted on to turn out mass support.[16] By far, the most divisive issue in the nationalist movement was the question of Sudan's future relationship with her imperial powers. Practically, this question centered on the potential diplomatic and economic associations between Great Britain, Egypt, and the future Sudanese state. Philosophically, the debate raised concerns about what it meant to be Sudanese and what path the new nation would follow.

After the Second World War, the attentions of the imperial powers returned to the business of Sudan's status, self-government, and eventual independence. In 1947, after decades of battling the British Government for control within Sudan, the Egyptian Government brought its grievances before the United Nations Security Council. The case was rejected. Taking advantage of this setback, British administrators of the Sudan Government unilaterally proposed the creation of a new elected administrative body, the Legislative Assembly. The Assembly would be composed of representatives from all parts of the country and would thus quash any accusations that the British were governing Sudan without the consent of the Sudanese. Sayyid Abd al-Rahman and the Umma Party welcomed the Assembly as an initial step to self-rule. But Ismail al-Azhari and the Ashiqqa claimed that the Assembly had been proposed without Egypt's approval and called for a boycott of the elections. (In the meantime, Egypt found herself distracted by a much more immediate crisis on her eastern border: the declaration of the State of Israel on May 14, 1948, and the ensuing Arab-Israeli War.) In agreement with al-Azhari, Sayyid Ali al-Mirghani also refused to endorse the Legislative Assembly. Although he favored an increased role for his fellow Sudanese in government positions, al-Mirghani argued that heavy British handling and mixed electoral guidelines that allowed for a large number of indirectly elected seats could not possibly result in a truly representative body.

Al-Mirghani's prediction proved correct. On November 15, 1948, direct elections were held for just ten out of a total of seventy-five Legislative Assembly seats. The remaining spots were filled by appointment or indirect elections by electoral colleges. South Sudan was allotted thirteen seats in the Assembly, a significant departure from the Southern Policy that had separated northern and southern affairs; however, because the British judged the south to be too politically immature for direct elections, all of the southern representatives were voted in by provincial councils. Election day in the capital saw violent demonstrations that left ten people dead. When the dust cleared, the Umma Party had carried the day and held twenty-six seats—the largest single party within the Assembly. But it was a hollow victory, as everyone knew of the strength of the Ashiqqa boycott and al-Mirghani's refusal to endorse the elections. Burdened with a clearly unrepresentative Legislative Assembly, the Sudan Government struggled to court its political opponents in hopes of lending credence to the entire exercise.

The first years of the Legislative Assembly were marked by procedural frustrations and mounting threats from the Egyptian Government. The Assembly adopted British rules of order, but its more inexperienced, and sometimes illiterate, members were often confused over basic points of procedure. More crucially, the Assembly suffered from a lack of legislative issues needing to be addressed. J. W. Robertson wrote of the second session, held in late 1949, "As usual, we have insufficient work." The third session, in 1950, was postponed for a month for lack of anything to do.[17] In the meantime, high-level British and Egyptian officials continued to stall in their debates over the future of Sudan. Of specific concern was the possibility of drafting a constitution that would place further governing authority in the hands of the Sudanese. Writing home in December 1950, Geraldine Culwick expressed her anxieties over an uncertain future: "I wish the Condominium would get a move on and let us have our new Constitution and elections. We are in an impossible interregnum now, every day's delay doing untold harm. The old regime is creaking and groaning, and its machinery is running down. . . . [I]t jams at every turn. Whatever the defects of the new regime are going to be, the sooner it comes into operation the better."[18]

In Cairo, the Egyptian Government decided to act. In November 1950, in a speech to the Egyptian Parliament, King Farouk announced his intention to abrogate the Condominium Agreement of 1899. Alarmed, the Umma-led Legislative Assembly quickly proposed a motion for Sudanese self-government by the end of 1951; the motion carried by one vote. This marginal victory in Sudan created major waves in Egypt. Furious that such a vote had been allowed to take place, on October 8, 1951, the Egyptian Prime Minister made good on Farouk's threat. He announced the end of the Condominium Agreement and introduced legislation that proclaimed Farouk "King of Egypt and Sudan." Anglo-Egyptian relations were at a dangerous impasse. Then, in July 1952, in a sudden and celebrated coup, prompted in part by "Egyptian impotence" in Sudan, a group of Egyptian army officials known as the "Free Officers" toppled King Farouk. The new government, led by Muhammad Naguib and Gamal Abdel Nasser, were willing to abandon old policies in favor of new negotiations.[19] Renewed bilateral talks resulted in the 1953 Anglo-Egyptian Agreement on Sudan Self-Government, a much-anticipated piece of legislation that established a three-year transitional period of self-governance to be followed by a vote of self-determination.

For the next three years, through a program known as "Sudanisation," Sudanese men systematically replaced British civil servants. The process of phasing out British officials had informally begun years earlier, but now there was a concentrated push to place Sudanese men in positions of responsibility. Critically, Sudanese women were largely excluded from this process. Due to the specialized training needed in the fields of education, nursing, and midwifery, few women were prepared to take on the role of headmistress of a school or principal of a nurses' training college. As late as 1955, British women still held the majority of leadership positions in these fields, and as they retired, men filled the top offices.[20] Throughout Sudan, the transition to self-government had come sooner than many expected, and Britons struggled to find and train qualified replacements. As a result, confusion, mistranslations, and delays troubled all levels of Sudan's government and infrastructure. Speaking of the logistical problems that accompanied the transition, one district commissioner warned, "At best Sudanisation is a very risky business."[21] There were missteps to be sure; but at the end of three muddled years, the country would vote on its future.

⌢

Women's activism took root in these heady times, when much was uncertain but much more seemed possible. The Sudanese Women's Union was neither the first nor the only association for women's progress. The first attempt at a formal organization for Sudanese women started in 1947 when two of Gordon College's earliest female graduates formed the League of Cultured Girls. Both women had been educated in missionary schools and felt the "great difference" in their own educational opportunities and those of most Sudanese women. The League's goals centered on improving literacy and promoting cultural activities. To that end, it opened a kindergarten as well as a night school, which offered classes in reading, writing, childcare, and home economics.[22] Despite a promising beginning, the League split over the issue of the proposed Legislative Assembly, with some members supporting the boycott and others in favor of the elections.[23] Unable to overcome partisan politics, the League dissolved.

More successful were the Republican Sisters, the female branch of Mahmoud Mohamed Taha's Republican Brothers reform party. For his actions in leading the antigovernment protests in Rufa'a in 1946, Taha was arrested and jailed for two years. There in his cell, Taha began to develop his philosophy of "The Second Message of Islam," which promoted a universalist interpretation of Islam for the modern age. Women's rights and gender equity were a critical component of this imagined new society, and Taha was often quoted as saying, "My daughters [female followers] are my work."[24] Like other women's associations, the Republican Sisters emphasized the importance of literacy programs and religious instruction. But they also had the advantage of the cooperative work with the Republican Brothers, which allowed for ideas of equity and reform to be put into practice without waiting for government-directed change.[25]

Although the League of Cultured Girls, Republican Sisters, and SWU spanned the political spectrum, Sudanese today collectively remember this initial generation of women activists as "pioneers" (al-ra'dat), the first to venture out in favor of women's rights and progress. The term is rich with metaphoric meaning. It powerfully evokes the challenges faced by Sudanese women who dared to move beyond the boundaries of social convention and demand a place within public debates. Pioneers were not simply the first; they were also conscious trailblazers who cleared obstacles, forged paths, and staked claims for the women who would follow. And as pioneers described new terrain, they located their actions within the broader political moment. One activist explained, "If we want to talk about the motives behind such work [activism], we can not ignore the political and social situation in Sudan at that time. It played an important role in motivating us to engage in the public arena. We were politically mature and we knew that since we were struggling for our country's independence, we would have to work hard to improve our society."[26] With the end of empire in sight, women wove their needs into the larger narrative of national liberation.

Pioneers' political maturity and interest in national affairs were nurtured at home. In fact, those who took on leadership roles in women's activism would be considered adolescents by today's standards. Of the ten initial members of the Sudanese Women's Union, all but two were younger than twenty.[27] For these young women, family influence and childhood experiences provided the foundation for later activism. While no single woman's story is typical, the backgrounds related here are representative. Nimat, a leader of the Nurses Trade Union and active member of the Communist Party, was raised in Omdurman by a father who worked as an engineer and a mother who was a teacher. She recognized her father's influence in her political life: "My father was a democratic man and since early childhood he discovered and encouraged my attitudes towards democracy, equality, and love of work." Suad, a leader in the Communist Party, also born in Omdurman, had a politically active father who "believed that educated people have a debt to repay, especially in voluntary service. . . . I would do what I thought I was right."

A civic spirit filled many houses. Founding member of the SWU, Nafisa Ahmed el Amin remembered the lessons learned from her brother, a member of the Graduates' Congress: "From my brother I learned many things about colonizers and their aims in Sudan and he told me about the national movement against colonization to get national independence."[28] Their Omdurman home was located near the Congress headquarters, and many members came by the house for conversation and debate. As a young girl Nafisa served them tea and snacks and was often invited to sit with

her father as the men sang "songs of the national movement."[29] Like early
activists in other areas of the Middle East, Sudan's pioneers belonged to
economically and educationally privileged families. Fathers and brothers instilled an appreciation for education in their daughters and sisters.
Equally important, men brought home intangible ideals of democracy and
nationalism and made them real through shared, familial practices of civic
responsibility, hospitality, and song.

Seeded by nationalist activity at home, interest in establishing a broad
organization for Sudanese women revived in the wake of both local and
global political demonstrations. Nafisa Ahmed and her peers watched with
great interest as the female nursing staff of the Khartoum Hospital joined
their male colleagues on strike in 1952. Even as Girl Guides rushed in to
care for patients, the sight of the demonstrating nurses "kindled a new fire
among Sudanese women."[30] In her history of the movement, Haga Kashif
Badri connects women's nascent activism in Sudan with nationalist and
feminist events around the Middle East. She cites the nationalization of
petroleum companies in Iran, Egyptian women's calls for suffrage, and the
establishment of the Pakistani Women's League in Karachi all as inspira-
tion for the creation of the Sudanese Women's Union.[31]

The SWU's mission reflected this atmosphere of political idealism. Its
constitution called for elevating the position of Sudanese women and expanding their national consciousness; struggling for the social, economic,
and political rights of women; and active philanthropy.[32] A global awareness colored Union goals as well. Elected General Secretary, Nafisa Ahmed
recalls, "From the start, the Sudanese Women's Union aimed at creating a
strong, effective, wide universal movement in order to serve family, working
women, school girls, and women on the whole. . . . The union intended to
demand the social and political rights of its members and to work in cooperation with women in the world at large."[33]

This enthusiasm for a global sisterhood was not always matched by efforts to unite all Sudanese women. Initial SWU guidelines required that its
members be over the age of sixteen and literate. Facing a limited pool for
membership, the literacy restriction was lifted after six months. Even so, the

SWU retained its character as an association of educated, urban women. Similarly, although branches of the SWU sprang up across northern Sudan, political cooperation with southern women was minimal and sporadic at best. Sondra Hale theorizes that had activism between northern and southern women been more integrated, the more permissive gender relations of the south might have influenced the north in mediating or "modifying the impact of European and Arab patriarchal structures."[34] Instead, the activities of the SWU and organizations like it remained focused on the local, particular concerns of women in the north.

On the whole, there was widespread enthusiasm for the idea of a women's organization. SWU activities were supported by student groups, trade unions, and the Sudan Communist Party, the only political party to permit female members. Many women belonged to both organizations, and thus a close relationship developed between the two. The independent press also maintained an interest in women's progress. Since the 1930s, girls' education, marital concerns, and proper gender roles were recurrent topics in newspaper editorials.[35] By the 1950s, the issue of women's progress had made a significant migration from the editorial pages to the news sheets. Four months after the SWU's founding, the popular biweekly *al-Saraha* featured an extensive cover story on the Union.[36] Accompanying the article was a large illustration of a smiling woman carrying a lit torch in one hand and a book in the other (Fig. 8). Her tobe has the words "The Union of Sudanese Women" inscribed upon it. She leads a long procession of women and is cheered on by a diverse crowd of men. The caption, taken from the Union's own literature, reads: "For the sake of education; For the sake of respectable life in marriage and work; For the sake of mothers and healthy children; For the sake of society moving forward with men and women together." The illustration depicts a bold vision, not an actual event. Wrapped in a tobe and illuminated by the fire of knowledge, women marched toward respectability and modernity, encouraged on by cheers.

As it happened, women's activism faced far greater social and political resistance than the illustrated crowds in *al-Saraha* would suggest. Opposition was centered in the conservative, religious elements of Sudanese society,

FIGURE 8. "The Union of Sudanese Women," *Al-Saraha*, August 1, 1952.

such as the Muslim Brothers, who worried that women activists were over-turning vital traditions and cultural values. Nafisa Ahmed characterized the critics as "a few, but very loud, voices."[37] Yet they were numerous and loud enough. Under a culture of conservatism, even those who supported the Union in theory urged moderation in practice. As a result, the SWU quickly dismissed its initial goal of large-scale equity as "over ambitious" and "impractical."[38] It is perhaps more accurate to judge their objectives as too vague and ill-defined for Sudan's current sociopolitical context. As a result, in its first years, the organization focused heavily on expanding reforms already begun under the government, namely adult literacy programs and an information campaign to bring an end to pharaonic circumcision. It would not be until after independence that the SWU took up more systemic (and more disruptive) issues such as wage equity and the introduction of maternity leave; more lenient custody laws that would allow children to remain with their mothers longer; and the prohibition of *bayt al-ta'a*, a practice that permitted husbands to forcefully, and even violently, compel the return of runaway wives to their home.

Like their male counterparts, pioneers held differing opinions on what women's progress looked like. The question of women's political participation proved particularly divisive and caused the earliest internal split in the SWU. Two of its founding members, Soad el Fatih and Thurayya Umbabi, believed that while Sudanese women needed to advance culturally and socially, they did not require full political rights. They and a number of other members left the politically progressive SWU to join the newly established and more conservative Women's Cultural Revival Society. Also based in Omdurman and run by women of Sayyid Abd al-Rahman al-Mahdi's family, the Revival Society worked to improve the social position of women while keeping in accordance with Islamic practices.[39]

After the 1953 Agreement for Self-Government, the SWU sent a memorandum to the transitional elections committee demanding women's right to stand for election and to vote.[40] The resulting election laws allowed both men and women, age thirty years and older, to stand for election to the lower House of Representatives, provided they were not bankrupt; had not, in the last seven years, been sentenced to prison for more than two years; and were literate and of sound mind. Voting rights were given to men of at least twenty-one years who possessed a sound mind and had resided in their voting district for at least six months prior to the election. Women's suffrage was governed by entirely different parameters. The only women permitted to vote were those twenty-five and older who had graduated from secondary school.[41] Though an important ideological step, these limited allowances for women's political participation had negligible effect. No woman stood for election, and the number of eligible female voters amounted to less than a thousand.[42]

The reluctance to grant political rights to all women was confirmed a year after independence, when Sudan's permanent constitution was being drafted. At a conference attended by all major political parties, the SWU presented a comprehensive platform demanding women's right to suffrage and political participation as well as greater protection for families and equitable wages. Excepting the support of the Sudan Communist Party, all other organizations rejected the proposal for women's political rights, but agreed in principle to the other issues.[43] This halfhearted support demonstrates the limited tangible successes of early women's activism. Although the theory of women's progress was roundly supported and even idealized, Sudan's emerging political leaders were resistant to specific calls for practical, measurable reform.

If Sudanese women's actual sociopolitical gains were slow in coming, the symbolism of forward progress remained powerful. Awash in the nationalist sentiment that flooded the country, Sudanese women from across the political spectrum were inspired to begin their own organizations to match their needs. Nafisa Ahmed explains that the multiplying groups were not "the fruit of conflict, but it was the result of wholesome competition, which aimed at spreading the cause of Sudanese women as much as possible."[44] Her words are not a naive attempt to explain away the existence of other organizations. Rather, she draws attention to the fertile ground of the early 1950s in which women's progress and national advancement grew together. In fact, it was the Women's Awakening Society of Khartoum (and not the characteristically progressive Sudanese Women's Union) that made the first explicit, visible connection between these joint projects. To commemorate the Agreement of Self-Government, the Women's Awakening Society organized a march from Khartoum to Omdurman. This was the first entirely women's political demonstration, and the scene was impressive. "The demonstration consisted of hundreds of women, the majority of them veiled, shouting 'Long live Sudan,' 'Independence,' and 'Long live the Sudanese woman.'" Looking back, Haga Kashif called the march "courageous."[45] And it certainly was. Women accustomed to remaining protected and shielded had taken to the streets to raise their voices in celebration. The parameters of Sudan's independence, whether union with Egypt or complete autonomy, had not been determined. Nor had the bounds of Sudan as a nation been defined. But pioneers had taken a critical first step in adding their voices to the democratic process. Just two years after the strike at the Omdurman Girls' Secondary School, Sudanese women were on the march.

PUBLIC WOMEN AND RIVAL GEOGRAPHIES

The above imagery of celebratory activists striding toward Omdurman is in many ways misleading. It too easily mimics the illustration of progress in *al-Saraha* or even the photograph of Girl Guides on parade mentioned in the previous chapter. In doing so, it obscures the roughness and unevenness of the paths that women traveled in the 1950s. If the first generation of activists were pioneers, then Khartoum and Omdurman were their frontiers. Closer and more tangible than an idealized point on the horizon, the frontier was the terrain under their feet. As the movement for independence gained momentum, Sudan's changing physical and social landscapes created new spaces for women to participate in national debates.

Structurally, roads, railways, and telegraph lines connected towns and provinces like never before. And schools and housewife cooperatives brought women out of their homes and into conversation about their domestic and civic responsibilities. At the center of these social and political worlds stood the city. Like other urban centers in the twentieth-century Middle East, Khartoum presented conflicting visions of challenge and opportunity. As an unregulated site of crowds, temptation, and criminal activity, the city was no place for an unchaperoned lady. And yet, as the seat of government, Khartoum was the focus of women's activism. These political and urban spaces stood as the uncharted outer limit of Sudanese women's participation in public life. Facing prejudices, insults, and physical threats, pioneers picked their way through the rocky terrain, discovering small pockets of opportunity, expanding where they could and conforming to the landscape when they could not.

Scholarly treatments of the rise of modern urban space have cast the (admittedly, Western) city as a site of contact, upheaval, and male pleasure. Roland Barthes underscores the unsettled nature of the city by noting that it is the place where we encounter the "other," a site where "subversive forces, forces of rupture, ludic forces act and meet."[46] The central character for these encounters is the urban explorer: an idle, well-to-do gentleman, more comfortable in the anonymity of the crowd than in the solitude of his home.[47] The urban explorer mingled and jostled with day laborers, merchants and sailors, prostitutes and thieves. Yet his movement though the crush of people was far from casual. As Anne McClintock argues, "Walking bespoke leisure and male class power."[48] Indeed, it was the presumed right of the urban explorer, just like his imperial counterpart, to cross established boundaries in search of visual excitement and promises of pleasure mixed with danger.

Women who walked through the city rarely exercised the same power. And scholars' continued focus on the male explorer overlooks, if not outright denies, women's unique urban experience.[49] If the city is a tangible space where opposing forces meet and social relationships play out, then it follows that a woman's experience of the city—who she meets, the distances she crosses, how fast she travels and in what mode of transport—would be distinct from that of her male counterparts. Simply put, gender determines how people move through the city.[50] While elite men's encounters emphasized playfulness and boundary crossing, women's urban behaviors were often determined by strict sociocultural rules that directed their movement. Unwritten and yet keenly felt, these guidelines formed a moral geography, determining where and how an individual might travel through space. In the case of Sudan, while the modest covering of the tobe facilitated journeys from home to schoolhouse, it did not release women and girls from the social codes of protection and enclosure. To claim the city as their own, women would have to rechart its moral geography, asserting their own definitions of which behaviors were acceptable and which public or semipublic spaces were safe (and what made them so).[51] To do so, Sudanese women traced "rival geographies" through the city: alternate maps with paths and movements that were distinct from the routes of their husbands, brothers, and sons.[52]

Khartoum was a city of multiple geographies. The downtown administrative and political center was built around a strict grid of streets and carefully placed diagonal thoroughfares. But the farther one got from the city's core, the more irregularities crept in. Building regulations relaxed and infrastructure diminished or disappeared altogether. Housing for the city's residents was similarly segregated into discrete zones based on race, class, and proximity to power. There was a zone for Europeans and persons "living in accordance with European standards," a suburban zone for "better class natives," and the native cantonment, "some distance outside of town but accessible to it, for occupation by the native laboring classes."[53]

Colloquially known as the *deims*, the residential area for the Sudanese working class housed construction workers, day laborers, rural migrants, and a large number of manumitted slaves. Overcrowding and sparse sanitation facilities contributed to frequent outbreaks of malaria, cholera, and dysentery. In the explosion of urban development after WWII, the government instituted a massive relocation program for the deims. Homes and neighborhoods were demolished to make room for commercial ventures and better-quality homes. A "New Deims" was built farther south, outside the ring of the railroad, which until then had served as the southernmost border of the city. From 1949 to 1953, approximately thirty thousand Sudanese were forced to move from their homes.[54] The new deims was constructed with a "monotonous uniformity": rectangular blocks composed of rectangular plots were broken up at regular intervals by open spaces and designated sites reserved for schools, shops, a health center, police station, and cinema. In this "native" part of Khartoum, aesthetics were not the goal. Instead, uniformity made for "simplicity and effectiveness of control."[55]

The lives of working women often fell outside these structural methods of control. While the growing city offered numerous employment opportunities for men, women's labor was confined to the informal economy, where they worked as domestic servants, street hawkers, beer and tea sellers, and prostitutes. Collectively, these women provided "domestic comforts" to the male urban labor force that served the imperial administration. Notably, while men commuted in and out of the city according to a regular workday schedule, women's movements in and out of the deims were much less predictable. This informality, in their movements and their work, made women vulnerable. In the recent past, a female slave had been subject to the physical and sexual authority of her owner and his family. Now host to a new population of working men, a woman's independent livelihood on street corners and in market stalls subjected her to anonymous scrutiny and violence. Outside the boundaries of the home, women in the city opened their reputations to social censure and their bodies to physical danger. These were "public women" in the truest sense of the word, ones whose highly visible bodies were marked by the harsh elements of urban life: dirt, crowds, commerce, glaring sun, and the intrusive male gaze.

Yet urban women could just as easily become sources of danger as victims to it. Within conservative Arab-Islamic cultures, mobile female bodies are often considered potential sources of *fitna*, a concept of upheaval and social and moral chaos. In the nineteenth century, fears of fitna were associated with marginal female characters such as prostitutes, dancers, healers, and midwives, whose work was considered improper or morally ambivalent. These professions yielded "women without men," women who moved about at will, unsupervised by a male guardian and for whom family obligations seemed secondary.[56] In Sudan in the twentieth century, when students, teachers, midwives, and activists began to enter urban spaces, they challenged the notion that a mobile body was a chaotic, destabilizing body. Fatima Ahmed Ibrahim remembers that in the first years of the women's movement the only other women sharing the city were beggars. Often as she and her colleagues approached passersby on the streets, men would presumptively apologize for having no spare change to give.[57]

Such cases of mistaken identity were especially demeaning in a culture where a woman's honor and familial ties were her most valuable assets. In becoming urban actors, Sudanese women risked forfeiting their social status. Public visibility rendered social distinction and identity *in*visible, and pioneers were reduced to women without family, status, or money. Thus activists' determined entry into Khartoum and Omdurman was an integral part of two related sociogeographic projects. The first was the assertion of women's rightful presence in public spaces. The second, by extension, was their entrance as respected actors on the political stage. Though undoubtedly warned against the dangers of the city, in truth it was this new generation of public women who held the potential to disrupt and overturn the existing urban landscape.

BEAUTY, RIGHTNESS, VIOLENCE

Overcoming cultural boundaries and establishing rival geographies required Sudanese women activists to engage in a delicate project of self-fashioning. Activists understood that achieving gender parity necessitated measured movements, both in their politics and in their bodies. As longtime president and one of the most influential leaders of the SWU, Fatima Ahmed describes the progressive philosophy of the organization as one that was grounded in tradition. She writes,

> We do not consider men our enemies. We do not consider Islam our opponent. . . . We demanded political, economic, and social rights for women, equal opportunities for employment, and an equal role for women within the family. . . . We held that feminism is indigenous to our culture, and full equality can be reached on the basis of our own religious and cultural precepts. We knew we must reassure our people that we did not mean to change the basic tenets of our traditions.

Her words have been referenced often, and most stop quoting her there. In fact, Fatima Ahmed ends her recollection with this line: "We stressed the beauty and rightness of our national costume, the toab [*sic*]."[58] In omitting Fatima's words on the tobe, previous scholars have overlooked the intimate connection between activists' bodily praxis and their reformist projects. The messages of authenticity carried on the one, affirmed the rightfulness of the other. In Fatima's vision of an indigenous feminism, the tools of the women's movement did not need to be borrowed from other countries or regions, but could readily be found within Sudan's own religious and cultural structures. Similarly, Sudanese women did not need to look elsewhere for other modes of dress or standards of behavior. The tobe sheltered women's bodies in a way that was beautiful and right.

A vital cultural transference was at work here. As it had with the earliest generations of schoolgirls, the tobe functioned as its own form of enclosure by shielding activists from the dangers and uncertainty of the streets. Wrapped around the body, the tobe echoed the protected spaces and objects, such as harem walls, ostrich eggs, sealed food tins, and circumcised genitalia, that held deep meaning in the intimate economies of the home. Thus even as it took them away from the harem, the tobe broadcast activists' access to valuable "resources" of family, tradition, and cultural authenticity.[59] For women like Fatima Ahmed, the symbolic strength of the tobe lay in its continuity—not its innovation. Amid the chaos of union strikes and mass demonstrations, the continued use of the tobe provided a crucial counterbalance. In deploying the domestic resources of the tobe, activists presented themselves as neither unadorned nor unattached; the garment physically bound them to their families and community. Now, however, the concept of family was widening to include the imagined nation. Pioneers styled themselves not as women without men, but as women whose commitments to home, family, health, and Sudanese culture had expanded exponentially to become endowed with national purpose.

Male politicians were also using dress to assert their access to resources of power and authenticity. In the 1924 uprisings, anti-imperialist demonstrators discarded their traditional jallabiyya in favor of Western dress in order to signal their equity with the British.[60] Over the next two decades, as more of Sudan's intelligentsia joined the administration they too adopted button-down shirts and trousers to demonstrate their modernity and readiness to rule. By contrast, Sayyid Abd al-Rahman al-Mahdi and Sayyid Ali al-Mirghani consciously drew upon the symbolism of local dress and wore jallabiyyas, turbans, and cloaks in all of their public appearances. Each man's choice of jallabiyya was distinct, but "in terms of their common pursuit of independence, their dress styles showed more similarities than differences. . . . These distinctive styles of dress put the two traditional leaders in mediatory positions by maintaining contact and influence over their followers and the general Sudanese public on the one hand, and by simultaneously dealing with the colonial administrators on the other hand."[61]

In the same way that a woman's tobe signaled her access to domestic resources and responsibilities, the men's jallabiyyas were equally recognizable signs of familial and religious authority. The mediatory effects of the jallabiyya were of critical importance. Slight differences in style distinguished the two men from one another. But as both men became entangled with the governance of the imperial state, their common use of historically and religiously influenced dress distanced them from their British counterparts and reassured followers of the two leaders' allegiance to Sudanese values. For his part, Ismail al-Azhari, who had no dynastic claims and worked his way to political prominence through the secular Graduates' Congress, always wore a Western-style business suit. Thus the fashion strategies of politicians were not so different from those of pioneers. Both used dress to define a space for themselves between local standards of authenticity and imperial measures of modernity.

Negotiating the demands of enclosure and the risks of visibility, women activists manipulated their bodies and behaviors to speak from a position of strength. The Republican Sisters were known for their modest appearance and employed a strict dress code when in public of a white tobe, with no accompanying makeup, gold jewelry, or henna.[62] Similarly, Nafisa Ahmed and other members of the SWU emphasized their respected family connections by ensuring that they were always well dressed and refraining from wearing bright colors.[63] In a parallel to imperial reformist logic, modest bodies were outward signs of inward discipline. Accordingly, the SWU's constitution required that its members be of "good moral repute." In her history of women's activism, Sudanese feminist Azza Anis describes "a 'stoic morality', almost akin to religious duty, [that] was thus embedded in the organizational culture of the SWU's norms, structures and practices." Critical of this strict policy, Anis contends that the attention to morals and appropriate behavior detracted from the more important work of challenging patriarchal culture and prevented women's full political power from being realized.[64] Yet Anis's judgment of social conservatism fails to recognize that establishing authority over the messages of their bodies was a critical component of early activism.

No one was more conscious of the connection between bodies and politics than Fatima Ahmed Ibrahim. Upon being elected the first woman to serve in Sudan's Parliament in 1965, she observed, "I had chosen to uphold an image of myself as a traditional, respectable, family-oriented woman in my private life. This image gained me the credibility that allowed me to be radical and outspoken in my public life." To avoid the possibility of rumors that would have destroyed her image and thus her effectiveness, Fatima Ahmed never traveled alone in a car with male colleagues, nor attended a meeting in which there was no other woman present.[65]

Body practices made women's political praxis visible. In the hands of Fatima Ahmed and her peers, the tobe and modest behaviors were instruments of activism that created a literal space for women's bodies on the political stage. Such manipulation of the tobe was not out of step with the garment's more quotidian functions. Although the tobe was designed for modesty, Sudanese women were well versed in adjusting its folds to show off their best features. By drawing the fabric tightly under her bottom, a woman could emphasize her hips and buttocks when she walked. Or she might choose to swing her arms exaggeratedly, so that the tobe, draped over her shoulder, swung as well.[66] Thus, Sudanese women had a great deal of practice in rendering their bodies visible while remaining concealed. Mirroring this conscious use of tobe-as-accessory, activists strategically drew upon the modest intentions of the garment to enhance their own position. The "beauty and rightness" of the tobe was simultaneously protective and permissive: it shielded activist bodies while making space for radical demands.

⌢

Women's voices and opinions entered public space alongside carefully dressed bodies. In the past, the seclusion and segregation of Sudanese women had implied their silence. As Beth Baron argues, "People without a public presence were certainly not expected to have a public voice."[67] But a public voice was critical if women were to make real social and political progress. As bodies entered the city, pioneers turned to journalism as another means of entering national politics and debates. Much has been written on the ways in which the popular press constructs feelings of community and solidifies shared values and goals. As expressed in a 1919 appeal for a Sudanese-run newspaper that would address local issues and promote native authors, one Sudanese journalist wrote, "A Nation without a Paper is a Heart without a Tongue."[68] Working under a similar sentiment, activists used an emerging women's press to vocalize the values and goals of the women's movement. The first woman's magazine, *Bint al-Wadi* (Daughter of the Valley), was established in 1947. Widely distributed in schools, the magazine was largely edited by men, with women contributing only a few articles.[69] And although the magazine was short-lived, it provided a model of intellectual space where women's issues could be openly discussed.

In establishing a viable women's press, the Sudanese were about half a century behind other women in the Middle East. In Egypt, the first women's magazine appeared in 1892, with new journals appearing at the rate of one a year until the First World War.[70] Much lower literacy rates accounted in part for Sudan's slower start, but so too did the country's strict culture of enclosure. As late as the 1940s, staunch conservatives believed that the sound of a woman's voice was equivalent to the exposure of her breasts. Though not spoken, an article authored by a woman was considered an extension of her voice. Women who were courageous enough to write often chose pen names to avoid scandal. Nafisa Ahmed, for example, wrote under the hopeful moniker "Daughter of Light."[71] Thus similar conventions governed bodies and voices. Even in an intangible discursive space, a woman's presence was simultaneously vulnerable and destabilizing.

In 1954, Fatima Ahmed Ibrahim founded a monthly women's magazine, *Sawt al-Mar'a* (The Woman's Voice)—a particularly subversive title given the suggestion of the forbidden blazoned across its cover. A popular tobe carried the same name. And both challenged the silence expected of Sudanese women. Averaging fifty pages an issue, *Sawt al-Mar'a* reported on an impressive array of social, national, and international topics.[72] Women's progress in educational and medical fields was celebrated. Editorials condemned female genital cutting and other traditions that contributed to women's "backwardness." Readers submitted letters seeking advice or offering suggestions and corrections. And a regular leftist column, "Women of the World," which ran short pieces on women in Russia and China or popular uprisings in Africa and Latin America, appeared alongside articles on childrearing and cooking. Inspired, other women activists established cultural and political magazines of their own.[73] But it was *Sawt al-Mar'a* that claimed pride of place as the mouthpiece for Sudanese women. Circulation estimates vary from 12,000 to 17,000 readers at the height of its popularity.[74] In 1960, a British observer staunchly opposed to the SWU cited a smaller number, but was no less convinced of the magazine's reach: "The official circulation of Sawt El Mar'ra [*sic*] is nine thousand," she wrote, "but the number of readers, and women generally, reached by the magazine must be three times that number."[75] This sizable readership put *Sawt al-Mar'a* on par with one of the most popular Sudanese magazines, *al-Sibyan* (Youth), which was read by both young people and adults and was subsidized by the government and sold in schools. In contrast, Sudan's largest daily newspapers had circulations of only approximately four thousand each.[76]

More important than numbers was the sense of community fostered by the women's press. In 1956, female literacy was estimated at 4 percent, while male literacy reached 23 percent.[77] With rates this low, one might wonder why activists directed their energy, time, and finances toward journalism at all. Clearly, *Sawt al-Mar'a* could not claim to be speaking to the majority of the population. But for those women it did reach, the magazine linked them in a fellowship of readers. Journalism is a curious institution: it functions as a public broadcast, but can also be consumed in the comfort and privacy of one's home. The movement of the printed word between private and public spaces connected women to public debates as well as to a widening collective of other readers. In Sudan, as elsewhere in the Middle East, editors of the women's press envisioned themselves as engaged in acts of dialogue, not monologue.[78] Through reciprocal acts of reading and writing, editors and subscribers formed a supportive imagined community through which women gained their first taste of a public voice. The hope, of course, was that active readers might one day become activists.

Pens and bodies worked in concert to define a political presence. But pen names and modest behaviors could not always guarantee complete protection. While activists spoke of a "new fire" and editorials championed a global sisterhood, women in public still risked misidentification and harm. Twenty years after Mabel Wolff had first petitioned for second-class travel warrants for MTS staff midwives, propriety while traveling continued to be a concern. In 1953 the Schoolmistresses Union sent a list of demands to the Ministry of Education asking for a pension, reduction in teaching loads, a cost of living raise, and pay equity with male teachers. Concerned about the safety and reputation of its members, the union also asked that chaperones for young teachers be permitted to travel in the same class of carriage as their charges and that school inspectresses be given first-class privileges in train and air travel.[79] Distinguishing which bodies were permitted in public remained as critical in the 1950s as it had been a generation earlier. As before, the request for a better class of travel was meant to recognize women's professional status and protect vulnerable bodies. Travel warrants, midwives' blue scarves, schoolgirls' borrowed tobes, and measured movements all sent messages of stability. No one was to mistake these women for their lower-class sisters in the deims. Even so, public respectability often lagged far behind the distances that women were now traveling.

Thirty years after independence, as a conservative government cracked down on political protesters, activist women continued to defy easy classification. In 1983, soon after imposing sharia law in Sudan, President Gaafar

Numeiri's regime arrested key members of the Republican Brothers, who had argued that Islamic law should not be instituted in a country where 30 percent of the population was non-Muslim. Four Republican Sisters were also arrested for speaking out. This was one of the first instances in which the state detained female political prisoners, and the question immediately arose as to where to house them. While the Republican Brothers were held in a special political wing of the central prison, the Sisters were placed in cells with prostitutes and impoverished women charged with illegally brewing alcohol. The close contact with women convicted of immoral behavior must have been jarring for the activists, who had devoted their lives to spreading a reformed version of Islam. Nevertheless, the Sisters made the best of the situation and spent their two years in prison teaching their cellmates to read and introducing them to spiritual poetry.[80] It is an uplifting story. But the state's lack of designated cells for female political prisoners is indicative of a continued deafness toward women's political voices. The absence of planned space for female dissidents presumed a corresponding lack of action on the part of real bodies.

Women's ambiguous public position opened the door to violence. Throughout the 1950s, imams in Khartoum's largest mosques used their Friday sermons to accuse activist women of violating the tenets of Islam. On the streets, men hurled taunts and insults at women walking by. Haga Kashif remembers one occasion in which a group of men beat women activists with a stick as they gathered for a public meeting.[81] Harassment and social pressures grew so great that the Khartoum branch of the Sudanese Women's Union disbanded and reinvented itself as a purely social club.[82] Such critiques were not against the SWU solely, but opposed any program that drew women out of the house and away from their domestic roles. Asma Mahmoud Mohamed Taha, the daughter of Mahmoud Mohamed Taha and an active member of the Republican Sisters, has memories of a similar attack. While Asma was speaking outside a market in Omdurman on the need for social and political reform under Islam, a man approached and hit her on the head with a large stick.[83] The similarity between the two accounts suggest that there may be other stories of abuse and harassment that have not been shared or recorded. Yet acknowledging even these isolated cases is critical, for they remind us that women's progress was a physical journey and not simply a social or intellectual transformation. The concept of fitna, chaos, gained expression as painful reality as Sudanese men's anxieties violently played out on women's bodies.

Violence against women's visibility was not limited to city streets or even strangers. The life of schoolteacher and author Malakat al Dar is evidence that danger and chaos could just as easily be found at home. Born in 1922 in the town of El Obeid, as a young girl Malakat al Dar wanted to attend the local khalwa but was forbidden by her family. Refusing to be discouraged, she disguised herself in her brother's shirt and turban and attended classes anyway. Her memorization of the Quran was so impressive that Malakat's teacher encouraged her to continue her education. Knowing of her family's disapproval, Malakat snuck away from home and enrolled in the Omdurman Teachers' Training College. According to her sister, when Malakat returned home during a school holiday, she "suffered physical violence" at the hands of her brother. After graduating, Malakat easily established herself as a popular teacher. She arranged competitions between girls' and boys' schools, and her girls always won. Working with a colleague, Malakat also organized a women's society to teach reading and sewing to adult women. This drew further objections from her brother, who claimed that the classes were held too close to the market. Undeterred, Malakat "continued and walked in the street to and from the society." Her hard work and strong character brought her to the attention of government administrators. Ina Beasley remembers Malakat as "a striking personality much liked and respected by the mistresses in other parts. A bit above average in build, good looking with strong features and a very deep voice, and a skin of a beautiful coppery color . . . she was evidently a woman of such force and personality. This was recognized by the people of the town, for the officials spoke of her with respect."[84]

As Malakat's career progressed, the resistance from her family intensified. Promoted to Inspectress for the Education Office in El Obeid, Malakat was allowed the use of a government car and driver. To hide this privilege from her brother, Malakat ordered the driver to park some distance from her house, where she would walk to meet him. Around this time, Malakat and popular MTS Staff Midwife Sitt Batul crossed paths; in 1946 the two women traveled together through rural provinces, giving lessons on the dangers of pharaonic circumcision. In the mid-1950s, Malakat married and moved to Khartoum. When she discovered that her husband had stolen her jewelry and a portion of her teaching salary, she sued for a divorce. Malakat soon married again, and the first years were happy ones; however, her second husband developed a dependence on alcohol, and the relationship turned sour. In 1969, Malakat al Dar was granted a transfer from Khartoum back to El Obeid. She was optimistic on the day of her move and told her sister how excited she was to be returning home. That day, Malakat and her husband had a heated argument. A short time later, Malakat al Dar was found dead; she was forty-seven years old.[85]

Malakat al Dar's life is first and foremost a story of one woman's courage and determination in the face of fierce opposition. Yet her experiences also vividly attest to the ways in which professional Sudanese women were beginning to negotiate who had access to and control over their bodies and labor. As a young woman, Malakat chose to remain in El Obeid—a town where her disapproving family exercised some level of influence. Still, she found means of mapping her own resistance. She walked unaccompanied to and from the women's society and schemed to keep the government car out of her brother's sight. In fact, this superior form of transportation, along with her promotion, released Malakat from the usual limits on women's mobility and placed her body and actions outside of men's control.

Malakat further used her ties with the Sudan Government to regulate her personal life. In order to avoid early marriage to a man her family had selected for her, Malakat approached Ina Beasley asking for a contract stating that she was in the employ of the government. Although Sudanese teachers did not have formal contracts, Beasley understood that Malakat "wanted a piece of paper with the government heading to wave in the face of her family." Using official Sudan Government letterhead, Beasley drafted a very unofficial letter stating that Malakat al Dar could not get married at that time because she was needed for "extra service."[86]

This minor domestic drama was evidence of the valuable resources the young schoolteacher held in her hands. Employment granted Malakat access to the authority of the state, which superseded that of her father or future husband. Later on, it was her steady salary that enabled Malakat to seek and receive a divorce from her first husband and then live comfortably on her own. Income and access to support networks beyond her family ensured Malakat's mobility. Even on the eve of her death, Malakat had negotiated a return to her hometown without the aid of her husband. Such freedom of movement, both professionally and personally, would have been unimaginable a generation earlier.

Malakat al Dar's use of a car and fictitious contract hint at the ways in which Sudanese women had begun to capitalize upon shifts from patriarchal authority to state power. From the 1950s on, professional Sudanese women developed ongoing relationships with the modern state. Inspired by the union activities of their male counterparts, working women, too, petitioned the government for equitable and just treatment. Malakat went a step further and looked to the government to protect her person outside the workplace. In effect, she invited the state into her home, asking it to serve as a mediator between harsh familial control and her own movements and desires. This was not so different from the campaigns of women activists who called upon the state to protect women's domestic rights by expanding custody laws or preventing husbands from forcing their wives to return home. Yet Malakat al Dar's untimely and violent end is tragic evidence of the limits of state power and the strength of patriarchal boundaries that still circumscribed women's lives.

The fear of women without men was, at its core, a concern about women's linked physical and political mobility. For opponents of women's activism, it was not the city that posed an inherent danger, but rather unregulated (and unidentified) women's bodies that threatened existing social order. For many Sudanese women, visibility made their bodies vulnerable—open to criticism and attack. All understood that women's physical entry into public space was the first step (for good or ill) in establishing a recognized presence in the political sphere. Thus, the real movements of women's bodies through the city could not be separated from the simultaneous political movement in which women, as a social category, gained new ground.

⌢

The messages that women sent with their bodies and dress could be just as powerful as their words. At a national conference on literacy in 1969, Fatima Ahmed Ibrahim gave a speech arguing that women's rights and education were wholly in keeping with Islam and Sudanese tradition. As evidence of her sincerity, Fatima Ahmed asked the audience to compare her choice of clothing, the tobe, to the Western business suits of President Numeiri and the other male politicians who stood next to her. She walked a fine philosophical line—for her tobe, too, was imported. But the audience well understood her distinction. It was not the place of manufacture that mattered, but the relationships and meanings crafted around the tobe that granted the garment cultural resonance. Numeiri's choice of a business suit gave him an air of First World authority that was recognized at global levels. Fatima Ahmed's tobe harnessed a different kind of power: one that drew upon long-standing threads of modesty, discipline, domesticity, and tradition.

Ever astute, the lifelong activist highlighted pervasive postcolonial anxieties about authenticity and in doing so challenged Numeiri's commitment to a national progress that was grounded in Sudanese values and systems. Fatima Ahmed's critique of the business suit was meant to draw attention to a crisis of categories, a moment of social and cultural "dissonance" and permeability in the new state.[87] She tacitly asked, "If our President imports his clothes, what other foreign influences is he bringing into our country? What else is crossing our borders, unseen and unacknowledged?" The weight of her critique was confirmed in the negative attention she received from the government. Three years later, after an aborted coup supported by her husband and the Sudan Communist Party, Fatima Ahmed Ibrahim, one of the most visible and vocal women in Sudan, was arrested and forced into exile.[88]

(CHAPTER 5)

KHARTOUM AT NIGHT

Global Politics and Personal Pleasures

Sittana Babikr Bedri has devoted the latter years of her life to documenting the history of fashion in Sudan. Her Omdurman home is filled with dolls, bolts of cloth, and furniture upholstered in eye-catching patterns. Dominating the entryway, just inside her front door, is a long work table and sizable shelf holding colorful paints. This is where, in 2010, Sittana sits and works, designing tobes for herself and on commission. Her painted samples are sent to a company in Switzerland to be printed on cotton fabric and shipped back to Sudan. In a notebook, Sittana has carefully recorded the names and descriptions of the more popular tobes from decades past. Many of the names evoke sensory pleasure and the luxury of the fabric. Her voice is soft as she reads: "Sugar," "Khartoum at Night," and "So Soft it Will Make You Weep." As Sittana speaks about her life and work, it is clear that she and her tobes are telling a much larger story.

At the dawn of independence, women's bodies and fashion possessed incredible political capital. Beyond the strategic choreography of dress and movements employed by activists, nonactivist women were also using fashion to craft their own lessons of belonging, modern progress, and beauty. For these women, the tobe was not a conscious political instrument, but a central component of their everyday lives. And yet its ordinariness did not leave the garment without meaning. On the contrary, as nationalist fervor swelled and older body rites fell out of favor, women turned to fashion and dress to locate themselves, their experiences, and their desires in a rapidly changing world. Twining the bustle of the streets with the intimacies of adornment, women used the personal pleasures of their bodies to articulate global lessons of politics and place.

BRIGHT CITY, DARK HAREM

After fifty years of imperial rule, Sudan's capital cities had changed along with their women. Depictions of Khartoum and Omdurman were nearly unrecognizable from those of two generations before. Describing "Modern Omdurman," Edwin Sarsfield-Hall wrote: "Flies do not swarm; stenches are not encountered; every street is swept and garnished and no rubbish is seen lying about. Its inhabitants are clean and alert and everywhere one encounters life and movement and progress." Movement, progress, and the trappings of empire were even more obvious in reconstructed Khartoum. The tree-lined Kitchener Avenue ran east to west along the banks of the Blue Nile; Gordon Avenue was one block south. The ubiquitous Victoria Avenue served as the city's north-south axis, framed by a footpath, a double row of trees, and electric lighting. The city was laid out along a standard grid pattern, with diagonals cutting through city blocks at regular intervals. And though it is only apocryphal that this street design was meant to mimic the Union Jack, there could be no doubt that the city had been shaped to meet imperial standards. Again Sarsfield-Hall boasted, "There is something almost European about modern Khartoum with its airy spaciousness, its greenery, its Clubs and football grounds, its shops and stores, its garages, and its electric tramways. It is difficult to realize that it is really a remote African town which came into existence only 40 years ago."[1] The city's European feel came as a pleasant surprise to new bride Dawn Arthur; in her first letter home she assured her mother, "Khartoum is far nicer than I imagined, all the residential part is very green with trees and very nice gardens and nice houses too." The merchants all spoke English and their shops were "full of everything imaginable so its [sic] all very easy."[2]

More than anything else, new public spaces for leisure affirmed Khartoum's status as a modern city. Under the leadership of Sarsfield-Hall in the 1930s, the city initiated a systematic build-up of social and cultural spaces, so that by the 1950s Khartoum boasted multiple public gardens, a sailing club, three cinemas, grass tennis courts and polo grounds, officers' clubs, dance halls, and a beloved zoo. Exquisite shops run by Greeks, Armenians, and Syrians carried all manner of foreign goods, from delicate cotton voile to silver platters and fountain pens. These well-ordered stores were a major departure from the dusty jumble of the sprawling Omdurman market or the modest offerings of neighborhood stalls. When shoppers got tired, they could duck into one of the numerous cafes or bakeries for a pastry and a cup of sweet tea.[3]

If these pleasurable pursuits weren't enough, a handful of Sudanese girls were treated to further delights. The city's two most prestigious social clubs, the Sudan and the Khartoum, each had their own pool and sunning deck. Membership in either club was reserved for British officials, but in 1950 Evelyn Simpson found a way to arrange swimming lessons one morning a week at the Khartoum Club for her students from the Unity Girls' School. Before the lessons began, a concerned father took Simpson aside and asked what type of swimsuit he should purchase for his daughter. "She was all for a modern cut-away model but he thought it would be immodest! I knew the young lady in question well and knew she would be immodest in any case, but I gave my vote for an old-fashioned black model with a skirt, and that is what she got . . . to her extreme annoyance."[4]

Tree-lined boulevards and sun-drenched pools stood in sharp contrast to the darkening imagery of the harem. The unexpected sight of adolescent girls splashing in the Khartoum Club pool was a striking reminder of how many women's bodies remained hidden. From the beginning, imperialists argued that the secrets of women's spaces prevented them from knowing (and reforming) the hearts of the Sudanese. Half a century later, the harem and its accompanying rituals continued to be a dominant force in women's and girls' lives.

Even as more women and girls appeared in public, the foundational experiences of Sudanese womanhood remained private body practices of scars, tattoos, and genital cutting. All of these rites, some more visible than others, celebrated a woman's beauty, belonging, and sexual preparedness. A tradition of scarring the cheeks, *shillukh*, with three vertical lines was practiced on both girls and boys to indicate tribal origins. In some areas parents also scarred the cheekbones of their marriageable daughters with a small, rounded "T." The shape resembled the footprint of water birds on the sand and was considered a mark of grace and desirability.[5] In another beauty enhancing technique, on the eve of her marriage, a bride's lower lip was stuck repeatedly with pins dipped in dye to create a distinct pattern. The darkened color of tattooed lips highlighted the whiteness of the bride's teeth to her best advantage. Though the process could take hours, young women were expected to remain silent throughout.[6] Once married, a woman maintained her good appearance and sexual attractiveness through regular waxing of body hair and intense exfoliating smoke baths. Thus female genital cutting was just the beginning; subsequent rites of shillukh, tattooing, smoke baths, and re-infibulation after childbirth all affirmed the beauty and fertility of female bodies.

As shared experiences, body rituals determined who was or was not a part of one's social world. In ways that could not be denied, gender expectations, obligations, and responsibilities were written on the body. In her work on colonial Mozambique, Heidi Gengenbach identifies a vital connection between body marks and community membership. "Women used their skin to map a social world in which boundaries of belonging were rooted ... in shared feminine culture, bodily experience, and geographic place."[7] Likewise, Sudanese women used a variety of body rites to forge their own social maps of belonging. Pain and discomfort were accompanied by the assurance that one now belonged to a select community. Cheek scars and lip tattoos were not just beauty marks, they marked belonging.

But by the 1950s, Sudanese women activists began to voice concerns that the very rituals and traditions that defined their community were in fact impeding women's social and political progress. Activist Zeinab el Fateh el Badawi paints a vivid picture of the ways in which Sudanese customs fell heavily upon the bodies of young women and girls.

> When the women's movement started in 1947 we felt at the time that the Sudan was the most disagreeable of all countries in which to be a woman. Women in mass were isolated in the hareem [*sic*] ... with no education and with superstition as a dominating power in their lives. ... Girls, backward and uneducated, had to endure the inhumane operation of pharaonic circumcision. Their right nostrils were pierced to hold heavy wedding rings, their lips were tattooed, and they had to go through the agony of the eventful forty days of the marriage.[8]

El Badawi's words describe a community of women that was hidden, threatening, and mysterious. A world away from trained midwives walking briskly to a patient or orderly schoolgirls practicing their lessons, the harem was a place of isolation and superstition. Weighed down by wedding rings and backward traditions, girls appeared to have little hope of escape.

Commanding the harem was the figure of the Sudanese grandmother, who possessed immense cultural authority and directed much of the behavior of younger generations. It was grandmothers who needed to be convinced of the value of imperial programs. Edith Jackson commented that her students at the Girls' Training College were "shocking 'intellectual snobs,'" when in fact the girls' educational privilege had little to do with their own talents and was instead a consequence of "their luck to have liberal-minded parents strong enough to stand up to Grandmama."[9] But many felt that it was far more likely for grandmothers' conservative values to win out. Ina Beasley expressed concern that schoolgirls who completed their four years of elementary education would return home with few books to read or opportunities for further intellectual stimulation. Even more worrisome, back home girls were once again ruled by a generation of older women whose, as Beasley described it, "petty rivalries and jealousies ... [and] slovenly and dirty habits were obstacles in the way of bringing about an improvement in ways of living."[10]

Grandmothers became easy scapegoats for Sudan's cultural obstinacy. In a speech on the harms of pharaonic circumcision, one MTS midwife cried, "Where are mothers who revolt against traditions and break to pieces the ideal of ignorance? Where are those wise brave mothers who pay no attention to old, out-of-date grandmothers and put at the top their loyalties to their daughters, the country, their religion and humanity?"[11] Thus the dangers of the harem were cast as a generational problem—one that could not be solved overnight. As one British schoolmistress conceded, "No true progress would be made until the present educated girls became grandmothers."[12]

The call for loyalty to daughters and country was a successor to an imperial rhetoric. In 1898, when Britons claimed to redeem Sudan for Charles Gordon, they invoked an imperial *moralpolitik*: a rationale for control based on the presumed moral deficiencies of the colonized region. Couched in the euphemism of a "civilizing mission," the moralpolitik forced conquered nations to assert their political readiness for self-rule by adhering to imported cultural codes of health, hygiene, femininity, and civility.[13] As a result, private behaviors became irrevocably bound up with political maturity. In 1944, Sayyid Abd al-Rahman declared cheek scars and lip tattoos to be "a survival from barbarous times, and a characteristic of backward nations."[14] Similarly, women activists consciously positioned themselves in opposition to the burdens of the harem. In a combination of religious and modernizing arguments, activists maintained that pharaonic circumcision, lip tattoos and shillukh, excessive mourning rituals, and the zar spirit cult were contrary to the laws of Islam and responsible for Sudanese women's inferior status.

Some traditions had already begun to fade away. The practice of scarring cheeks to denote tribal origins noticeably declined as large numbers of Sudanese intermarried and moved to the cities. As Heather Sharkey suggests, such expressions of tribalism would have been conspicuously out of place during an era of intense nation-building.[15] Other cultural critiques, however, had to be proffered more carefully. Nafisa Ahmed remembers the contradictory aim to move "gradually but fast."[16] Many considered it "shameful" (*'ib*) to openly discuss women's body rites, especially as they related to sex and reproduction. This need for discretion meant that activists could not mount public campaigns against body traditions. Instead, night schools, housewife associations, and Girl Guide meetings became the sites for reformist lessons and instruction. Even the semipublic location of these discussions carried meaning: in traveling to class or a meeting, the modern woman distanced herself from the harmful behaviors that rooted her in her home and the past.

Activism itself suggested a new type of community and belonging that was not directly tied to bodies. It offered solutions to women's problems that were structural rather than individual. In a 1988 interview, Fatima Ahmed Ibrahim recalled, "The [zar] ceremony gave women a false sense of being helped, when only a socialist revolution would change their condition, not *zar* type collective therapy."[17] From a modernist standpoint, the zar drummings that had been traditionally used to address infertility, illness, depression, and marital strife were a misuse of women's energy. Real improvements in women's lives were only possible through sustained social and political action. Civic engagement and eventual full citizenship were intended to replace the zar's "collective therapy" in sustaining Sudanese women. In effect, Fatima Ahmed and her peers represented a new form of women's collective: one that was united by ideas, not kinship or bodily practices, and one that sought reform at a societal rather than individual level.

The imported language of the moralpolitik had very real, very intimate consequences. When the younger generation of activist women spoke out against traditional body practices, they disavowed many of the social maps and behaviors that had historically defined them (and their mothers and grandmothers before) as Sudanese women. Pharaonic circumcision was barbaric. Tribal cheek scars were primitive. And the zar cult was a waste of energy for women who needed real, practical help. Young women's move to a new cultural morality threw long-standing indicators of femininity and sexual maturity into disarray. But while rituals could be modified or abandoned, past body modifications were permanent and could not be so easily cast aside. No amount of imported soaps or powders could scrub them away. As beauty marks turned to scars of shame, Sudanese women searched for new signs of womanhood and belonging to replace those now deemed uncivilized.

THE POLITICS OF FASHION

The reshaping and restyling of women's bodies and behaviors was closely connected to imperial economies. Scholars of consumerism and empire have convincingly argued that the consumption of imported goods by colonized populations was a crucial component of imperial systems. Adding nuance to classic theories of economic imperialism, John and Jean Comaroff suggest that Africans were made to need a host of new, imported products: "Imperialists and their mercantile associates tried to conquer by implanting new *cultures* of consumption . . . promoting trade that might instill needs which only they could satisfy, desires to which only they could cater, signs and values over whose flow they exercised control."[18] Anne McClintock draws the relationship between economies and cultural reform with much darker strokes, arguing, "The inscription of Africans as dirty and undomesticated . . . served to legitimize the imperialists' violent enforcement of their cultural and economic values, with the intent of purifying and thereby subjugating the unclean African body and imposing market and cultural values more useful to the mercantile and imperial economy."[19] Capitalist consumption and civilization went hand in hand. The perception of dirt created difference, but it also produced desires for goods that would make colonized bodies clean. It is no coincidence that imperialists introduced imported soaps, clothing, hats, hairpins, shoes, and packaged foods as requisite accompaniments to civility.

Women, more often than men, were the focus of these new markets. Newly schooled in modern domestic arts, colonized women found themselves the targets of dual campaigns of modernity and consumption. As Timothy Burke writes, "Women bore the burden of ensuring their own purity and the purity of their households through the use of soap and cleansers. Equally, the 'beauty' of their bodies and the 'modernity' of their manners were a major subject of domestic and hygienic training."[20] In some ways, this lesson was not new. With their traditions of enclosure and genital cutting, northern Sudanese women already subscribed to a close relationship of pure bodies, homes, and souls. Now, however, it was women's responsibility to ensure that bodies and homes matched imperial standards.

Again, foreign products were pivotal as they altered the largely feminine behaviors of cooking, cleaning, laundering, and adornment.

Yet scholars' continued emphasis on the overarching power of imperial markets denies a vital agency on the part of the consumer. Rarely have we examined what control colonized populations did exercise or asked what meanings they granted to these imported goods.[21] Notably, merchants and manufacturers in the early twentieth century fully understood the importance of catering to local preferences. There were limits to the profitability of simply shipping European castoffs to African markets. Instead, European cloth manufacturers competed to anticipate and meet the tastes and whims of far-off consumers. Anthropologist Christopher Steiner explains, "There is a point in the Euro-African textile trade where good fortune or luck in the selection and design of a textile motif is replaced or, at least, coupled with sensitivity to African aesthetics—sensitivity being defined here not as the quality or state of being fully attuned to every subtlety of indigenous African stylistic cognition, but simply as the capacity to recognize the richness and complexity in styles of African adornment."[22] With this sensitivity, manufacturers imagined Africa not as a blank, passive space on the map, but as a diverse region with its own desires, signs, and symbols.

Looking back on his career, George Ainscrow, a textile designer in Manchester during the 1930s, noted, "Designing for the West African market was very specialised, requiring some knowledge of traditional African culture, as many of the designs were composed of tribal symbols whose meaning was important to the society." These skills were carefully honed, and designers who displayed a special knack for these kinds of patterns often spent their entire careers creating cloth for African markets. As with any changeable good, textile designers and manufacturers could never be certain whether new styles would be well received. As Ainscrow describes, Manchester factories bought pattern ideas, printed them onto cotton cloth, and shipped them out, all "with the hope that the design chosen would sell well in the markets of Africa."[23] The Manchester fabric furnished for tobes, with its subtle tone-on-tone stripes, dots, and tufts, did not reference the same repertoire of symbols as the more colorful cloth destined for other African countries. But this did not make its aesthetics any less fluid or complex. Dots or stripes that were deemed unflattering one season might suddenly be the height of fashion in the next. Thus Ainscrow's experiences shed light on the significant commercial (and often personal) investment that went into cloth design for the outskirts of empire. Manufacturers recognized Africans as active and complex consumers, exercising judgment and preference on the goods laid before them.

In Sudan, the market for foreign fabrics took off in the economic boom of the late 1940s and early 1950s. After years of wartime austerity, an explosion of global demand for cotton, Sudan's leading export, pushed cotton prices ever higher and led to routine surpluses in national revenue. The cost of living rose, and the government struggled to counter inflation. But it could not stifle Sudanese demand for foreign goods. The value of imported cotton-piece goods, of which tobes were a part, quadrupled from 1946 to 1952. Imports of coffee, tea, sugar, ready-made clothes, shoes, synthetic textiles, cigarettes, and beer similarly rose in value. This rush to prosperity set Sudan apart. Daly writes that although worldwide conditions necessitated a "slow transition" after the war, "Sudan's economic and political situation required rapid change."[24] In fact, new tastes and the rise in consumerism wove themselves into Sudan's national story.

Women's public mobility and a new command of cash dramatically altered the pace of fashion trends in Sudan. Historically, Sudanese men purchased tobes and other clothing for the women in their family. With men managing the purse strings, styles and trends were slow to evolve. Now, as part of a growing class of professionals with disposable income of their own, women for the first time were both consumers and purchasers of their own clothing and accessories. As a result, style, friendship, peer pressure, and envy drove markets like never before. On occasion, the eagerness and haste with which some women adopted new styles bordered on the comedic. When certain materials became unavailable, savvy consumers and merchants made quick substitutions. To meet demand during the Korean War, shopkeepers reached for irregular lengths of fabric, never before used for tobes, and hastily joined them by sewing machine, producing unusually sized garments whose edges were unfinished. The woman who adopted this wartime style would claim that her tobe was so new and she was so eager to wear it that she didn't have time to sew it properly.[25]

Speed and adaptability were the hallmarks of the most fashionable women. Joining this trend, goldsmiths, who normally traded in the most stable products, promoted new styles of rings and bracelets in hopes that women would melt down their old jewelry to be set in new shapes.[26] Thus, even permanent forms of women's wealth were being transformed into malleable fashion accessories. No longer dependent on the lax consumptive practices of their fathers and husbands, by the mid-1950s women translated their desires directly into the purchase of new products.

Within this energized atmosphere, tobes and their unique labels gained sociopolitical currency. Over the past fifty years, the function of tobe names had remained relatively unchanged. Merchants selected appealing and culturally relevant monikers to identify new styles, which continued to be advertised through word of mouth and in wedding songs. But economics and politics changed the scale and significance of this process. When fashion markets expanded, so too did the number of tobe styles needing to be named. Wrapped up in the projects of nationalism and independence, men and women used the abundance of tobes as a blank canvas for a range of political expression. Names became self-consciously editorial, rather than merely commemorative. And for women especially, they joined the pleasures of fashion to the most pressing issues of the day.

The use of tobe names as historical evidence is more art than science. Today, physical examples of tobes or descriptions of specific styles are largely lost. The link between a tobe's name and its pattern was most often one of chance rather than design. And because of the myriad of slight variations in style, it is rarely possible to identify a particular tobe shown in old photographs. Nor do we have shopkeeper inventories, documenting how many tobes of a particular type were sold in a given period or one style's popularity relative to another. What have been preserved are the names— and even these could prove slippery as evidence. As informal inventions, what was to ensure that labels remained the same across different towns or regions? Could a dishonest merchant claim to sell a woman one style while, in fact, giving her another? Yet remarkably, with very minor exceptions, the tobe names recollected in anthropological works and the memories of Sudanese men and women overlap.[27] Certainly there were instances in which a single style received different appellations from town to town. But the most popular names, the ones that resonated most intimately with women and their world, remained true across regions. As for the imagined unscrupulous merchant, his attempts at substitution only demonstrate further the importance that women attributed to fashion labels. The signifier carried just as much meaning as the signified.

Although the material facts of individual tobes are lost, we are left with a rich rhetoric of names. And it is here in the collection of names that we find historical value and women's stories, separate from any one garment's fabric or pattern. Griselda el Tayib, a folklorist and former teacher at the Omdurman Girls' Intermediate School, has carried out extensive research on Sudanese women's fashion. She writes, "Topical names represent a sort of amusing and daring statement of the women of their awareness of the men's world from which they were excluded."[28] El Tayib is right to note how witty and daring names could be; however, she undervalues the social and political power of naming. Women used fashion to remark not upon a world that was separate from theirs, but rather one to which they belonged. In the hands of educated, civic-minded consumers, the tobe served not just as commentary on the world of men but as an actual site for constructing Sudanese *women's* worldview. Thus, in the collection of tobe names we catch a glimpse of women's interests, values, ambitions, and even humor that have not been preserved elsewhere.

As Britons and Sudanese alike counted the days until self-determination, a widening variety of tobe styles was matched by an increasing complexity of message. In the early 1950s, tobes such as "Sudanisation," "The Political Corps," and "The Diplomatic Corps" marked the transition between the imperial and independent governments and heralded the arrival of foreign consuls and envoys for the new state.[29] These nationally minded tobes marked a critical shift in sentiment. Earlier labels had often been whimsical, such as the "Son of the Steel Blade," or referenced specific social moments, such as the achievements of doctors or the first generation of schoolmistresses. In contrast, this new category of tobe names drew attention to major political processes whose final outcomes had not yet been determined. Wearing these tobes, Sudanese women were not marking what was past, but rather inserting themselves into the national conversations of an ongoing and active present.

⌒

There was much to discuss. The 1950s brought dramatic political shifts in Sudan, though not necessarily a change in the way politics was conducted. The transitional period of self-government from 1953 to 1956 was meant to provide an opportunity for internal state-building, but in fact the newly created governing bodies remained hampered by external affairs, intractable party politics, and domineering personalities. Ismail al-Azhari and the pro-Egyptian National Unionist Party carried the first parliamentary elections in 1953—a result that was more a vote against British intervention than for union with Egypt.[30] This ambiguity toward Egypt was confirmed in March 1954, when Sayyid Abd al-Rahman's Umma Party organized a mass demonstration to coincide with the visit of Egyptian President Muhammad Naguib. President Naguib was a well-known and popular figure in Sudan; born in Khartoum to a Sudanese mother and an Egyptian father, Naguib came of age and studied in Sudan while his father served in the Egyptian army. Cheering crowds met Naguib at the airport. But a swarm of angry protestors made ready to rush Naguib on the steps of the Governor-General's palace. The riots left thirty people dead and many more wounded. Naguib was quickly ushered out of the country in order to avert further violence.[31]

Self-government had brought the Sudanese no closer to consensus, and it was difficult to predict which way the political winds were blowing. Later that year, Gamal Abdel Nasser ousted Naguib from office and assumed the role of President of Egypt. Watching the political upset from Khartoum, al-Azhari realized that union with Egypt was no longer likely and considered changing tactics. In November 1955, al-Azhari was narrowly reelected

Prime Minister, but it was clear he had lost much of the confidence of the general public. A series of unprecedented meetings between rivals Sayyid Abd al-Rahman and Sayyid Ali al-Mirghani were enough to convince al-Azhari that opposition toward him was steadily growing. Without the support of either of the two largest political factions, al-Azhari would have to rely on his own charisma and cunning to maintain his place in Sudan's new government.

On December 19, 1955, in a stunning about-face, Ismail al-Azhari, the most vocal proponent of unity with Egypt, introduced a resolution in Parliament calling for the immediate recognition of Sudan as an independent sovereign state. The resolution passed unanimously. Just days earlier, Governor-General Sir Knox Helm had left the country for the Christmas holiday. Within two weeks, the United Kingdom and Egypt agreed to recognize Sudan's independence. On January 1, 1956, the flags of Egypt and the United Kingdom were lowered and al-Azhari raised the blue, yellow, and green flag of Sudan over the Governor-General's palace. With his office removed out from under him, Governor-General Helm never returned to Sudan.

Sudanese women were eager participants in the political fervor. They celebrated the end of empire with tobes named "Freedom," "Independence," and "The Republic." The existence of (at least) three tobes commemorating the same event is indicative of the excitement that coursed through the new state. They are also strong evidence for the tobe's rise as a fashion object. We cannot say what distinguished "Freedom" from "The Republic." As with other luxury goods, woman's choice between the celebratory tobes would have been informed by cost and individual preferences in patterns or fabric. Critically, then, women were not limited to a single sartorial form for expressing their enthusiasm for the new chapter in Sudan's history. Instead, messages of independence could be woven into personal style.

Two more curiously named tobes also captured the promise and energy of the new nation. The first, "Azhari at the Airport," combined the allure of rapid transit with the hope of independence politics. For over a decade, Ismail al-Azhari had been one of the most recognizable faces of the nationalist movement. Always a volatile figure, he was imprisoned more than once for demonstrating against British rule. As Sudan's Prime Minister, al-Azhari was compelled to work alongside British administrators and eventually abandon his long-held position of Nile Valley unity in order to secure his country's independence. With these political negotiations in mind, "Azhari at the Airport" carried a message much more nuanced than simple nationalist sentiment. Al-Azhari's personal history traced a particular path to statehood that was antagonistic to Western interference and also in opposition to the political preferences of thousands of Sudanese. Thus, al-Azhari's politics color this pale, tufted tobe. This is not to suggest that only women of his National Unionist Party purchased and wore this particular tobe, but rather that the garment and its name were an ever-present reminder of Sudan's evolving political landscape. The route to statehood had not been linear or predetermined. Alliances shifted; compromises were struck, and strategies abandoned. No one knew this more fully than Ismail al-Azhari.

The location of al-Azhari "at the airport" is a bit of a puzzle. As Prime Minister both before and after independence, al-Azhari made a number of journeys by air, and any one of these may have made an impression on the public. Given the themes of novelty and newness that were so often celebrated in tobe fashions, it is equally likely that the imagery of the airport was symbolic of the country's forward movement. It took only a small leap of imagination to find parallels between this modern, rapid means of transport and the momentum of Sudanese politics.[32]

There is no doubt as to the events surrounding the second tobe, "The Agreement of the Two Sayyids." On November 30, 1955, bitter political opponents Sayyid Ali al-Mirghani and Sayyid Abd al-Rahman met to momentarily put aside their differences and announce their support for immediate independence for Sudan. The agreement took everyone by surprise and was pivotal in securing independence a month later. The rapprochement between the two men referenced in the tobe was an idealized vision of moving past sectarian politics and on toward a joint effort of national progress. Yet critically, for Sudan's most progressive women the joining of the two campaigns made little difference in their own sociopolitical position. Neither political party permitted female members. And in neither scenario—unity with Egypt or tutelage and cooperation with the British— were women guaranteed increased rights or social status. Nor did the commitment to political cooperation last. Al-Azhari was voted out of office just seven months after independence. At the same time, heightened Cold War politics reopened the divides between the two Sayyids: Al-Rahman continued to argue for closer ties with the West, while al-Mirghani and his supporters sought to follow Egypt's lead in courting the Soviet Bloc. Divisive party politics had returned.

⌒

Fashion afforded women the means for participating in the uneven and complex processes of nation-building and global citizenship. Just as tobes had physically mediated women's movement in public space, editorial tobe names provided women's intellectual entry into social and political debates. Together, tobe names comprised a political vocabulary. Notably, this was not a subversive language or one reserved just for women. As buyers and sellers of tobes, men, too, traded in names and their attendant messages. Names' primary function as advertisements remained; as such, labels were selected to be easily remembered and, most importantly, spoken aloud. This catchphrase quality operated as a method of shorthand. To invoke the name of a tobe called forth its accompanying politics. And it was within these threads of conversation that women voiced their opinions on larger themes of sociopolitical change, national progress, and personal expectation. Fashion, like politics, was fluid. A woman who first donned the "Agreement of the Two Sayyids" in a spirit of optimism may have paused for reflection a few months later when she realized how fleeting the moment of political cooperation had been.

The rhetorical function of the tobe challenges existing presumptions that Sudan's political sphere was an entirely male space. To date, historians have paid little attention to Sudanese women's sociopolitical consciousness, arguing that low levels of education and a conservative harem culture limited their civic engagement. Admittedly, the paucity of preserved written sources has made women's experiences and opinions difficult to track. But arguments that women were politically passive make little sense in a world in which they were clothed in garments named after political leaders. As activists worked to secure a physical foothold in urban landscapes, tobe names served as intellectual nodes of contact between women's culture and the political realm. Even a woman who may not have considered herself an activist or reformer could find room for expression or commentary in a particularly witty tobe. Fashion rendered women's political praxis visible and conveyed bodies and philosophies, both, into public space.

Sudanese women's use of their tobes for political commentary did not go unnoticed. Sometime in the late 1950s, an agent of Tootal, Broadhurst, and Lee, a high-end tobe manufacturer, approached members of the Sudanese Women's Union and solicited suggestions for tobe names that would reference local issues and current topics of interest. Unlike all other tobe names, which were born from interactions between women and merchants after a new style had come to market, these preselected names were sewn in English and Arabic onto the Tootal label during production. Advance models of these exclusive new tobes were then shipped to select members of the SWU.[33] In a savvy marketing move, the Tootal agent realized that his most desired customers, elite, educated Sudanese women, had something to say, and he was happy to let them use his merchandise to say it.

The opportunity to choose names in advance of production does not seem to have been repeated, and neither Sudanese nor Tootal company archives have preserved a record of the names suggested by the Union. However, we may be able to venture a guess. Records show that popular tobes from the same period were boldly named "The Women's Union," "The Week of Women," and "The Woman's Voice."[34] Like the multiple tobes that marked Sudan's independence, this collection leaves no doubt that women's activism had become a recognized, and indeed celebrated, part of Sudan's political scene.

Even as they sought to improve their own positions in their new state, Sudanese women increasingly affirmed their connections to women in other postcolonial countries. In April 1955, leaders from twenty-nine nations, including a not-yet independent Sudan, assembled in Bandung, Indonesia. The purpose of the conference was to protest spreading Cold War tensions and craft a viable collective Third World identity that could stand up to imperialism and its legacies. Coming just eight months before Sudan's vote for independence, the conference signaled to the Sudanese that they were part of a global movement for progress and change. The revolutionary energy of Bandung traveled six thousand miles and wrapped itself around Sudanese women in the form of two tobes named "Asia and Africa" and "The Bandung Conference."[35] This sense of international connection was repeated in the pages of *Sawt al-Mar'a*, where a regular "Women of the World" feature carried brief blurbs on women's activities across the globe. A single column might include stories on women in Iraq, Lebanon, and China, giving the impression that all were united in a common purpose.[36]

Global sisterhood was the order of the day, and Sudanese women eagerly sought opportunities for cross-cultural visits and exchange. The 1957 national Women's Week celebrations hosted two women from India and one each from Lebanon, Iraq, Egypt, and Finland.[37] And in 1960, a British anti-Communist watch group reported, "Iron Curtain countries have made several efforts to woo the Sudanese women. An invitation for three women to visit Red China was handled skillfully by the Sudanese Authorities, who refused to allow the Chinese nominees to go, substituting instead three non-political housewives, who were stolidly unimpressed by what they saw."[38] Impressed or not, these "non-political" housewives must have been struck by the extraordinariness of their journey and the speed with which Sudanese women's horizons had expanded beyond the home or even national borders. For those without an opportunity to travel, the excitement of Bandung and a global sisterhood could be found no farther away than the Omdurman market.

Fashion offered expansiveness and fluidity of identity that was not possible with other body marks. Scars were permanent, and tattoos constrained by the stubbornness of the flesh. In contrast, white tobes offered a rhetorical palette of infinite possibilities, whose messages could be refreshed each season. In fact, some claim that by the middle of the 1950s the annual meetings of the SWU had taken on the air of a "fashion show" as members proudly wore the latest in tobe designs. Women who were "coming out more and more in the public eye" eagerly searched for new patterned effects of white on white and the "chance to express their individualism."[39]

This variety in tobes was more than a frivolous show of vanity. Tobes displayed one's personal style, yes; but they also located Sudanese women within the contemporary landscape. As Jean Allman reminds us, fashion is not a "universal language," but "deeply vernacular."[40] By which she means that sartorial practices and symbols derive their meaning from local contexts. It is no surprise then that Sudan's most politically active women delighted in new styles. New tobes and new names demonstrated fluency in current events and confirmed one's presence in the political moment. Fashion registered women's historic and geographic place as they watched the arrival of foreign envoys or joined in partnership with women in Asia and Africa. This does not mean that body marks were dull, static, or had lost their meaning. Genital cutting remained a powerful and foundational part of Sudanese womanhood. But the increased attention to dress and adornment expanded the social maps and boundaries of belonging that could be described by women's bodies. And did so in a way that was acceptable to "modern" sensibilities and in keeping with narratives of sociopolitical progress. When reformers rejected women's traditional body rites, they were rejecting identities that marked them solely as wives and mothers. Instead, women "more and more in the public eye" used their dress to attest to beliefs, values, and connections that went far beyond their bodies.

BEAUTY IN AN ERA OF MISSILES AND SATELLITES
Expanding horizons gave beauty a new face. Despite frequent claims to "naturalness," beauty is not universal. It relies only in part on symmetrical facial features and pleasing body proportions. The core essence of beauty, rather, lies in its reflection of local cultures and values. Bodies that measure up to (or exceed) social expectations are judged beautiful. In contrast, "ugly" bodies are disruptive, unkempt, and marginal. By the 1950s, hygiene lessons in government schools, a problematic campaign against pharaonic circum-

cision, and a host of imported styles and goods from the West changed the way men and women viewed women's bodies and left open the question of what modern Sudanese beauty should look like. Recall that Fatima Ahmed Ibrahim celebrated the tobe for being both beautiful *and* right, meaning it was both visually appealing and culturally appropriate. But her words are perhaps redundant. For beauty as an ideal is, like so much else about the body, a locator of self and place. As empire waned and Sudanese women struggled to establish themselves on national and international stages, balancing beauty and rightness was critical.

Even as women enjoyed the freedom of new fashions, some expressed concern that overindulgence in foreign trends led to weakness and cultural instability. Thus beauty became a factor in the debates over women's progress. Editors of the progressive women's magazine *Sawt al-Mar'a* ran a regular "Style and Beauty" column. And in other magazines, editorials appeared on topics such as "Clothing, Customs, and Sudanese Traditions," "Manners of Young Sudanese Women," "Coiffeur and Its Role in the Adornment of Women," and "Hairstyles from the Ponytail to the Hoopoe's Crest."[41] Despite their simplistic titles, these articles reveal the sense of urgency that women felt in addressing and guiding rapidly shifting notions of beauty. In April 1961, *Sawt al-Mar'a* featured a comic strip narrating the story of a woman who seeks to rise above her place (Fig. 9). Reading right to left, the first panel shows a woman in a tobe observing another woman, DeeDee, who walks down the street in a tight dress and high heels. The protagonist states that she must have shoes like DeeDee's and sets out for

FIGURE 9. A cautionary tale of beauty and elegance, *Sawt al-Mar'a*, April 1961.

the crowded Bata shoe store. After making a purchase, she puts on her new high heels and takes a few tentative steps. The folds of the tobe get in her way and she yells, "My veil!" just before she falls to her knees. In the final frame, she stands barefoot with her head down in shame: her old sandals are in her hand, and the troublesome high heels are nowhere to be seen. She had made a costly mistake.

Grace and innate beauty were prized traits for Sudanese women. The article that accompanied the comic strip of the unfortunate high-heeled shoes opened with two simple equations: "Neatness and tidiness + simplicity = elegance" and "Sound body + care = gracefulness and beauty." The piece continued, "Be assured that elegance never means exaggeration and affectation in dress, or blind imitation in the choice of colors and dress preferences. Beauty does not mean exaggeration in adornment or affectation in walking or movements or attempts to imitate the stars of the cinema."[42] As women entered public space, activists (and editors) were highly aware of the body's role in walking the fine line between propriety and progress. Bata Shoes, a Czechoslovakian company, was one the first to market inexpensive footwear in Africa and the Middle East. It was a prime symbol of the globalization and homogenization of fashion. At the time of the article, a Bata manufacturing plant had recently opened in Khartoum North.[43] Yet for *Sawt al-Mar'a* readers, beauty could not be found in modern stores behind panes of glass. Sudanese women's beauty was to be local and authentic. It did not need to be constructed or enhanced or blindly copied from abroad.

Other forms of imitation were also proving worrisome. Due to expanding markets and lowered prices, more and more middle- and working-class women were able to afford good-quality tobes, which had historically been reserved for elites. Young girls were also pushing against established sartorial boundaries: Even those who did not attend school begged to wear a tobe like their school-bound peers, in order to appear sophisticated and "grown up." Others experimented with imported makeup and cosmetics. In response to these new classes of consumers, well-to-do women exclaimed with dismay that the very best shops and hair salons were now patronized by unmarried girls and even prostitutes.[44] The prevalence of prostitutes in high-end stores may have been exaggerated, but it was true that it was becoming increasingly difficult to gauge a "good" Sudanese woman by her appearance alone.

Shopping itself, however, was not to be dismissed outright. The same magazine issue that featured DeeDee's cautionary story ran an advertisement from an Omdurman merchant calling for "The Woman Concerned with Her Elegance" and announcing the arrival of a large selection of "renowned Tootal" tobes in "new fabrics" and "beautiful colors."[45] The language of the blurb and the quality of the product made clear that shopping was not a base or unrefined pastime. Rather, readers were valued for their appreciation of color and texture as well as their desire to present an elegant appearance. Advertisements in *Sawt al-Mar'a* were rare. This one stands as a first attempt to speak directly to women's tastes and preferences. The fact that the advertisement was entirely text-based with no accompanying image suggests that the merchant was confident in the literacy skills of his potential customers. His message also complements that of the rest of the magazine, namely that Sudanese women were to look to themselves for images of beauty and elegance. Imitating the exaggerated gestures of film stars or women like DeeDee resulted in a false beauty and false movements, both of which were easily and literally overturned as a woman tried to move throughout her day.

Finding balance between the fast pull of fashion and the conservative anchor of tradition wasn't easy. Noted editorialist Fauzia al-Yemeni made a name for herself writing about the cultural implications of rapidly shifting beauty standards. In one impassioned piece, titled "The Tobe, Shillukh, and Baqudi [Hairstyle]," she acknowledged the immense pressure to conform to European standards: "[In this] period of haste and era of missiles and satellites . . . [the Sudanese woman] feels she is behind the bandwagon by tens of years. Behind the women of Russia and France and England or of the world generally, and the stars of Hollywood especially." But, al-Yemeni laments, "I saw her already rushed pace . . . and I saw her fall. I heard the women of the world laughing, but I cried. I cried for you, my sisters, because in haste there is regret."[46]

Here again were anxieties about improper movement and bodies being upset. Though some women moved too fast, others worried about moving too slowly and falling—not down, but behind. Their bodies still bore the scars and tattoos of earlier traditions, but the marks that resulted from "shameful habits" did not release women from the responsibility to dress and behave appropriately. Over and over again, al-Yemeni chastises women's misuse of the tobe—a garment that she claims "holds the world's attention in its beauty and elegance"—in the name of modern fashion. "I see scarred Sudanese women that remove the tobe because it is a sign of backwardness or because the tobe hides in its folds the 'pocket' dress that costs dearly. . . . And second, those that maintain the tobe, but gather all the hair on top of her head into a hairstyle called *baqudi*. And third, those that wear the tobe of transparent [material] to reveal what is underneath." Signs of Sudanese femininity and beauty were in disarray. Women with out-of-date tribal marks discarded the tobe because it seemed to them uncivilized or old-fashioned. Others manipulated the garment to reveal intricate hairstyles or an expensive new dress underneath. Such women had misidentified the marks of backwardness on their bodies. It was not the tobe, but lingering scars and a rush to imitation that kept Sudanese women behind their peers in Russia and France. Al-Yemeni ends with a familiar refrain: "Development does not mean extremes and handsomeness does not mean display. And beauty does not mean not mean pretending. Beauty is in knowledge alone through your discipline."[47]

Fauzia al-Yemeni's words are more than a simple anti-imperial resistance to Western dress. Instead, she and her peers were attempting to define themselves in relation to other women around the world. In their discussions of hemlines and Hollywood starlets, Sudanese women were not retreating from the modern world, but rather seeking to establish their proper place within it. Tobes themselves were imported garments, whose fabrics had traveled from India, England, and Japan to reach Sudan. Yet for all the discussions of local beauty, no one accused the tobe of being foreign or inauthentic. Quite the opposite. Even as they condemned other traditions, reformers seized upon the tobe as the proper icon of modern Sudanese womanhood. For them, the materiality of the fabric mattered far less than the message of the garment, which combined modesty and fertility with ordered and disciplined movement. But embracing the tobe did not mean rejecting the momentum of the modern age. In two poetically named styles, "Khartoum at Night" and "The Russian Satellite," Sudanese women expressed their excitement for moving beyond established boundaries, whether that be exploring their capital city at night or the edges of space. In this atmosphere of cultural and political change, Sudanese women were asking themselves, quite explicitly, "How do we keep our balance?"

As pioneers had painfully learned when they first entered the streets, public visibility had to be tempered with impeccable private morals. But as more women entered public space, signs and signals crossed. Young girls dressed and made up their faces just like their married counterparts. And those who should know better got tripped up on imported, flashy trends. In response, activists like Fatima Ahmed Ibrahim and Fauzia al-Yemeni insisted that the tobe would maintain women's equilibrium. In doing so, they asserted their authority over what was beautiful, authentic, and right. Foreign films, high heels, and satellites were hallmarks of a fast-paced world that held the power to corrupt women's bodies just as tattoos and scars had done to earlier generations. True beauty in such an age required thoughtful negotiation between backwardness, tradition, and new global trends.

Khartoum at night was a real place, but it was also an imagined space of romance, progress, and risk. While Omdurman was home to most reformers and activists, Khartoum was the city of opportunity and the unexpected. It was the site of Sudan's first women-led political demonstration in favor of independence. It was home to Gordon Memorial College—renamed the University of Khartoum—where nationalist leaders received an advanced education and where Nafisa Ahmed el Amin first laid eyes on her future husband. In Khartoum, political rivals reconciled—if only briefly—and young girls swam in the British officers' pool. After the sun went down, the excitement of missiles and satellites was closer than one might expect. Open-air cinemas, the Blue Nile and the Coliseum, played the latest Hollywood films (subtitled in both French and Arabic) and provided cool and refreshing spots for an evening's entertainment.[48] More sensuous pleasures could be found at the Gordon Cabaret, where champagne flowed, a live band played, acrobats from Baghdad tumbled, and young Spanish and Austrian women danced.[49]

But this was not a city of Hollywood endings. Long-standing, meaningful birth rituals were upended by government and biomedical intervention. Mushatas who had spent days carefully plaiting hair lost much of their livelihoods to modern salons. Working-class Sudanese struggled to rebuild their lives in the "new deims" after being forcibly relocated to the far southern edge of the city. And activists suffered insults and attacks on the street. Much farther south, a civil war was brewing. Whether one felt a part of the city or spurned by its transformations, there was no denying that Khartoum was no longer a remote outpost of empire, but a central node in a world of immense and intimate exchange.

⌒

Knowing the names of tobes opens a small window into the lives of thousands of Sudanese women whose own names we cannot know. Tobes adorned women of all shapes, sizes, and convictions, and gave voice to experiences that have not been preserved in any other way. And although particularly provocative names undoubtedly held an appeal, we must acknowledge that women selected their tobes with their best possible appearance in mind. Thus, without knowing more about individual women, we cannot begin to decipher between political agendas and personal taste.[50] Instead, within the limits of the existing archive, it is far more instructive to consider tobes as collaborative markers of global and intimate place, where the garment's dual strands of politics and pleasure oriented Sudanese women to particular moments in a rapidly changing landscape.

A 1954 photograph of a sewing class captures this sartorial place-making, as ever more tobe styles were exclaimed over, exchanged, and brought home (Fig. 10). In this image, more so than in many others, the range of fabric patterns is clear: polka dots and stripes abound, though in each the density of the dots or thickness of the stripe is different. One particularly fashion-forward woman's white tobe is decorated with colored dots—anticipating

FIGURE 10. Sewing and chatting at a social welfare class in a Gezira village, 1954, SAD 428/3/257 (G. M. Culwick Collection). Sudan Government photograph: Crown copyright. Reproduced by permission of Durham University Library.

by a number of years the explosion of colored tobes in the 1960s. One can easily imagine the eager exchange of gossip and news as the women plied their needles or searched for just the right thread. But the photograph's true value lies not in the variety of styles displayed, but in how the tobes are collected together. In truth, the way that tobes have been presented in this book, either singly or in groups of two or three, only partially conveys the narrative work that this versatile garment performed. Like the women who wore them, tobes existed in community, not in isolation. Shifting trends in texture, pattern, and cuts of fabric were used to make sense of a dizzying array of political figures, international events, and popular culture. Nor was a woman limited to the messages of tobes in her wardrobe. The tobes of relatives and friends, outmoded styles of the past, and exorbitant tobes that hung unattainable in the shop window all provided opportunities for discussion and consideration of the world around her. And as a woman moved through her day, her tobe brushed and bumped up against those of neighbors and strangers. Thus, the stories that women wove in their clothing were not linear, moving determinedly from one significant moment to the next. Instead, tobes and their accompanying politics existed in tandem: alongside and layered upon one another in ways that mirrored the texture of women's lives.

We cannot fully know what crossed Sudanese women's minds as they dressed. Yet in a culture in which gender and sex roles were surgically cut into the body, the physiological link between an evocative name and the caress of imported fabric over the skin would have been all too real. Indeed, Carole Turbin reminds us of the power of dress as a means of "tactile communication." Like other body rituals, fashion is constructive, "giving shape and meaning" to bodies and politics.[51] Imagination came to life in foreign fabrics and fanciful names, rendering global connections that were both intellectual and sensual. When we turn our attention to shared body practices, the story moves beyond the voices of a few elite women and envelops a wider population of ordinary, but no less worthy, women. Excluded from other modes of public expression, the simple act of dressing was made complex as Sudanese women wrapped themselves in garments that spoke of a world that combined luxury, humor, civic engagement, and national pride. For those who listen carefully, echoes of that world sound in the tobe as Sittana Bedri recites their names.

CONCLUSION

In Leila Aboulela's novel *The Translator*, a story about multiple loves and belonging, the protagonist, Sammar, carries sensuous memories of her childhood in Sudan. She attempts to recapture these feelings while talking to a friend,

> "We have a winter in Sudan, a cold that stays on the skin, does not punch inside the bones, is content to crack people's skin, turn it into the color of ash." . . . [She remembered] tasteless Vaseline, in plastic tubs, with grains of sand, brown and coarse in the thick silver mess. Or Nivea cream, the blue tin of luxury that came with a German ad on TV.
>
> He asked her, "Which is bluer: the Nile or Nivea tins?"[1]

The question goes unanswered. But it is not foolish. The German "blue tins of luxury" were as central to Sammar's childhood as the waters of the Nile that flowed around her city. Years later, Sammar still recalled how special lotions had soothed her chafed skin. Sensuality, pleasure, and pain are not subjects that historians frequently measure and, indeed, are hard to quantify. But when we turn our attention to physical sensibilities and the tactile qualities of historical experience, we uncover depths and textures that might otherwise go unnoticed. On the surface, the above scene offers evidence for the popularity of foreign products. Yet Aboulela is making a point not of global consumption, but of global place, in which the blue of the Nile and the blue of Nivea tins were equal parts of young women's lives.

This is a story of how bodies record history and place. Like the harsh effects of winter, imperial codes of hygiene, biomedicine, reproductive health, and modern beauty impressed themselves on skin, hair, hands wrapped around imported bars of soap, and genitalia. Using a rhetoric of reform and progress, the Anglo-Egyptian Government exercised social and political dominance by dictating the behaviors and presentation of Sudanese bodies. Women, especially, were considered measures of civility and progress, and only when their bodies had been disciplined and civilized according to Western standards would Sudan be judged ready for self-rule. But bodies also talked back. Northern Sudanese women discarded certain traditions, clung fast to others, and redefined what was beautiful and right—all in the name of maintaining their balance amid the uneven terrain of empire.

Very few Sudanese women have left written records. Instead, they registered their response to imperial rule in the names of their tobes, the steps they took to school, the government uniforms they kept clean, and debates over how to circumcise their daughters. Critically, women's bodies were not merely reactive, but generative—constructing identities of self, community, and place. Tattoos, cut genitalia, Nivea'ed limbs, and high heels were plotted points on maps of belonging that let a woman know where she stood geographically, socially, and historically. Following the contours of the body and the topographies of these maps, we can begin to trace women's opportunities and anxieties, joys and concerns, pleasures and politics in the age of empire.

This is also a history of women's bodies in motion. Previous scholarship has kept Sudanese women in the first half of the twentieth century fixedly at home, unconnected to the political world around them. In truth, women's experiences of imperialism were staged in a variety of locales: in birthing rooms and government classrooms; on dangerous streets and at activist meetings; in high-end shops and private moments of dressing. When women's activism began in the 1950s, it enfolded two related forms of movement and progress. The first and most straightforward was a political program that advocated for women's improved social status and the rights of political participation. The second, which was in some ways a pre-requisite for the first, was the sustained physical entry of women's bodies into public space. For the success of political voices was dependent on the acceptance of public bodies.

Leading the way was a generation of young women who had grown into adulthood and their bodies under the oftentimes brutal contradictions of Anglo-Egyptian rule. Performing a strategic choreography, pioneers combined authenticity and domesticity with a bold public presence and expressive fashions to enact a new model of visible, progressive, civic-minded woman-hood. In tangible, observable ways, women understood how the movements of their bodies were both constituted by and constitutive of broad social and political transformations. The measures of morality and civility that shaped their behaviors and gestures informed the literal and figurative pathways that guided their steps. And as these standards altered and shifted, the directions that women traveled changed as well.

The attention to fully fleshed bodies and movement affirms the intimacy of the imperial experience. Sudanese men and women belonged to empire; they were not simply subject to it. In the half century that it was ruled by the dual powers of the Condominium, Sudan was part of a dynamic network of international trade, cultural exchange and appropriation, and political action. Day to day, these big systems were felt and experienced as small acts, which the Sudanese variously negotiated, resisted, accommo-dated, and welcomed. Bryan Turner writes of the body that it is "at once the most solid, the most elusive . . . ever present and ever distant thing."[2] The same might be said of empire. Though the locus of control and boundaries of influence exceeded the grasp of any single individual, its philosophies and effects were ever solid, ever present, ever personal.

Nothing expressed women's sense of belonging and global imagination so well as their fashions. An anthropologist herself, Janice Boddy has com-mended Sudanese women for being "unconscious anthropologists," able to "filter, interpret, and obliquely put to use information about the world beyond their courtyard walls—information passed on to women by local men when the former were unable to observe for themselves."[3] But when

Sudanese women moved beyond their courtyard walls and entered public space as teachers, nurses, and activists, they acted, in fact, as highly conscious *archivists,* recording sociopolitical milestones in their steps and in each new style of tobe. By way of illustration, the tobes selected as chapter titles for this book provide a narrative arc of northern life in Anglo-Egyptian Sudan. It opens with the uncertain beginnings of imperial rule, the darkness of the harem, and seeds of girls' education that promised the use of a "Post Office Pen" connecting Sudanese women and men to the farthest reaches of empire. Soon, large numbers of sensible white tobes clothed the first generation of state-certified midwives, who mediated between the tradition of purity and enclosure and government standards of hygiene and reproductive health. In the 1940s, "The Schoolmistresses' Ribs" celebrated advances in education and simultaneously shielded the bodies of young women and girls as they made their way to school, housewife associations, and Girl Guide meetings. The 1950s saw the increase in women's public and political presence as activism provided outlets for "The Woman's Voice." Finally, as the sun set on the age of empire, Sudanese women eagerly participated in new cultures of beauty and fashion and the cosmopolitan adventure of "Khartoum at Night." Yet this is but one narrative possibility; another selection of tobes would yield a story shaded and patterned in a different way.

It is as a collective that tobes find their full archival and historical power. It is difficult to determine the precise dates that a specific tobe was in vogue. Nor did styles exist singularly, moving in neat linear progression from one to the next. As a result, individual tobes provide only a partial view of the world in which they were made. As a group, however, they form a broad landscape of signs, symbols, and messages. For example, Ali Ali-Dinar, conducting fieldwork in 1990, recorded "The Russian Satellite" as a notable tobe of the 1960s. When this date is taken at face value, Sudanese women appear woefully behind in celebrating Sputnik well after its launch in 1957. Yet what is more important for historians is the placement of "The Russian Satellite" alongside other popular tobes of that era. "The Nightingales," "The Lonely Pillow," "Azhari at the Airport," "The Bandung Conference," and "Freedom" were all remembered as 1960s tobes by Ali-Dinar's respondents, though here again certain actors and events, like Ismail al-Azhari and Bandung, rose to prominence in the 1950s.[4] Examples of these tobes do not survive, and precise descriptions of fabrics and patterns have faded with time. What remain are the names. These fragments of memory collected by Ali-Dinar document associative experience rather than a strict chronicle of events. In fact, it is the very persistence of these fanciful labels, when the material itself is gone, that stands as the strongest evidence of fashion's rhetorical importance in measuring and marking women's and men's lives. It is the recollective links between tobes, between the Bandung Conference, the lonely pillow, and the Russian satellite, and not the garments themselves, that give shape to Sudan's vibrant and charged atmosphere in the mid-twentieth century.

Unlike other archival forms, which are overwhelmingly institutional and often inaccessible, these records of national and personal history were touched, desired, and consciously worn on display. The tobe's increased editorial functions did not diminish its domestic or sensory significance. Grooms continued to send tobes to their brides on the eve of their wedding and husbands presented tobes to their wives on the birth of a child. As the twentieth century progressed, politically minded tobe names brought themes of modernity and national progress deep into the intimacy of the harem. A gift of a tobe such as "The Diplomatic Corps" bound narratives of national progress to family milestones. A woman's collection of tobes provided a tangible dual accounting of sociopolitical change and reproductive cycles. As the tobe draped over her skin, its soft folds anchored an expectant bride or exhausted mother within overlapping spheres of the global and the intimate. Through this lived coupling of private acts and broad politics, Sudanese woman made sense of the uncertain landscape of empire. Each tobe narrated a part of the imperial experience and each woman found a thread of her own story running through it.

⌒

Some of the arguments presented here require a scholarly act of faith, a willingness to accept that which we cannot know with certainty. As Saidiya Hartman writes of her struggles to locate slave voices in the archive, "I have endeavored to represent the lives of the nameless and the forgotten, to reckon with loss, and to respect the limits of what cannot be known."[5] Similarly engaged scholars must navigate between their desire to reconstruct the lives of the forgotten and the acknowledgment that too liberal an interpretation does further violence to individuals, groups, and narratives already obscured in standard archives. It is my hope that my research has successfully walked this fine line, providing provocative arguments for the global and intimate experiences of Sudanese women while respecting voices and differences that remain unknown. The histories of far too many Sudanese women cannot be recovered. And yet a spectrum of fabrics, poetic names, body cuts, and tattoos offer invaluable remnants of women's historical experience. Following these strands has been its own form of labor and sensory experience, as my body has traveled, feasted, rested, sweated, walked, and danced from Kansas to Khartoum to London and back again.

Today, the tobe's popularity among Sudan's younger generations has diminished; nevertheless, it remains an evocative outlet for women's voices. In 2008, the most highly sought after tobe was called "Ocampo," named for the chief prosecutor of the International Criminal Court, Luis Moreno-Ocampo, who, earlier that year, called for an arrest warrant for Sudan President Omar al-Bashir, accusing him of genocide, war crimes, and crimes against humanity. The Ocampo tobe, supposedly made of silk with a beautifully detailed design, was so precious and so controversial that its very existence may have been no more than a rumor. Still, at the height of the shopping season Sudan's fashion elites lined up to request the fantastical Ocampo tobe in hushed tones. More important than the actual fact of the Ocampo tobe were the daring women who searched for it, the conservative shopkeepers who refused to stock it, and the ambitious merchants who claimed they were waiting for a consignment to arrive from Dubai any day.[6]

Even with so many other outlets for expression in the twenty-first century, fashion remains a catalyst for discussion and debate. Indeed, the tobe's enduring appeal stems from its ability to tell multiple stories about global relationships and place. In August 2011, one month after the Republic of South Sudan seceded from the north and claimed its independence, and eight months into the Arab Spring, women in southern Darfur Province headed to the crowded marketplace to buy clothing and supplies for the Ramadan holidays.[7] Far from the elite urban centers of Khartoum and Omdurman, two tobes captured everyone's imagination. The first was "Zanga Zanga," named for the catchy refrain of a hiphop song celebrating Libya's uprising against the regime of Colonel Muammar Gaddafi. The phrase was borrowed from a televised speech given by Gaddafi in which he vowed to track down antigovernment protestors, "inch by inch, house by house, home by home, alleyway by alleyway [*zenga bi zenga* in Libyan dialect], person by person." Noy Alooshe, an Israeli journalist and musician, overlaid the video and audio of Gaddafi onto an existing track of music by an American rapper and posted his creation on the internet—where it became an instant hit. The story of "Zanga Zanga" didn't take long to reach the women in Darfur, and the celebrated tobe of the same name placed them at the nexus of revolution, viral internet videos, and global music. The second tobe also commemorated revolution, though one much longer and more bloody. It was named "Al-Infisal," meaning secession, and marking the end of the politically united Sudan that the women in the marketplace had always known, and the beginning of a new chapter.

POSTSCRIPT

There are thousands for whom the tobe does not narrate their experience of empire. From the onset of the Condominium, southern Sudan's numerous ethnic groups and forbidding geography meant that the region was ruled quite differently from the Arab-Muslim north. The 1927 Southern Policy intentionally closed southern Sudan to "radical" nationalist influences, drawing a line that prevented the circulation of northern merchants, businessmen, and educators. At the same time, foreign missionaries were permitted to evangelize in the south and establish their own schools and medical centers. When the policy was lifted in 1946, south Sudan had a sizable minority of converted Christians, spoke English as the lingua franca, and was far behind the north in terms of education, economics, and infrastructure. As the possibility of independence drew near, both southern Sudanese and sympathetic British officials expressed concern that northern politics and culture would overwhelm the south.

In the summer of 1955 fighting broke out. On August 14, the Sudan Government ordered the Equatoria Corps, the oldest, entirely southern, branch of the Sudanese military, to travel to Khartoum to witness the evacuation of imperial troops from the country. Many southerners suspected that the order to go north was a trap intended to leave the southern provinces open and vulnerable to occupation by the northern units of Sudan's army. In response, in the garrison town of Torit, four officers devised a plan to mutiny and claim independence for south Sudan. They hoped to enlist the help of the British-led King's African Rifle Company of East Africa, with whom the Equatoria Corps had a long, cooperative relationship. On August 18, the troops in Torit refused to board the trucks that were to take them to Khartoum. After breaking into the armory to secure guns and ammunition, the Equatoria Corps attacked their northern commanding officers and looted and burned the officers' homes. Within a day, the mutiny spread to troops in other towns. Yet the expected outside support did not arrive.

A flurry of telegrams between Torit and the King's African Rifles in Nairobi revealed that the rebelling troops would get no help from East Africa.[1] Surprised by the uprising, the British officers of the King's African Rifles urged an end to the mutiny and assured the soldiers that Britain would ensure their fair treatment. Additional telegrams came from government officials in Khartoum guaranteeing the troops that no harm would come to them while under arrest and that each would have a chance to explain his actions. Still, the mutineers showed no sign of surrender.

Facing a stalemate, the still British-led Sudan Government sent eight thousand northern troops south. On August 27, the men at Torit surrendered. With little regard for the earlier assurances of fairness and full inquiry, three hundred soldiers were arrested, summarily tried, and executed. The men who refused to lay down their arms fled over the border into Uganda, where they became insurgents, continuing to fight against northern dominance. The civil war between north and south Sudan had begun. It would last for fifty years, killing an estimated two million people and displacing four million more.[2]

Like religion, race, language, and infrastructure, dress created and affirmed boundaries between the people of northern and southern Sudan. Less culturally unified than the north, the south featured more diverse styles of dress, ranging from broad-leaf skirts to leather thongs but also including cotton shirts, pants, and skirts. Even so, both British officials and the northern Sudanese considered the men and women of the south to be undressed. Southerners' perceived nakedness was just one more sign of their supposed backwardness and difference. And as northern nationalists increasingly adopted the imperial moralpolitik, they identified southern bodies as sites of necessary reform. In keeping with the civilizing rhetoric playing out in the capital region, the Sudanese Women's Union and other women's associations routinely organized drives to send clothes to their presumably less fortunate sisters in the south.[3]

The exoticism of southerners and attempts to introduce new fashions were in keeping with the north's political and military dominance over the south. After independence the north continued its efforts to bring un-ruly bodies in line with its own cultural and sartorial standards. The new government enacted legislation that criminalized nakedness and forbade foreigners from photographing "undressed" Sudanese. Such laws didn't stop renowned actress and infamous filmmaker Leni Riefenstahl, who in 1962 traveled to the Nuba Mountains in southern Sudan to document the fading tradition of naked Nuba wrestling. She writes, "Our group had gained a new recruit in Kadugli: a young Sudanese policeman who had to accom-pany us, not to protect us—which was unnecessary among the peace-loving Nuba—but to prevent us from photographing unclad Nuba. Fortunately, our likeable 'guard' was diverted by the pretty Nuba girls, so we had few problems taking pictures."[4] In fact, the likable guard exercised critical forms of power and prejudice when he expanded his responsibilities of surveil-lance into acts of voyeurism. For the Nuba girls appeared as exotic others, not just to Leni Riefenstahl but also to the northern policeman. In the eye of the camera and the policeman, the Nuba girls were reduced to objects of curiosity within their own country.

As we've seen fashion construct identities, new clothes could just as easily obscure them. When northern women activists spoke of the tobe as their national costume, they invoked a singular vision of nationhood that centered on an urban, Arab-Muslim identity with particular gen-der values and a particular imperial history. Southern women would have struggled to locate their experiences and their stories in tobes such as the "Post Office Pen," "Azhari at the Airport," or "Freedom." For those outside the northern nationalist narrative, the tobe and its accompanying messages were not authentic and local, but foreign and imposed. To declare the tobe as "national" disregarded southern women's sartorial practices and values, non-Arab identities and cultures, and alternate conceptions of Sudanese nationality. With imperial bonds breaking, violence in the south rising, and their sisters to the north drawing new maps of social and political belonging, women in southern Sudan faced essential questions about their identities and their place in the world. Their story has not yet been told.

NOTES

INTRODUCTION

1. M. W. Daly's foundational surveys of Sudanese history, *Empire on the Nile: The Anglo-Egyptian Sudan, 1898–1934* (Cambridge: Cambridge University Press, 2003) and *Imperial Sudan: The Anglo-Egyptian Condominium, 1934–1956* (Cambridge: Cambridge University Press, 2002), make no mention of women as historical actors. Heather Sharkey has written a thoughtful survey on the issues and successes of Sudanese women's social progress under Anglo-Egyptian rule, "Chronicles of Progress: Northern Sudanese Women in the Era of British Imperialism," *Journal of Imperial and Commonwealth History* 31 (2003): 51–82. However, her larger work on the acculturation of nationalism among educated elites, *Living with Colonialism: Nationalism and Culture in the Anglo-Egyptian Sudan* (Berkeley: University of California Press, 2003), excludes women's experiences, stating that women's lack of education precluded their participation in politics.

2. Janice Boddy's work on the imperial campaign to end female genital cutting is a notable exception. See Janice Boddy, *Civilizing Women: British Crusades in Colonial Sudan* (Princeton: Princeton University Press, 2007). More typical anthropological surveys include Marjorie Hall and Bakhita Amin Ismail, *Sisters under the Sun: The Story of Sudanese Women* (London: Longman, 1981); and Susan M. Kenyon, *Five Women of Sennar: Culture and Change in Central Sudan*, 2nd ed. (Long Grove, IL: Waveland Press, 2004).

3. Nafisa Ahmed el Amin, Director, Documentation Unit for Women's Studies, conversation with author, Ahfad University, Omdurman, July 22, 2013.

4. Sarah Deutsch, *Women and the City: Gender, Space, and Power in Boston, 1870–1940* (Oxford: Oxford University Press, 2000), 6.

5. Geraldine Pratt and Victoria Rosner, eds., *The Global and the Intimate: Feminism in Our Time* (New York: Columbia University Press, 2012), 2–3.

6. The robust scholarship on imperialism and women's bodies is far too extensive to list here. Those studies most salient for this work are Tony Ballantyne and Antoinette Burton, eds., *Bodies in Contact: Rethinking Colonial Encounters in World History* (Durham, NC: Duke University Press, 2005); Boddy, *Civilizing Women*; Sarah Graham-Brown, *Images of Women: The Portrayal of Women in Photography of the Middle East, 1860–1950* (New York: Columbia University Press, 1988); Nancy Rose Hunt, *A Colonial Lexicon of Birth Ritual, Medicalization, and Mobility in the Congo* (Durham, NC: Duke University Press, 1999); Adeline Masquelier, *Dirt, Undress, and Difference: Critical Perspectives on the Body's Surface* (Bloomington: Indiana University Press, 2005); and Anne McClintock, *Imperial Leather: Race, Gender, and Sexuality in the Colonial Contest* (New York: Routledge, 1995).

7. Edward Said argues this most clearly: *Orientalism* (New York: Vintage Books, 1994), 6. See also Malek Alloula, *The Colonial Harem*, trans. Myrna Godzich and Wlad Godzich (Minneapolis: University of Minnesota Press, 1986).

8. Ann Laura Stoler, *Carnal Knowledge and Imperial Power: Race and the Intimate in Colonial Rule*, 2nd ed. (Berkeley: University of California Press, 2010), 42.

9. Timothy Mitchell, *Colonising Egypt* (Berkeley: University of California Press, 1991), xi.

10. Hunt, *Colonial Lexicon*, 11.

11. Kathleen Canning provides a thorough introduction to "the body" as a historical concept in "The Body as Method? Reflections on the Place of the Body in Gender History," *Gender & History* 11 (1999): 499–513. For a reflection on bodies, sensation, and analysis, see Marie Grace Brown, "In Touch: The Body and Sensibility as Historical Text," *International Journal of Middle East Studies* 48 (2016): 565–69.

12. For a discussion on how bodily movements are culturally specific, see Marcel Mauss, "Techniques of the Body," *Economy and Society* 2 (1973): 70–88.

13. Terence S. Turner, "The Social Skin," in *Not Work Alone: A Cross Cultural View of Activities Superfluous to Survival*, ed. Jeremy Cherfas and Roger Lewin (Beverly Hills, CA: Sage Publications, 1980), 112.

14. Tony Ballantyne and Antoinette Burton, eds., *Moving Subjects: Gender, Mobility, and Intimacy in an Age of Global Empire* (Urbana: University of Illinois Press, 2008), 4.

15. Properly transliterated as *thawb*, the garment is pronounced as "tōb" in Sudan. As a result, the phonetic rendering *tobe* is one of the most common trans-

literations and will be used throughout this book. Other popular spellings include *thobe*, *toob*, and *taub*.

16. For a discussion of tobes and Sudan's international trade, see Marion Johnson, "Calico Caravans: The Tripoli-Kano Trade after 1880," *Journal of African History* 27 (1976): 95–117; George Michael La Rue, "Imported Blue Cotton Cloth: Status Clothing for Rural Women in Pre-Colonial Dar Fur" (paper presented at the African Studies Association annual meeting, Boston, 1993); and Terence Walz, *Trade between Egypt and Bilad as-Sudan, 1700–1820* (Cairo: Institut Français d'Archéologie Orientale du Caire, 1978).

17. A central text is Timothy Burke, *Lifebuoy Men, Lux Women: Commodification, Consumption, and Cleanliness in Modern Zimbabwe* (Durham, NC: Duke University Press, 1996). See also Jean Allman, ed., *Fashioning Africa: Power and the Politics of Dress* (Bloomington: Indiana University Press, 2004); "Fashioning the Colonial Subject," in John L. and Jean Comaroff, *Of Revelation and Revolution: The Dialectics of Modernity on a South African Frontier*, vol. 2 (Chicago: University of Chicago Press, 1997), 218–73; Hildi Hendrickson, ed., *Clothing and Difference: Embodied Identities in Colonial and Post-Colonial Africa* (Durham, NC: Duke University Press, 1996); Phyllis M. Martin, "Contesting Clothes in Colonial Brazzaville," *Journal of African History* 35 (1994): 401–26; and Leslie W. Rabine, *The Global Circulation of African Fashion* (Oxford: Berg, 2002).

18. Griselda el Tayib, "Women's Dress in the Northern Sudan," in *The Sudanese Woman*, ed. Susan Kenyon (Khartoum: Graduate College, University of Khartoum, 1987), 42, 48.

19. Antoinette Burton, *Dwelling in the Archive: Women Writing House, Home, and History in Late Colonial India* (Oxford: Oxford University Press, 2003), 5.

20. Natalie Zemon Davis, *The Return of Martin Guerre* (Cambridge: Harvard University Press, 1983), 5.

CHAPTER 1. THE POST OFFICE PEN

1. Babikr Bedri, *The Memoirs of Babikr Bedri*, vol. 2, ed. and trans. Yusuf Bedri and Peter Hogg (London: Ithaca Press, 1980), 138.

2. Heather J. Sharkey, "Chronicles of Progress," 59.

3. R. C. Stevenson, "Khartoum during the Turco-Egyptian Occupation," in *Urbanization and Urban Life in the Sudan*, ed. Valdo Pons (Khartoum: Development Studies and Research Centre, University of Khartoum, 1980), 133.

4. Robert S. Kramer, *Holy City on the Nile: Omdurman During the Mahdiyya, 1885–1898* (Princeton, NJ: Markus Wiener Publishers, 2010), 51.

5. Jay Spaulding and Stephanie Beswick, "Sex, Bondage, and the Market: The

Emergence of Prostitution in Northern Sudan, 1750–1950," *Journal of the History of Sexuality* 5 (1995): 527.

6. Guiseppe Cuzzi and Hans Resener, eds., *Fifteen Years Prisoner of the False Prophet*, trans. Hildegund Sharma (Khartoum: Sudan Research Unit, University of Khartoum, 1968), 36–37; P. M. Holt, *The Mahdist State in the Sudan, 1881–1898*, 2nd ed. (Oxford: Clarendon Press, 1970), 130.

7. Quoted in Kramer, *Holy City on the Nile*, 100.

8. Holt, *The Mahdist State in the Sudan*, 131.

9. Ali Bahr Aldin Ali-Dinar, "Contextual Analysis of Dress and Adornment in Al-Fashir, Sudan" (PhD diss., University of Pennsylvania, 1995), 27–30.

10. Daly, *Empire on the Nile*, 1.

11. Bedri, *Memoirs of Babikr Bedri*, 2:80.

12. Babikr Bedri, *The Memoirs of Babikr Bedri*, vol. 1, trans. Yousef Bedri and George Scott (London: Oxford University Press, 1969), 241.

13. Quoted in Daly, *Empire on the Nile*, 18.

14. Quoted in Harold MacMichael, introduction to *Sudan Political Service, 1899–1956* (Oxford: Oxonian Press, 1958), 1.

15. Robert Collins, "The Sudan Political Service: A Portrait of the 'Imperialists,'" *African Affairs* 71 (1972): 296.

16. A. H. M Kirk-Greene, "The Sudan Political Service: A Profile in the Sociology of Imperialism," *International Journal of African Historical Studies* 15, no. 1 (1982): 28.

17. MacMichael, introduction to *Sudan Political Service*, 3.

18. Collins, "Sudan Political Service," 300.

19. Odette Keun, "A Foreigner Looks at British Sudan," *The Nineteenth Century*, September 1930, 307–8.

20. Francis M. Deng and M. W. Daly, *Bonds of Silk: The Human Factor in the British Administration of the Sudan* (East Lansing: Michigan State University Press, 1989), 6, 19, 120.

21. Official Papers, E. Sarsfield-Hall Papers, SAD 682/12/53.

22. Ibid., SAD 682/13/10–11.

23. G. W. Steevens, *With Kitchener to Khartum* (New York: Dodd, Mead, and Co., 1898), 300.

24. "Stationing of Forces at Khartoum or Omdurman: Expenditure Involved and Fears of High Incidence of Disease among Troops," War Office Correspondence, WO 32/5552.

25. Official Papers, 1939–1953, E. D. Arbuthnot Papers, SAD 849/7/4.

26. Medical Papers, 1909–1910, J. B. Christopherson Papers, SAD 407/9/11–12.

27. Keun, "A Foreigner Looks at British Sudan," 297.

28. Steevens, *With Kitchener to Khartum*, 301.

29. Daly, *Empire on the Nile*, 6–7.

30. Masquelier, *Dirt, Undress, and Difference*, 10.

31. Ina Beasley, *Before the Wind Changed: People, Places, and Education in the Sudan*, ed. Janet Starkey (Oxford: Oxford University Press, 1992), 14.

32. MacMichael, introduction to *Sudan Political Service*, 5.

33. Collins, "Sudan Political Service," 300.

34. Collected Memoirs, R. Kenrick Papers, SAD 890/7/11.

35. Ibid., SAD 890/8/29.

36. Ibid., SAD 890/9/5.

37. Ibid., SAD 890/7/71.

38. Deng and Daly, *Bonds of Silk*, 40.

39. Ibid., 114.

40. Ibid., 55.

41. Paul S. Landau, "Empires of the Visual: Photography and Colonial Administration in Africa," in *Images and Empires: Visuality in Colonial and Postcolonial Africa*, ed. Paul S. Landau and Deborah Kaspin (Berkeley: University of California Press, 2002), 157.

42. Rosemary Kenrick, *Sudan Tales: Recollections of Some of the Sudan Political Service Wives, 1926–1956* (Cambridge: Oleander Press, 1987), 56.

43. Deng and Daly, *Bonds of Silk*, 44.

44. Ibid., 35.

45. Daly, *Empire on the Nile*, 27.

46. Ibid., 242.

47. Ibid., 243.

48. Haga Kashif Badri, *Women's Movement in the Sudan*, 2nd ed. (Omdurman: MOB Center for Sudanese Studies, 2009), 51.

49. This agreement did not apply to southern Sudan, where, as a result, missionary groups played a much larger role in the development of the region.

50. Lilian M. Sanderson, "Some Aspects of the Development of Girls' Education in the Northern Sudan," *Sudan Notes and Records* 42 (1961): 96–97.

51. Bedri, *Memoirs of Babikr Bedri*, 2:112, 116–17, 119.

52. Ibid., 127.

53. Ibid., 132.

54. Ibid., 127.

55. Ibid., 132.

56. Haga Kashif Badri, "My Experience as a Female Researcher" (unpublished essay, 1987), 12–13.

57. Griselda el Tayib, "An Illustrated Record of Sudanese National Costumes" (Master's thesis, University of Khartoum, 1976), 306.

58. Ismail Suleiman, Professor, University of Khartoum, conversation with author, June 24, 2013.

CHAPTER 2: "FORTY WHITE TOBES"

1. Eileen Kendall, "A Short History of the Training of Midwives in Sudan," *Sudan Notes and Records* 33 (1952): 52.

2. A. Cruickshank, "The Midwives Training School and the Development of a Midwifery Service in the Sudan During the Anglo-Egyptian Condominium, 1899–1956," in *The Condominium Remembered: Proceedings of the Durham Sudan Historical Records Conference 1982*, vol. 2, ed. Deborah Lavin (Durham, UK: Centre for Middle Eastern and Islamic Studies, University of Durham, 1982), 131.

3. Kendall, "A Short History of the Training of Midwives," 43.

4. "Female Circumcision in Sudan, 1949," Foreign Office Correspondence, FO 371/73668.

5. Daly, *Empire on the Nile*, 288.

6. Ibid., 309–12.

7. Ibid., 379–87.

8. Ibid., 246, 387.

9. Salma Ahmed Nageeb, *New Spaces and Old Frontiers: Women, Social Space, and Islamization in Sudan* (Lanham, MD: Lexington Books, 2004), 24.

10. Sophie Zenkovsky, "Marriage Customs in Omdurman," *Sudan Notes and Records* 26 (1945): 242. See also, J. W. Crowfoot, "Wedding Customs in the Northern Sudan," *Sudan Notes and Records* 5 (1922): 1–28.

11. Janice Boddy, *Wombs and Alien Spirits: Women, Men, and the Zar Cult in Northern Sudan* (Madison: University of Wisconsin Press, 1989), 93–94.

12. Ibid., 55.

13. Collected Memoirs, R. Kenrick Papers, SAD 890/9/6.

14. Boddy, *Civilizing Women*, 112.

15. Boddy, *Wombs and Alien Spirits*, chap. 2.

16. Official Papers, 1921–1937, M. E. and G. L. Wolff Papers, SAD 580/1/8.

17. Susan M. Kenyon, *Five Women of Sennar*, 51.

18. Official Papers, 1921–1937, M. E. and G. L. Wolff Papers, SAD 580/1/8.

19. Balghis Yousif Bedri, "Food and Differential Roles in the Fetiehab Household," in Kenyon (ed.), *The Sudanese Woman*, 88.

20. Kenyon, *Five Women of Sennar*, 57.

21. Official Papers, 1921–1937, M. E. and G. L. Wolff Papers, SAD 580/1/58–59.

22. It is unclear whether (though unlikely that) the "Sitt Batul" mentioned here is the MTS's own Sitt Batul Muhammad Isa, discussed later in the chapter. If so, then this entry, dated 1937, is Sitt Batul's recollection of her confinement with her son from years earlier.

23. Official Papers, 1921–1937, M. E. and G. L. Wolff Papers, SAD 580/1/55.

24. Ahmad Sikainga, "Shari'a Courts and the Manumission of Female Slaves in the Sudan, 1898–1939," *International Journal of African Historical Studies* 28 (1995): 11.

25. Ahmad Alawad Sikainga, *Slaves into Workers: Emancipation and Labor in Colonial Sudan* (Austin: University of Texas Press, 1996), 112–13.

26. Boddy, *Wombs and Alien Spirits*, 190.

27. Official Papers, 1921–1937, M. E. and G. L. Wolff Papers, SAD 579/3/5.

28. Kendall, "A Short History of the Training of Midwives," 44.

29. Official Papers, 1921–1937, M. E. and G. L. Wolff Papers, SAD 579/3/15.

30. Heather Bell, *Frontiers of Medicine in the Anglo-Egyptian Sudan, 1899–1940* (Oxford: Clarendon Press, 1999), 204.

31. Official Papers, 1921–1937, M. E. and G. L. Wolff Papers, SAD 580/3/6–7, 15.

32. Bell, *Frontiers of Medicine*, 208.

33. Midwives Register, 1921–1934, M. E. and G. L. Wolff Papers, SAD 579/8/5–33.

34. Quoted in Bell, *Frontiers of Medicine*, 52–53.

35. Ibid., 202.

36. Ibid., 206.

37. For a full discussion of the fluctuations of the term "Sudany," see chapter 2 in Sharkey, *Living with Colonialism*.

38. Personal Papers, 1924–1946, M. E. and G. L. Wolff Papers, SAD 582/7/10–12, 16.

39. Ibid., SAD 582/7/24–25.

40. Robert O. Collins, *Shadows in the Grass: Britain in the Southern Sudan, 1918–1956* (New Haven: Yale University Press, 1983), 174–75.

41. Official Papers, 1921–1937, M. E. and G. L. Wolff Papers, SAD 582/3/34.

42. Bell, *Frontiers of Medicine*, 216.

43. Personal Papers, 1924–1946, M. E. and G. L. Wolff Papers, SAD 582/7/52.

44. Official Papers, 1921–1937, M. E. and G. L. Wolff Papers, SAD 579/3/15.

45. Ibid., SAD 581/1/2.

46. Kendall, "A Short History of the Training of Midwives," 44.

47. Bell, *Frontiers of Medicine*, 217.

48. Boddy, *Civilizing Women*, 219.

49. Quoted in Kendall, "A Short History of the Training of Midwives," 46.

50. Ibid., 47.

51. Official Papers, 1921–1937, M. E. and G. L. Wolff Papers, SAD 581/5/18.

52. "Female Circumcision," I. M. Beasley Papers, SAD 657/4/98.

53. Boddy, *Civilizing Women*, 210.

54. Quoted in Kendall, "A Short History of the Training of Midwives," 47.

55. Boddy, *Civilizing Women*, 196.

56. Official Papers, 1921–1937, M. E. and G. L. Wolff Papers, SAD 580/3/10–14.

57. Ibid., SAD 579/3/28.

58. Ibid., SAD 580/1/9.

59. Personal Papers, 1924–1946, M. E. and G. L. Wolff Papers, SAD 582/7/37.

60. James Ryan, *Picturing Empire: Photography and the Visualization of the British Empire* (Chicago: The University of Chicago Press, 1997), chap. 5.

61. Official Papers, 1921–1937, M. E. and G. L. Wolff Papers, SAD 579/3/28.

62. Ibid., SAD 579/3/11.

63. Ibid., SAD 582/2/73.

64. Quoted in Kendall, "A Short History of the Training of Midwives," 50.

65. Personal Papers, 1924–1946, M. E. and G. L. Wolff Papers, SAD 582/7/45.

66. Official Papers, 1921–1937, M. E. and G. L. Wolff Papers, SAD 582/3/28.

67. Kendall, "A Short History of the Training of Midwives," 43.

68. Official Papers, 1921–1937, M. E. and G. L. Wolff Papers, SAD 579/3/28.

CHAPTER 3: THE SCHOOLMISTRESSES' RIBS

1. Personal Correspondence, T. R. H. Owen Papers, SAD 414/15/35.

2. Beasley, *Before the Wind Changed*, 351.

3. "Sudan Days," T. R. H. Owen Papers, SAD 769/11/49–56.

4. Working Papers, L. P. Sanderson Papers, SAD 60/5/40.

5. In 1944, just over 6,600 girls were enrolled in government-sponsored elementary schools. A further 3,300 girls attended non-government schools. *Report by the Governor-General on the Administration of the Sudan, 1942–1944* (Khartoum: Sudan Government, 1950), 118–24.

6. El Tayib, "Illustrated Record of Sudanese National Costumes," 306.

7. Daly, *Imperial Sudan*, 82.

8. Note by the Graduate General Congress on Education, July 1939, C. M. W. Cox Papers, SAD 662/15/18–19.

9. Ibid.

10. *Report by the Governor-General on the Administration, Finances, and Conditions of the Sudan in 1938* (London, 1939), 84.

11. Note by the Graduate General Congress on Education, July 1939, C. M. W. Cox Papers, SAD 662/15/36.

12. *Gordon College Magazine* (Khartoum), March 12, 1938, 35.

13. Ibid., 31-32.

14. Beasley, *Before the Wind Changed*, 331.

15. See, for example, Firoozeh Kashani-Sabet, *Conceiving Citizens: Women and the Politics of Motherhood in Iran* (Oxford: Oxford University Press, 2011); Hanan Kholoussy, *For Better, For Worse: The Marriage Crisis that Made Modern Egypt* (Stanford: Stanford University Press, 2010); and Lisa Pollard, "From Housewives and Husbands to Suckers and Whores: Marital-Political Anxieties in the 'House of Egypt,' 1919–1948," *Gender & History* 21 (2009).

16. Report of Lord De La Warr's Educational Commission, 1937, Foreign Office Correspondence, FO 371/21998.

17. Beasley, *Before the Wind Changed*, 1–2.

18. Official Papers, I. M. Beasley Papers, SAD 658/4/3.

19. Ibid.

20. Collected Memoirs, R. Kenrick Papers, SAD 890/8/12.

21. Quoted in Sharkey, *Living with Colonialism*, 59.

22. Beasley, *Before the Wind Changed*, 357.

23. Ibid.

24. Comaroff and Comaroff, *Of Revelation and Revolution*, 227.

25. Sharkey, *Living with Colonialism*, 47–50.

26. Magdalen King-Hall, *Somehow Overdone: A Sudan Scrapbook* (London: Peter Davies, 1942), 9.

27. Deng and Daly, *Bonds of Silk*, 102.

28. The resulting garment is sometimes credited as the first "polo shirt" style. See Collins, *Shadows in the Grass*, 262.

29. Diaries, I. M. Beasley Papers, SAD 204/9/83.

30. Beasley, *Before the Wind Changed*, 184–185.

31. El Tayib, "Illustrated Record of Sudanese National Costumes," 278.

32. Beasley, *Before the Wind Changed*, 185.

33. Ibid., 262–63.

34. Comaroff and Comaroff, *Of Revelation and Revolution*, 235.

35. Beasley, *Before the Wind Changed*, 30.

36. Ibid.

37. Comaroff and Comaroff, *Of Revelation and Revolution*, 240.

38. Diaries, I. M. Beasley Papers, SAD 204/9/59.

39. Ibid., SAD 204/9/67.

40. Ibid.

41. Beasley, *Before the Wind Changed*, 242.

42. Diaries, I. M. Beasley Papers, SAD 204/9/25, 55–57.

43. Working Papers, L. P. Sanderson Papers, SAD 60/5/42.

44. "Female Circumcision," I. M. Beasley Papers, SAD 657/4/87.

45. Ibid., SAD 657/4/97–98.

46. Ibid., SAD 657/4/27.

47. Rogaia Mustafa Abusharaf, "'We Have Supped So Deep in Horrors': Understanding Colonialist Emotionality and British Responses to Female Circumcision in Northern Sudan," *History and Anthropology* 17 (2006): 212.

48. "Female Circumcision," I. M. Beasley Papers, SAD 657/5/29–30.

49. Ibid., SAD 657/4/27.

50. Personal Papers, 1924–1946, M. E. and G. L. Wolff Papers, SAD 580/3/27–28.

51. Elaine Hills-Young, "The Surgical Seal of Chastity," p. 2 in "Female Circumcision in Sudan, 1949," Foreign Office Correspondence, FO 371/73668.

52. "Female Circumcision in Sudan, 1949," Foreign Office Correspondence, FO 371/73668.

53. Ibid.

54. "Third Session of the Advisory Council for Northern Sudan," Foreign Office Correspondence, FO 371/45894.

55. "Female Circumcision," I. M. Beasley Papers, SAD 657/4/71.

56. Ibid.

57. Ibid., SAD 657/4/217.

58. Abusharaf, "'We Have Supped So Deep in Horrors,'" 210.

59. Personal Papers, 1924–1946, M. E. and G. L. Wolff Papers, SAD 581/4/18–19.

60. Diary, W. Johnson Papers, SAD 751/11/3–5.

61. W. Stephen Howard, "Mahmoud Mohammed Taha and the Republican Sisters: A Movement for Women in Muslim Sudan," *Ahfad Journal* 23 (2006): 40; Abusharaf, "'We Have Supped So Deep in Horrors,'" 224–25.

62. "Female Circumcision," I. M. Beasley Papers, SAD 657/4/217.

63. Badri, *Women's Movement in the Sudan*, 25–26.

64. Collected Memoirs, R. Kenrick Papers, SAD 890/8/12.

65. Beasley, *Before the Wind Changed*, 12.

66. Personal Correspondence, G. M. Culwick Papers, SAD 428/3/134.

67. Fadwa El Guindi, *Veil: Modesty, Privacy, and Resistance* (Oxford: Berg, 1999), 78–81.

68. "Girl Guides in Sudan," Small Donations, SAD 866/8/3.

69. Collected Memoirs, R. Kenrick Papers, SAD 890/9/10.

70. Personal Papers, E. Jackson Papers, SAD 769/14/17.

71. "Girl Guides in Sudan," Small Donations, SAD 866/8/4.

72. Ibid., SAD 866/8/4–6.

CHAPTER 4: THE WOMAN'S VOICE

1. Fatima Ahmed Ibrahim, *Hasduna khilal 'Ishrin 'Aman* (Khartoum: Sudanese Women's Union, 1986), 9–10.

2. See, for example, the account of the Omdurman Girls' Intermediate School striking in sympathy with boys in El Obeid. Personal Papers, K. M. E. Wood Papers, SAD 82/4/134–37, 161–62.

3. Official Papers, L. P. Sanderson Papers, SAD 739/6/3, 10–15.

4. Ibid., SAD 739/6/1–2.

5. Personal Papers, K. M. E. Wood Papers, SAD 82/6/82–91.

6. Official Papers, K. M. E. Wood Papers, SAD 80/4/16.

7. Haga Kashif Badri, *Al-Haraka al-Nisa'iyya fi al-Sudan*, 2nd ed. (Khartoum: University of Khartoum Press, 2002), 112.

8. F. A. Ibrahim, *Hasduna khilal 'Ishrin 'Aman*, 7.

9. Badri, *Al-Haraka al-Nisa'iyya fi al-Sudan*, 112.

10. Personal Papers, K. M. E. Wood Papers, SAD 82/7/63.

11. Nafisa Ahmed el Amin, "The Democratic Advance and Women's Movement in the Sudan" (paper presented at the 16th World Congress of the International Political Science Association, Berlin, 1994), 11.

12. In Arabic, the name *Itihad al-Nisa'i al-Sudani* translates as the "Union of Sudanese Women," but the name is most commonly rendered in English as the "Sudanese Women's Union." This causes some difficulty because in 1971 President Gaafar Numeiri's government banned the Union of Sudanese Women and established in its place, *Itihad Nisa' al-Sudan*, "Sudan's Union of Women"—a name intentionally chosen to confuse Sudan's public. In keeping with general practice I will refer to the 1952 "Union of Sudanese Women" as the "Sudanese Women's Union" or "Union."

13. Sondra Hale provides a detailed look at the successes and challenges of the SWU and other activist groups in her definitive work *Gender Politics in Sudan: Islamism, Socialism, and the State* (Boulder, CO: Westview Press, 1996).

14. P. M. Holt and M. W. Daly, *A History of the Sudan from the Coming of Islam to the Present Day*, 6th ed (Harlow: Pearson Education Ltd., 2011), 100–101.

15. Ibid., 101–2.

16. Daly, *Imperial Sudan*, 277.

17. Ibid., 270.

18. Personal Correspondence, G. M. Culwick Papers, SAD 428/3/146.

19. Daly, *Imperial Sudan*, 280.

20. *Sudan Government List, 15 March 1955* (Khartoum: Sudan Government, 1955). For example, when Sylvia Clark retired as Controller of Girls' Education she was succeeded by Ahmed Mirghani.

21. Official Papers, 1939–1953, E. D. Arbuthnot Papers, SAD 849/7/75–76.

22. Badri, *Women's Movement in the Sudan*, 169.

23. Tim Niblock, *Class and Power in Sudan: The Dynamics of Sudanese Politics, 1898–1985* (Albany: State University of New York Press, 1987), 135.

24. Howard, "Mahmoud Mohammed Taha and the Republican Sisters," 33.

25. Asma Mahmoud Mohamed Taha, conversation with author, Alustadh Mahmoud M. Taha Cultural Center, Omdurman, October 23, 2010.

26. Ahfad University for Women Documentation Unit for Women's Studies, *Sudanese Pioneer Women*, Women in Development Series (Omdurman: Ahfad University for Women, 1993), 66.

27. Nafisa Ahmed el Amin, Director, Documentation Unit for Women's Studies, conversation with author, Ahfad University for Women, Omdurman, October 28, 2010.

28. Ahfad University for Women Documentation Unit for Women's Studies, *Sudanese Pioneer Women*, 71–79.

29. Nafisa Ahmed el Amin, Director, Documentation Unit of Women's Studies, conversation with author, Ahfad University for Women, Omdurman, September 21, 2010.

30. El Amin, "The Democratic Advance," 10.

31. Badri, *Women's Movement in the Sudan*, 174–75.

32. El Amin, "The Democratic Advance," 13.

33. Ibid.

34. Hale, *Gender Politics in Sudan*, 72.

35. Heather J. Sharkey, "A Century in Print: Arabic Journalism and Nationalism in Sudan, 1899–1999," *International Journal of Middle East Studies* 31 (1999): 539.

36. "Al-Mar'a fi al-Sudan," *Al-Saraha*, August 1, 1952, 1–2, 5–6.

37. Nafisa Ahmed el Amin, conversation with author, September 21, 2010.

38. El Amin, "The Democratic Advance," 13.

39. Badri, *Women's Movement in the Sudan*, 184.

40. F. A. Ibrahim, *Hasduna khilal 'Ishrin 'Aman*, 44.

41. "Sudan Elections for Self-Government, 1953," Colonial Office Correspondence, CO 1069/14. There was added layer of complexity in the requirements for who could stand for, and vote in, the Senate elections. As laid out in this document, it appears that women could vote and be candidates for the House of Representatives but could only vote for Senate seats.

42. This estimate is based on the limited number of girls, no more than 100–150 each year, who were enrolled in either the Omdurman Secondary School or Unity High School—the only schools to provide secondary education for girls.

43. El Amin, "The Democratic Advance," 17.

44. Ibid., 14.

45. Badri, *Al-Haraka al-Nisa'iyya fi al-Sudan*, 119. It is interesting to note that in the English edition of this account the demonstrators are described as wearing "their national toob." See Badri, *Women's Movement in the Sudan*, 182.

46. Roland Barthes, "Semiology and the Urban," in *Rethinking Architecture: A Reader in Cultural Theory*, ed. Neil Leach (London: Routledge, 1997), 171.

47. For a foundational definition of the male urban explorer and his city, see "The Flaneur" in Walter Benjamin, *Charles Baudelaire: A Lyric Poet in the Era of High Capitalism* (London: Verso, 1983), 96.

48. McClintock, *Imperial Leather*, 81.

49. Elizabeth Grosz, *Space, Time, and Perversion* (New York: Routledge, 1995), 100.

50. Tanu Priya Uteng and Tim Cresswell, eds., *Gendered Mobilities* (Farnham, UK: Ashgate, 2008), 2.

51. This idea is borrowed from Deutsch, *Women and the City*, 6, 78–79.

52. Here I am inspired by Stephanie Camp (in turn building off of Edward Said), who argues that slaves in the American South used "rival geographies" to exercise "mobility in the face of constraint." Stephanie M. H. Camp, *Closer to Freedom: Enslaved Women and Everyday Resistance in the Plantation South* (Chapel Hill: University of North Carolina Press, 2004), 7.

53. Official Papers, E. Sarsfield-Hall Papers, SAD 682/13/58.

54. G. Hamdan, "The Growth and Functional Structure of Khartoum," *Geographical Review* 50, no. 1 (January 1960): 27.

55. A. J. V. Arthur, "Slum Clearance in Khartoum," in *Urbanization and Urban Life in Sudan*, ed. Valdo Pons (Khartoum: Development Studies and Research Centre, University of Khartoum, 1980), 531, 536.

56. Karin Van Nieuwkerk, *"A Trade Like Any Other": Female Singers and Dancers in Egypt* (Austin: University of Texas Press, 1995), 6.

57. F. A. Ibrahim, *Hasduna khilal 'Ishrin 'Aman*, 146.

58. Fatima Ahmed Ibrahim, "Arrow at Rest," in *Women in Exile*, edited by Mahnaz Afkhami (Charlottesville: University Press of Virginia, 1994), 197–98.

59. Martin, "Contesting Clothes in Colonial Brazzaville," 419.

60. Ali-Dinar, "Contextual Analysis of Dress and Adornment in Al-Fashir, Sudan," 144.

61. Ibid., 164.

62. Asma Mahmoud Mohamed Taha, conversation with author, October 23, 2010.

63. Nafisa Ahmed el Amin, conversation with author, September 21, 2010.

64. Azza I. M. Anis, "Charting New Directions: Reflections on Women's Political Activism in Sudan" (PhD diss., Mount Saint Vincent University, 2001), 29–31.

65. F. A. Ibrahim, "Arrow at Rest," 199, 203.

66. El Tayib, "Women's Dress in the Northern Sudan," 51.

67. Beth Baron, *The Women's Awakening in Egypt: Culture, Society, and the Press* (New Haven: Yale University Press, 1994), 39.

68. Mahgoub Mohamed Salih, "The Sudanese Press," *Sudan Notes and Records* 46 (1965): 3.

69. Badri, *Women's Movement in the Sudan*, 152.

70. Beth Baron, "Readers and the Women's Press in Egypt," *Poetics Today* 15 (Summer 1994): 218.

71. Nafisa Ahmed el Amin, conversation with author, September 21, 2010.

72. There are only a handful of extant issues of *Sawt al-Mar'a* held at the National Records Office in Khartoum, with the earliest dating to 1959. My summary of the magazine's content is informed by a general reading of those later issues as well as commentary from contemporary and secondary sources.

73. Badri, *Women's Movement in the Sudan*, 153.

74. Carolyn Fluehr-Lobban, "The Women's Movement in the Sudan and Its Impact on Sudanese Law and Politics," *Ahfad Journal* 2, no. 1 (June 1985): 58; F. A. Ibrahim, "Arrow at Rest," 199.

75. "Sudan: Report on Women's Affairs 1960," Foreign Office Correspondence, FO 1110/1295.

76. Sharkey, "A Century in Print," 543.

77. Ibid.

78. Baron, "Readers and the Women's Press in Egypt," 233.

79. Official Papers, I. M. Beasley Papers, SAD 657/2/37.

80. Howard, "Mahmoud Mohammed Taha and the Republican Sisters," 46–47.

81. Badri, *Women's Movement in the Sudan*, 178.

82. Adullahi Ali Ibrahim, "The House That Matriarchy Built: The Sudanese Women's Union," *South Atlantic Quarterly* 109 (Winter 2010): 62.

83. Asma Mahmoud Mohamed Taha, conversation with author, October 23, 2010.

84. Official Papers, I. M. Beasley Papers, SAD 658/4/49–58.

85. Ibid.

86. Ibid., SAD 658/4/54.

87. Marjorie Garber, *Vested Interests: Cross-Dressing and Cultural Anxiety* (New York: Routledge, 1997), 16.

88. F. A. Ibrahim, "Arrow at Rest," 201.

CHAPTER 5: KHARTOUM AT NIGHT

1. Official Papers, E. Sarsfield-Hall Papers, SAD 682/13/30–34.

2. Personal Correspondence, A. J. V. Arthur Papers, SAD 707/16/8.

3. Nafisa Ahmed el Amin, conversation with author, July 22, 2013.

4. Collected Memoirs, R. Kenrick Papers, SAD 890/8/36.

5. Boddy, *Civilizing Women*, 62.

6. Anne Cloudsley, *Women of Omdurman: Life, Love, and the Cult of Virginity* (London: Ethnographica, 1983), 34.

7. Heidi Gengenbach, "Boundaries of Beauty: Tattooed Secrets of Women's History in Magude District, Southern Mozambique," *Journal of Women's History* 14, no. 4 (2003): 109.

8. Zeinab el Fateh el Badawi, *The Development of the Sudanese Women Movement* (Khartoum: Ministry of Information and Social Affairs, 1966), 1–3.

9. Personal Papers, E. Jackson Papers, SAD 769/14/21.

10. Official Papers, I. M. Beasley Papers, SAD 657/1/68. See also Marjorie Hall and Bakhita Amin Ismail, *Sisters under the Sun: The Story of Sudanese Women*, 107.

11. "Female Circumcision," I. M. Beasley Papers, SAD 657/4/106.

12. Ibid., SAD 657/4/217.

13. Lisa Pollard, *Nurturing the Nation: The Family Politics of Modernizing, Colonizing and Liberating Egypt* (Berkeley: University of California Press, 2005), 11.

14. Quoted in Sharkey, "Chronicles of Progress," 64.

15. Ibid.

16. Nafisa Ahmed el Amin, conversation with author, September 21, 2010.

17. Sondra Hale, "Activating the Gender Local: Transnational Ideologies and 'Women's Culture' in Northern Sudan," *Journal of Middle East Women's Studies* 1 (2005): 36.

18. Comaroff and Comaroff, *Of Revelation and Revolution*, 219.

19. McClintock, *Imperial Leather*, 226.

20. Burke, *Lifebuoy Men, Lux Women*, 194.

21. Jeremy Prestholdt's work on nineteenth-century African consumers' desires for global products has begun some of this important work. See Jeremy Prestholdt, *Domesticating the World: African Consumerism and the Genealogies of Globalization* (Berkeley: University of California Press, 2008), 8.

22. Christopher B. Steiner, "Another Image of Africa: Toward an Ethnohistory of European Cloth Marketed in West Africa, 1873–1960," *Ethnohistory* 32 (1985): 97.

23. Personal Papers, George F. Ainscrow, Archive of Art & Design (Victoria and Albert Museum, London), AAD/1993/12/1/1.

24. Daly, *Imperial Sudan*, 302, 315–16.

25. El Tayib, "Illustrated Record of Sudanese National Costumes," 249.

26. Griselda el Tayib, conversation with author, Khartoum, October 26, 2010.

27. The most comprehensive lists of tobe names and other fashions are found in Ali Bahr Ali-Dinar's doctoral dissertation, "Contextual Analysis of Dress and Adornment in al-Fashir, Sudan," and in two works by Griselda el-Tayib, her master's thesis, "An Illustrated Record of Sudanese National Costumes," and "Women's Dress in Northern Sudan," in Susan Kenyon's *The Sudanese Woman*. Although the works are separated by chronology and geography, the overlap in their findings affirms the national reach of tobe names.

28. El Tayib, "Illustrated Record of Sudanese National Costumes," 306.

29. Ali-Dinar, "Contextual Analysis of Dress," app. 1.

30. Holt and Daly, *History of the Sudan*, 110–11.

31. Daly, *Imperial Sudan*, 368.

32. Since the precise date of this tobe is unclear, it is also possible that it references an earlier period in Sudan's history. On December 30, 1949, to great fanfare at the Khartoum airport, al-Azhari and a delegation of the Graduates' Congress traveled to Egypt to strengthen their ties with the new Egyptian government and call for an immediate end of Condominium rule.

33. El Tayib, "Women's Dress in the Northern Sudan," 54.

34. Ali-Dinar, "Contextual Analysis of Dress," app. 1.

35. Ibid.

36. "Ma'a Nisa' al-'Alam," *Sawt al-Mar'a*, April 1959, 18.

37. Diaries, K. M. E. Wood Papers, SAD 85/3/1.

38. "Sudan: Report on Women's Affairs 1960," Foreign Office Correspondence, FO 1110/1295.

39. El Tayib, "Illustrated Record of Sudanese National Costumes," 247.

40. Jean Allman, "Introduction," in Allman (ed.), *Fashioning Africa*, 6.

41. *Al-Judhur al-Tarikhiyya li-l-Haraka al-Nisa'iyya al-Sudaniyya* (Cairo: Maktaba Madbuli, 1990), 37.

42. "Anaqa wa-Jamal," *Sawt al-Mar'a*, April 1961, 10.

43. Diaries, K. M. E. Wood Papers, SAD 85/3/34.

44. El Tayib, "Illustrated Record of Sudanese National Costumes," 230, 242.

45. "Al-Mar'a Tahtammu bi Anaqatiha," *Sawt al-Mar'a*, April 1961, 41.

46. Fauziya al-Yemeni, "Al-Thawb wa-l-Shillukh wa-l-Baqudi," *Sawt al-Mar'a*, May 1962, 11.

47. Ibid., 11–12.

48. Personal Correspondence, G. M. Culwick Papers, SAD 428/1/37.

49. Allan Arthur gives lively and detailed descriptions of the people who worked at the cabaret. Personal Correspondence, A. J. V. Arthur Papers, SAD 726/4/1–82.

50. I am responding in part to a question asked by Kathy Peiss in her own work on the political and cultural meanings of dress: When does fashion and adornment become political and how will we know it? Kathy Peiss, *Zoot Suit: The Enigmatic Career of an Extreme Style* (Philadelphia: University of Pennsylvania Press, 2011), 9.

51. Carole Turbin, "Refashioning the Concept of Public/Private: Lessons from Dress Studies," *Journal of Women's History* 15 (2003): 45.

CONCLUSION

1. Leila Aboulela, *The Translator* (Edinburgh: Polygon, 2003), 43.

2. Bryan S. Turner, *The Body and Society: Explorations in Social Theory*, 2nd ed. (London: Sage, 1996), 43.

3. Boddy, *Civilizing Women*, 79.

4. Ali-Dinar, "Contextual Analysis of Dress," app. 1.

5. Saidiya Hartman, "Venus in Two Acts," *Small Axe* 26 (2008): 4.

6. "Politics Inspires Fashion for Sudanese Women," *Al Arabiya News*, September 7, 2008, www.alarabiya.net/articles/2008/09/07/56130.html (accessed August 24, 2016).

7. Khalid Sharaf El Deen, "'Zanga Zanga' and 'Secession' Are Latest Names of Sudanese Female Traditional Dress," *Sudan Vision Daily*, August 27, 2011, www.sudanvisiondaily.com//modules.php?name=News&file=article&sid=79933 (accessed March 8, 2012).

POSTSCRIPT

1. The continued use of telegrams in 1955 is indicative of the limited technology and infrastructure in place in southern Sudan. No telephones or radios were available to the rebelling troops. See Scopas S. Poggo, *The First Sudanese Civil War: Africans, Arabs, and Israelis in the Southern Sudan, 1955–1972* (New York: Palgrave Macmillan, 2009), 46.

2. For an excellent overview of the local and global factors in Sudan's civil war, see Poggo, *First Sudanese Civil War*.

3. "Li-l-Fata," *Al-Saraha*, August 1, 1952, 5; Nafisa Ahmed el Amin, conversation with author, October 5, 2010.

4. Leni Riefenstahl, *The Sieve of Time: The Memoirs of Leni Riefenstahl* (London: Quartet Books, 1992), 471.

BIBLIOGRAPHY

ARCHIVAL RECORDS AND MANUSCRIPTS

Archive of Art and Design, Victoria and Albert Museum, London
George F. Ainscrow Papers

The National Archives, London

BW 90	Inter-University Council for Higher Education Oversees
FCO 95	Foreign and Commonwealth Offices: Information Department
FO 141	Foreign Office: Egypt Embassy Correspondence
FO 371	Foreign Office: General Correspondence
FO 1110	Foreign Office: International Research Department
WO 32	War Office: Registered Files

Sudan Archive, Durham University (SAD), England
A. J. V. Arthur Papers
E. D. Arbuthnot Papers
I. M. Beasley Papers
J. B. Christopherson Papers
C. M. W. Cox Papers
G. M. Culwick Papers
E. Cumings Papers
L. H. Gwynne Papers
R. Hassan Papers
E. Hills-Young Papers

E. Jackson Papers
W. Johnson Papers
R. Kenrick Papers
T. R. H. Owen Papers
J. W. Robertson Papers
L. P. Sanderson Papers
E. Sarsfield-Hall Papers
C. R. Williams Papers
M. E. and G. L. Wolff Papers
K. M. E. Wood Papers

NEWSPAPERS AND JOURNALS [YEARS CONSULTED]
Al-Saraha [1951–1953]
Sawt al-Mar'a [1959–1968]
Sudan al-Jadid [1944, 1954]
Sudan Notes and Records [1918–1983]

PUBLISHED AND UNPUBLISHED WORKS
Aboulela, Leila. *The Translator*. Edinburgh: Polygon, 2003.
Abd al-Rahim, Muddathir. *Imperialism and Nationalism in the Sudan: A Study in Constitutional and Political Development, 1899–1956*. Oxford: Clarendon Press, 1969.
Abusharaf, Rogaia Mustafa. *Transforming Women in Sudan: Politics and the Body in a Squatter Settlement*. Chicago: University of Chicago Press, 2009.
———. "'We Have Supped So Deep in Horrors': Understanding Colonialist Emotionality and British Responses to Female Circumcision in Northern Sudan." *History and Anthropology* 17 (2006): 209–28.
Ahfad University for Women Documentation Unit for Women's Studies. *Sudanese Pioneer Women*. Women in Development Series. Omdurman: Ahfad University for Women, 1993.
Ali-Dinar, Ali Bahr Aldin. "Contextual Analysis of Dress and Adornment in Al-Fashir, Sudan." PhD diss., University of Pennsylvania, 1995.
Allman, Jean, ed. *Fashioning Africa: Power and the Politics of Dress*. Bloomington: Indiana University Press, 2004.
Alloula, Malek. *The Colonial Harem*. Translated by Myrna Godzich and Wlad Godzich. Minneapolis: University of Minnesota Press, 1986.
el Amin, Nafisa Ahmed. "The Democratic Advance and Women's Movement in the Sudan." Paper presented at the 16th World Congress of the International Political Science Association, Berlin, 1994.

Anis, Azza I. M. "Charting New Directions: Reflections on Women's Political Activism in Sudan." PhD diss., Mount Saint Vincent University, 2001.

Appadurai, Arjun, ed. *The Social Life of Things: Commodities in Cultural Perspective.* Cambridge: Cambridge University Press, 1986.

Arthur, A. J. V. "Slum Clearance in Khartoum." In *Urbanization and Urban Life in Sudan,* edited by Valdo Pons. Khartoum: Development Studies and Research Centre, University of Khartoum, 1980.

el Badawi, Zeinab el Fateh. *The Development of the Sudanese Women Movement.* Khartoum: Ministry of Information and Social Affairs, 1966.

Badri, Haga Kashif. *Al-Haraka al-Nisa'iyya fi al-Sudan.* 2nd ed. Khartoum: Khartoum University, 2002.

————. "My Experience as a Female Researcher." Unpublished essay, 1987.

————. *Women's Movement in the Sudan.* 2nd ed. Omdurman: MOB Center for Sudanese Studies, 2009.

Ballantyne, Tony, and Antoinette Burton, eds. *Bodies in Contact: Rethinking Colonial Encounters in World History.* Durham, NC: Duke University Press, 2005.

————, eds. *Moving Subjects: Gender, Mobility, and Intimacy in an Age of Global Empire.* Urbana: University of Illinois Press, 2008.

Baron, Beth. *Egypt as a Woman: Nationalism, Gender, and Politics.* Berkeley: University of California Press, 2005.

————. "Readers and the Women's Press in Egypt." *Poetics Today* 15 (Summer 1994): 217–40.

————. *The Women's Awakening in Egypt: Culture, Society, and the Press.* New Haven: Yale University Press, 1994.

Barthes, Roland. "Semiology and the Urban." In *Rethinking Architecture: A Reader in Cultural Theory,* edited by Neil Leach, 166–72. London: Routledge, 1997.

Beasley, Ina. *Before the Wind Changed: People, Places, and Education in the Sudan.* Edited by Janet Starkey. Oxford: Oxford University Press, 1992.

Bedri, Balghis Yousif. "Food and Differential Roles in the Fetiehab Household." In *The Sudanese Woman,* edited by Susan Kenyon. Khartoum: Graduate College Publications, University of Khartoum, 1987.

————. "Pitfalls in Social Development: A Critical Review of a Training Center for Women." In *Women and the Environment: Environmental Research Paper Series,* No. 2, edited by Diana Baxter. Khartoum: Institute of Environmental Studies, University of Khartoum, 1981.

Bedri, Babikr. *The Memoirs of Babikr Bedri,* vol. 1. Translated by Yousef Bedri and George Scott. London: Oxford University Press, 1969.

———. *The Memoirs of Babikr Bedri*, vol. 2. Translated and edited by Yusuf Bedri and Peter Hogg. London: Ithaca Press, 1980.

Bell, Heather. *Frontiers of Medicine in the Anglo-Egyptian Sudan, 1899–1940*. Oxford: Clarendon Press, 1999.

Benjamin, Walter. *Charles Baudelaire: A Lyric Poet in the Era of High Capitalism*. London: Verso, 1983.

Boddy, Janice. *Civilizing Women: British Crusades in Colonial Sudan*. Princeton: Princeton University Press, 2007.

———. *Wombs and Alien Spirits: Women, Men, and the Zar Cult in Northern Sudan*. Madison: University of Wisconsin Press, 1989.

Brown, Marie Grace. "In Touch: The Body and Sensibility as Historical Text." *International Journal of Middle East Studies* 48 (2016): 565–69.

Burke, Timothy. *Lifebuoy Men, Lux Women: Commodification, Consumption, and Cleanliness in Modern Zimbabwe*. Durham, NC: Duke University Press, 1996.

Burton, Antoinette. *Dwelling in the Archive: Women Writing House, Home, and History in Late Colonial India*. Oxford: Oxford University Press, 2003.

Camp, Stephanie M. H. *Closer to Freedom: Enslaved Women and Everyday Resistance in the Plantation South*. Chapel Hill: University of North Carolina Press, 2004.

Canning, Kathleen. "The Body as Method? Reflections on the Place of the Body in Gender History." *Gender & History* 11 (1999): 499–513.

Cloudsley, Anne. *Women of Omdurman: Life, Love, and the Cult of Virginity*. London: Ethnographica, 1983.

Cohn, Bernard S. *Colonialism and Its Forms of Knowledge: The British in India*. Princeton: Princeton University Press, 1996.

Collins, Robert O. *Shadows in the Grass: Britain in the Southern Sudan, 1918–1956*. New Haven: Yale University Press, 1983.

———. "The Sudan Political Service: A Portrait of the 'Imperialists.'" *African Affairs* 71 (1972): 293–303.

Comaroff, John L., and Jean Comaroff. *Of Revelation and Revolution: The Dialectics of Modernity on a South African Frontier*, vol. 2. Chicago: University of Chicago Press, 1997.

Crowfoot, J. W. "Wedding Customs in the Northern Sudan." *Sudan Notes and Records* 5 (1922): 1–28.

Cruickshank, A. "The Midwives Training School and the Development of a Midwifery Service in the Sudan During the Anglo-Egyptian Condominium, 1899–1956." In *The Condominium Remembered: Proceedings of the Durham Sudan Historical Records Conference 1982*, vol. 2, edited by Deborah Lavin. Durham: Centre for Middle Eastern and Islamic Studies, University of Durham, 1982.

Cuzzi, Guiseppe, and Hans Resener, eds. *Fifteen Years Prisoner of the False Prophet.* Translated by Hildegund Sharma. Khartoum: Sudan Research Unit, University of Khartoum, 1968.

Daly, M. W. *Empire on the Nile: The Anglo-Egyptian Sudan, 1898–1934.* Cambridge: Cambridge University Press, 2003.

———. *Imperial Sudan: The Anglo-Egyptian Condominium, 1934–1956.* Cambridge: Cambridge University Press, 2002.

Daly, M. W., and Jane Hogan. *Images of Empire: Photographic Sources for the British in the Sudan.* Leiden: Brill Academic Publishers, 2005.

Deng, Francis M., and M. W. Daly. *Bonds of Silk: The Human Factor in the British Administration of the Sudan.* East Lansing: Michigan State University Press, 1989.

Deutsch, Sarah. *Women and the City: Gender, Space, and Power in Boston, 1870–1940.* Oxford: Oxford University Press, 2000.

Diyab, Mina Ahmed Ibrahim. *Dawr al-Mar'a al-Sudaniyya fi al-Haraka al-Ijtima'i wa-l-Siyasi fi al-Mujtama' (1900–1969).* Cairo: Al-Dar al-'Arabiyya li-l-Nashr wa-l-Tawzi'a, 2006.

El-Bakri, Z. B., and E. M. Kameir. "Aspects of Women's Political Participation in Sudan." *International Social Science Journal* 35 (1983): 605–23.

Ensor, F. Sidney. *Incidents on a Journey through Nubia to Darfoor.* London: W. H. Allen & Co., 1881.

Fluehr-Lobban, Carolyn. "Women and Social Liberation: The Sudan Experience." In *Three Studies on National Integration in the Arab World.* North Dartmouth, MA: Association of Arab-American University Graduates, Inc., 1974.

———. "The Women's Movement in the Sudan and Its Impact on Sudanese Law and Politics." *Ahfad Journal* 2, no. 1 (June 1985): 53–62.

Foley, Helen. *Letters to Her Mother: War-Time in Sudan, 1938–1945.* Somerset: Castle Cary Press, 1992.

Garber, Marjorie. *Vested Interests: Cross-Dressing and Cultural Anxiety.* New York: Routledge, 1997.

Gengenbach, Heidi. "Boundaries of Beauty: Tattooed Secrets of Women's History in Magude District, Southern Mozambique." *Journal of Women's History* 14 (2003): 106–141.

Graham-Brown, Sarah. *Images of Women: The Portrayal of Women in Photography of the Middle East, 1860–1950.* New York: Columbia University Press, 1988.

Grosz, Elizabeth. *Space, Time, and Perversion.* New York: Routledge, 1995.

el Guindi, Fadwa. *Veil: Modesty, Privacy, and Resistance.* Oxford: Berg, 1999.

Hale, Sondra. "Activating the Gender Local: Transnational Ideologies and

'Women's Culture' in Northern Sudan." *Journal of Middle East Women's Studies* 1 (2005): 29–52.

———. *Gender Politics in Sudan: Islamism, Socialism, and the State.* Boulder, CO: Westview Press, 1996.

———. "Mothers and Militias: Islamic State Construction of the Women Citizens of Northern Sudan." *Citizenship Studies* 3 (1999): 373–86.

Hall, Marjorie, and Bakhita Amin Ismail. *Sisters under the Sun: The Story of Sudanese Women.* London: Longman, 1981.

Hamdan, G. "The Growth and Functional Structure of Khartoum." *Geographical Review* 50, no. 1 (January 1960): 21–40.

Hartman, Saidiya. "Venus in Two Acts." *Small Axe* 26 (2008):1-14.

Hendrickson, Hildi, ed. *Clothing and Difference: Embodied Identities in Colonial and Post-Colonial Africa.* Durham, NC: Duke University Press, 1996.

Holt, P. M. *The Mahdist State in the Sudan, 1881–1898.* 2nd ed. Oxford: Clarendon Press, 1970.

Holt, P. M., and M. W. Daly. *A History of the Sudan from the Coming of Islam to the Present Day.* 6th ed. Harlow: Pearson Education Ltd., 2011.

House, William J. "The Status of Women in the Sudan." *Journal of Modern African Studies* 26 (1988): 277–302.

Howard, W. Stephen. "Mahmoud Mohammed Taha and the Republican Sisters: A Movement for Women in Muslim Sudan." *Ahfad Journal* 23 (2006): 31–49.

Hunt, Nancy Rose. *A Colonial Lexicon of Birth Ritual, Medicalization, and Mobility in the Congo.* Durham, NC: Duke University Press, 1999.

Ibrahim, Adullahi Ali. "The House That Matriarchy Built: The Sudanese Women's Union." *South Atlantic Quarterly* 109 (Winter 2010): 53–74.

Ibrahim, Fatima Ahmed. "Arrow at Rest." In *Women in Exile,* edited by Mahnaz Afkhami. Charlottesville: University Press of Virginia, 1994.

———. *Hasduna khilal 'Ishrin 'Aman.* Khartoum: Sudanese Women's Union, 1986.

———. "War in Empty Rooms and the Sudanese Women's Union." In *Common Ground or Mutual Exclusion? Women's Movements and International Relations,* edited by Marianne Braig and Sonja Wolte. London: Zed Books, 2002.

Ismail, Ellen T. *Social Environment and Daily Routine of Sudanese Women: A Case Study of Urban Middle Class Housewives.* Berlin: Dietrich Reimer Verlag, 1982.

Ismail, Sawsan Salim. *Al-Judhur al-Tarikhiyya li-l-Haraka al-Nisa'iyya al-Sudani-yya.* Cairo: Maktaba Madbuli, 1990.

Johnson, Marion. "Calico Caravans: The Tripoli-Kano Trade after 1880." *Journal of African History* 27 (1976): 95–117.

Jok, Jok Madut. *Militarization, Gender, and Reproductive Health in South Sudan.* Lewiston, NY: Edwin Mellen Press, 1998.

Kashani-Sabet, Firoozeh. *Conceiving Citizens: Women and the Politics of Motherhood in Iran.* Oxford: Oxford University Press, 2011.

Kendall, Eileen. "A Short History of the Training of Midwives in Sudan." *Sudan Notes and Records* 33 (1952): 42–53.

Kenrick, Rosemary. *Sudan Tales: Recollections of Some of the Sudan Political Service Wives, 1926–1956.* Cambridge: Oleander Press, 1987.

Kenyon, Susan M. *Five Women of Sennar: Culture and Change in Central Sudan.* 2nd ed. Long Grove, IL: Waveland Press, 2004.

———, ed. *The Sudanese Woman.* Khartoum: Graduate College Publications, University of Khartoum, 1987.

Keun, Odette. "A Foreigner Looks at British Sudan." *The Nineteenth Century,* September 1930, 292–309.

Kholoussy, Hanan. *For Better, for Worse: The Marriage Crisis That Made Modern Egypt.* Stanford: Stanford University Press, 2010.

King-Hall, Magdalen. *Somehow Overdone: A Sudan Scrapbook.* London: Peter Davies, 1942.

Kirk-Greene, A. H. M. "The Sudan Political Service: A Profile in the Sociology of Imperialism." *International Journal of African Historical Studies* 15, no. 1 (1982): 21–48.

Kramer, Robert S. *Holy City on the Nile: Omdurman during the Mahdiyya, 1885–1898.* Princeton, NJ: Markus Wiener Publishers, 2010.

La Rue, George Michael. "Imported Blue Cotton Cloth: Status Clothing for Rural Women in Pre-Colonial Dar Fur." Paper presented at the African Studies Association annual meeting, Boston, 1993.

Landau, Paul S., and Deborah Kaspin, eds. *Images and Empires: Visuality in Colonial and Postcolonial Africa.* Berkeley: University of California Press, 2002.

Langley, Michael. *No Woman's Country: Travels in the Anglo-Egyptian Sudan.* New York: Philosophical Library, 1951.

Lavin, Deborah, ed. *The Condominium Remembered: Proceedings of the Durham Sudan Historical Records Conference 1982,* vol. 2. Durham: Centre for Middle East and Islamic Studies, University of Durham, 1982.

Lutz, Catherine, and Jane Collins. *Reading National Geographic.* Chicago: University of Chicago Press, 1993.

MacMichael, Harold. Introduction to *Sudan Political Service, 1899–1956.* Oxford: Oxonian Press, 1958.

Mahmoud, Fatima Babiker. *The Sudanese Bourgeoisie: Vanguard of Development?* Khartoum: Khartoum University Press, 1984.

Martin, Phyllis M. "Contesting Clothes in Colonial Brazzaville." *Journal of African History* 35 (1994): 401–26.

Masquelier, Adeline. *Dirt, Undress, and Difference: Critical Perspectives on the Body's Surface.* Bloomington: Indiana University Press, 2005.

Mauss, Marcel. "Techniques of the Body." *Economy and Society* 2 (1973): 70–88.

McClintock, Anne. *Imperial Leather: Race, Gender, and Sexuality in the Colonial Conquest.* New York: Routledge, 1995.

Mitchell, Timothy. *Colonising Egypt.* Berkeley: University of California Press, 1991.

al Nagar, Sami Al Hadi. "Women and Spirit Possession in Omdurman." In *The Sudanese Woman,* edited by Susan Kenyon. Khartoum: Graduate College Publications, University of Khartoum, 1987.

Nageeb, Salma Ahmed. *New Spaces and Old Frontiers: Women, Social Space, and Islamization in Sudan.* Lanham, MD: Lexington Books, 2004.

Niblock, Tim. *Class and Power in Sudan: The Dynamics of Sudanese Politics, 1898–1985.* Albany: State University of New York Press, 1987.

Oyewumi, Oyeronke. *The Invention of Women: Making an African Sense of Western Gender Discourses.* Minneapolis: University of Minnesota Press, 1997.

Peiss, Kathy. *Zoot Suit: The Enigmatic Career of an Extreme Style.* Philadelphia: University of Pennsylvania Press, 2011.

Poggo, Scopas S. *The First Sudanese Civil War: Africans, Arabs, and Israelis in the Southern Sudan, 1955–1972.* New York: Palgrave Macmillan, 2009.

Pollard, Lisa. "From Housewives and Husbands to Suckers and Whores: Marital-Political Anxieties in the 'House of Egypt,' 1919–1948." *Gender & History* 21, no. 3 (2009): 647–69.

———. *Nurturing the Nation: The Family Politics of Modernizing, Colonizing, and Liberating Egypt.* Berkeley: University of California Press, 2005.

Pons, Valdo, ed. *Urbanization and Urban Life in the Sudan.* Khartoum: Development Studies and Research Centre, University of Khartoum, 1980.

Pratt, Geraldine, and Victoria Rosner, eds. *The Global and the Intimate: Feminism in Our Time.* New York: Columbia University Press, 2012.

Prestholdt, Jeremy. *Domesticating the World: African Consumerism and the Genealogies of Globalization.* Berkeley: University of California Press, 2008.

Rabine, Leslie W. *The Global Circulation of African Fashion.* Oxford: Berg, 2002.

Rich, Adrienne. "Notes towards a Politics of Location." In *Blood, Bread, and Poetry: Selected Prose 1979–1985.* New York: W. W. Norton, 1994.

Riefenstahl, Leni. *The Sieve of Time: The Memoirs of Leni Riefenstahl.* London: Quartet Books, 1992.

Ryan, James. *Picturing Empire: Photography and the Visualization of the British Empire.* Chicago: University of Chicago Press, 1997.

Said, Edward. *Culture and Imperialism.* First Vintage Books edition. New York: Vintage Books, 1994.

————. *Orientalism.* Twenty-fifth anniversary edition. New York: Vintage Books, 1994.

Salih, Mahgoub Mohamed. "The Sudanese Press." *Sudan Notes and Records* 46 (1965): 1–7.

Sanderson, Lilian M. "Some Aspects of the Development of Girls' Education in the Northern Sudan." *Sudan Notes and Records* 42 (1961): 91–101.

Schneider, Jane, and Annette B. Weiner, eds. *Cloth and Human Experience.* Washington, DC: Smithsonian Institution Press, 1989.

Sharkey, Heather. "A Century in Print: Arabic Journalism and Nationalism in Sudan, 1899–1999." *International Journal of Middle East Studies* 31 (1999): 531–49.

————. "Chronicles of Progress: Northern Sudanese Women in the Era of British Imperialism." *Journal of Imperial and Commonwealth History* 31 (2003): 51–82.

————. *Living with Colonialism: Nationalism and Culture in the Anglo-Egyptian Sudan.* Berkeley: University of California Press, 2003.

Sikainga, Ahmad. "Shari'a Courts and the Manumission of Female Slaves in the Sudan, 1898–1939." *International Journal of African Historical Studies* 28 (1995): 1–24.

————. *Slaves into Workers: Emancipation and Labor in Colonial Sudan.* Austin: University of Texas Press, 1996.

Spaulding, Jay, and Stephanie Beswick. "Sex, Bondage, and the Market: The Emergence of Prostitution in Northern Sudan, 1750–1950." *Journal of the History of Sexuality* 5 (1995): 512–34.

Steevens, G. W. *With Kitchener to Khartum.* New York: Dodd, Mead, and Co., 1898.

Steiner, Christopher B. "Another Image of Africa: Toward an Ethnohistory of European Cloth Marketed in West Africa, 1873–1960." *Ethnohistory* 32 (1985): 91–110.

Stevenson, R. C. "Khartoum during the Turco-Egyptian Occupation." In *Urbanization and Urban Life in the Sudan,* edited by Valdo Pons. Khartoum: Development Studies and Research Centre, University of Khartoum, 1980.

Stoler, Ann Laura. *Carnal Knowledge and Imperial Power: Race and the Intimate in Colonial Rule.* 2nd ed. Berkeley: University of California Press, 2010.

Sudan Government. *Reports on the Finances, Administration, and Condition of the Sudan.* [Continued as *Report by the Governor-General on the Administration, Finances, and Conditions of the Sudan.*] London: Sudan Government, 1902–55.

Sudan Women Union [*sic*]. *Sudan Women Union: An Outline Descriptive Report.* Khartoum: The Organizational and Management Office, Documentation Unit, 1981.

el Tayib, Griselda. "An Illustrated Record of Sudanese National Costumes." Master's thesis, University of Khartoum, 1976.

———. "Women's Dress in the Northern Sudan." In *The Sudanese Woman*, edited by Susan Kenyon. Khartoum: Graduate College, University of Khartoum, 1987.

Turbin, Carole. "Refashioning the Concept of Public/Private: Lessons from Dress Studies." *Journal of Women's History* 15 (2003): 43–51.

Turner, Bryan S. *The Body and Society: Explorations in Social Theory.* 2nd ed. London: Sage, 1996.

Turner, Terence S. "The Social Skin." In *Not Work Alone: A Cross Cultural View of Activities Superfluous to Survival*, edited by Jeremy Cherfas and Roger Lewin. Beverly Hills, CA: Sage Publications, 1980.

Uteng, Tanu Priya, and Tim Cresswell, eds. *Gendered Mobilities.* Farnham, UK: Ashgate, 2008.

Van Nieuwkerk, Karin. *"A Trade Like Any Other": Female Singers and Dancers in Egypt.* Austin: University of Texas Press, 1995.

Walz, Terence. *Trade between Egypt and Bilad as-Sudan, 1700–1820.* Cairo: Institut Français d'Archéologie Orientale du Caire, 1978.

Warburg, Gabriel. "Ideological and Practical Considerations regarding Slavery in the Mahdist State and the Anglo-Egyptian Sudan, 1881–1918." In *The Ideology of Slavery in Africa*, edited by Paul Lovejoy. Beverly Hills, CA: Sage Publications, 1981.

Willis, Deborah. *The Black Female Body: A Photographic History.* Philadelphia: Temple University Press, 2002.

Willis, Justin. "'The Nyamang Are Hard to Touch': Mission Evangelism and Tradition in the Nuba Mountains, Sudan, 1933–1952." *Journal of Religion in Africa* 33 (2003): 32–62.

Zenkovsky, Sophie. "Marriage Customs in Omdurman." *Sudan Notes and Records* 26 (1945): 241–55.

INDEX

Page numbers in *italics* indicate illustrations.

Benjamin, Walter, 197n47
bicycles, Sudanese midwives using, *75,*
    75–76
Bint al-Wadi (Daughter of the Valley),
    137
Blackley, Elizabeth, 30
Bluebirds, 108, 109. *See also* Girl Guides
Boddy, Janice, 50–51, 65, 66, 175, 185n3
body hair, waxing and exfoliation of,
    148
body politics, 1–14, 173–79; activism of
    women and, 133–37, 139–41, 144;
    centrality to women's history, 12–14;
    consumerism and imperialism,
    152–55; as indicator of community
    and place, 9, 148, 173–74; intimate
    nature of imperial experience, 6–9;
    midwives and imperial order, 66–74;
    national and global citizenship and,
    158–163; urban space and, 130–133.
    See also beauty; cleanliness and
    hygiene; gender identity in Sudan;
    harem culture; tobes
Britain. *See* Anglo-Egyptian
    Condominium
Browne, E. G., 24
"bucket men," 32
Burton, Antoinette, 8, 13; *Dwelling in
    the Archive* (2003), 12

caregiving, ideology of, 43, 58
Christie, Agatha, 113
circumcision, female. *See* female genital
    cutting and infibulation
Clark, Sylvia, 113–17, 196n20
cleanliness and hygiene: British impres-
    sions of Sudanese and, 28–29; con-
    sumerism and, 152–53; dress as sign

of, 67–68, 79–80; education of girls
    and, 88, 95, 97–98; in female genital
    cutting and infibulation, 44, 66; as
    moral imperative, 64–65; on MTS
    curriculum, 55, 56, 64–65
Clifton, D., 1–3, *2,* 6, 9, 13
clothing. *See* body politics and fashion;
    tobes; western dress
Cold War, 160, 162
Comaroff, John and Jean, 93, 152
Communist Party, 123, 125, 128, 144
consumerism and imperialism, 152–55
cotton clothing, 94–95
Cromer, Lord (Evelyn Baring), 22, 24,
    27, 33
Crowfoot, Mary Grace, 44, 103
Culwick, Geraldine, 107, 112, 120
Cumings, Lady Enid, 108, 109
Currie, Sir James, 33, 34, 37, 48

damuriyya tobes , 10, 39
al Dar, Malakat, 141–43
dayas: access to MTS supplies, 73; dress
    of, compared to MTS students and
    midwives, 67–74, *69, 70, 72;* female
    genital cutting and infibulation, role
    in, 44–45, 103; harem culture and,
    51–53, 55; as MTS students, 45, 55–56;
    registration and licensing of, 78–79;
    rope birthing method, and 62; sexu-
    ality and experience, 56, 58
De La Warr Commission, 86
deims, 131
Dickinson, Ernest, 15, 16
"The Diplomatic Corps" (tobe name),
    156
dirt. *See* cleanliness and hygiene
"The Doctors' Ribs" (tobe name), 83